Travel Notes from the New Literacy Studies

NEW PERSPECTIVES ON LANGUAGE AND EDUCATION
Series Editor: Professor Viv Edwards, *University of Reading, Reading, Great Britain*
Series Advisor: Professor Allan Luke, *Nanyang Technological University, Singapore*

Two decades of research and development in language and literacy education have yielded a broad, multidisciplinary focus. Yet education systems face constant economic and technological change, with attendant issues of identity and power, community and culture. This series will feature critical and interpretive, disciplinary and multidisciplinary perspectives on teaching and learning, language and literacy in new times.

Recent Books in the Series
Distance Education and Languages: Evolution and Change
Börje Holmberg, Monica Shelley and Cynthia White (eds)
Ebomics: The Urban Education Debate (2nd edn)
J.D. Ramirez, T.G .Wiley, G. de Klerk, E. Lee and W.E. Wright (eds)
Decolonisation, Globalisation: Language-in-Education Policy and Practice
Angel M. Y. Lin and Peter W. Martin (eds)

Other Books of Interest
Beyond the Beginnings: Literacy Interventions for Upper Elementary English Language Learners
Angela Carrasquillo, Stephen B. Kucer and Ruth Abrams
Bilingualism and Language Pedagogy
Janina Brutt-Griffler and Manka Varghese (eds)
Continua of Biliteracy: An Ecological Framework for Educational Policy, Research, and Practice in Multilingual Settings
Nancy H. Hornberger (ed.)
Language and Literacy Teaching for Indigenous Education: A Bilingual Approach
Norbert Francis and Jon Reyhner
Language Learning and Teacher Education: A Sociocultural Approach
Margaret R. Hawkins (ed.)
Language Strategies for Bilingual Families
Suzanne Barron-Hauwaert
Language Minority Students in the Mainstream Classroom (2nd edn)
Angela L. Carrasquillo and Vivian Rodríguez
Making Sense in Sign: A Lifeline for a Deaf Child
Jenny Froude
Multilingual Classroom Ecologies
Angela Creese and Peter Martin (eds)
A Parents' and Teachers' Guide to Bilingualism
Colin Baker
Power, Prestige and Bilingualism: International Perspectives on Elite Bilingual Education
Anne-Marie de Mejía
Understanding Deaf Culture: In Search of Deafhood
Paddy Ladd

For more details of these or any other of our publications, please contact:
Multilingual Matters, Frankfurt Lodge, Clevedon Hall,
Victoria Road, Clevedon, BS21 7HH, England
http://www.multilingual-matters.com

NEW PERSPECTIVES ON LANGUAGE AND EDUCATION
Series Editor: Viv Edwards

Travel Notes from the New Literacy Studies

Instances of Practice

Edited by

Kate Pahl and Jennifer Rowsell

MULTILINGUAL MATTERS LTD
Clevedon • Buffalo • Toronto

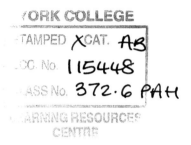

Library of Congress Cataloging in Publication Data
Travel Notes from the New Literacy Studies: Instances of Practice
Edited by Kate Pahl and Jennifer Rowsell.
New Perspectives on Language and Education
Includes bibliographical references and index.
1. Literacy. 2. Technological literacy. 3. Globalization.
I. Pahl, Kate. II. Rowsell, Jennifer. III. Series.
LC149.T73 2005
302.2' 244–dc22 2005021288

British Library Cataloguing in Publication Data
A catalogue entry for this book is available from the British Library.

ISBN 1-85359-862-3 / EAN 978-1-85359-862-3 (hbk)
ISBN 1-85359-861-5 / EAN 978-1-85359-861-6 (pbk)

Multilingual Matters Ltd
UK: Frankfurt Lodge, Clevedon Hall, Victoria Road, Clevedon BS21 7HH.
USA: UTP, 2250 Military Road, Tonawanda, NY 14150, USA.
Canada: UTP, 5201 Dufferin Street, North York, Ontario M3H 5T8, Canada.

Typeset by Techset Composition Ltd.
Printed and bound in Great Britain by the Cromwell Press Ltd.

Contents

Part 3: Crossings in Literacy Practices

Part 4: Multimodal Communicative Practices in Pedagogical Settings

Foreword

The editors of this volume bring together work from two fields of study, both relatively recent arrivals: Multimodality and New Literacy Studies. In the former there has been an attempt to redress the emphasis on writing and speech as the central, salient modes of representation, in favour of a recognition of how other modes – visual, gestural, kinaesthetic, three-dimensional – play their role in key communicative practices. So one major emphasis in work on multimodality is to develop a 'language of description' for these modes, that enables us to see their characteristic forms, their affordances and the distinctive ways in which they interact with each other. Likewise, those in the field of New Literacy Studies (NLS) have attempted to provide a language of description for viewing literacy as a social practice in its social environments. Again there is an intent to change many emphases of the past – especially in educational contexts of the most varied kinds – from literacy as a static skill and to describe instead the multiple literacy practices as they vary across cultures and contexts.

One key question addressed by the writers in this volume is how these approaches can 'speak to each other', in attempts to find correspondences and differences. All the authors here resist moves to polarize, looking instead for complementarities in theoretical aims and approach. For instance, in both approaches there is a worry about the stretching of the term *literacy* well beyond the NLS conception of *social practices of representation* to become a metaphor (and often much less than that) for any kind of skill or competence. One needs to ask whose interests are advanced and in what ways by the use of labels such as 'palpatory literacy' (skills in body massage), 'emotional literacy' (skills in affective massage?), 'cultural literacy' (skills in social massage??), and so on. Of course, one clear effect of such moves is that where 'a literacy' is identified, those with an interest in finding the corresponding illiterates are never far behind with their remedies. But even such uses where some aspects of literacy practices are involved – computer literacy, visual literacy – bring their own problems, not least of them the blunting of analytic and theoretical sharpness and power. Where there is a label there is already an answer; and where there is an answer, any need for questions has stopped. More significantly perhaps, there is the question of 'complementarity'. This poses quite simply an as yet thorny question: where does the 'reach' of one theory stop – or, maybe better, begin to attenuate, 'fizzle out'. A social semiotic theory (of multimodality) is interested in sign-makers, sign-making and signs. In being interested in signs it is interested precisely in what signs 'are made of', the affordances, the materiality and the provenance of modes and signs in that mode. In being interested in sign-makers and in sign-making necessarily it is interested in the social place, the history and formation of the sign-makers, and in the social environments in which they make their signs. A social semiotic theory of multimodality can attempt to expand its domain to include the features of the sign-maker and of the environment of sign-making; it would do so by treating all of the world as signs – the practices, the characteristics of social organization, and so on. And at times that is necessary. In most cases it is better by far to say: but look, there are those whose work is concerned precisely with these issues, who have their tools, different tools. Your own tools become ever less useful, and *their* tools are so much more effective – whether those of sociology, of anthropology, or the varieties of ethnographic methods.

A theory of literacy as social practice addresses similar questions but with, perhaps, a focus upon a narrower range of semiosis – the uses of reading and writing, although always in association with other modes, such as speech or visual representation. What NLS has added to traditional approaches has been the recognition that reading and writing vary across cultural time and space – the meanings associated with them vary for participants and are rooted in social relationships, including crucially relationships of power. Indeed, the very definitions of what counts as literacy already frame social relationships of literacy and what people can do with it – as we see in increasingly narrow Government demands on curriculum and assessment. How these schooled literacies relate to those of everyday social life, with its multiple literacies across different cultural and institutional contexts, is a key question raised by NLS and for which, at present, schooled literacy advocates are not providing answers. Researchers in NLS, with their ever expanding vision of literacy in society, have developed research methods and concepts for addressing such questions. They talk of literacy events – the immediate visible activities associated with literacy – and of literacy practices – the more hidden, underlying conceptions of what those events mean held by both participants and by observers and researchers. We can, then, talk of schooled literacy practice, or of academic literacy practise in the domain of education and, more broadly, of religious literacy practices or commercial literacy practices. NLS, then, is developing a language of description for addressing literacy in all its social variety.

But again the question arises of what are the limits and boundaries here and what does NLS not address that, for instance, a social semiotic theory of multimodality can better handle? Whose tools are better suited to different aspects of the broader task? The question of 'complementarity' addresses itself to that – not a matter of mere eclecticism, but of compatible competences. NLS and multimodality, in this sense, are well placed to explore each others' strengths and weakness, to develop a conversation that facilitates new growth and more powerful tools. It is that conversation into which the authors in this volume have entered.

This is timely and necessary, precisely because burning issues in representation and communication have proliferated along with the profound changes in the social, cultural, economic and technological world, issues for which there are as yet no answers. In that context the need is to open up questions; and bringing the compatible and complementary approaches of NLS and multimodality to bear, offers one means of getting further. For one thing, while both approaches look at broadly the same field, from each of the two positions the field has a distinctive look: one that tries to understand what people acting together are doing, the other tries to understand about the tools with which these same people do what they are doing. Each has defined its objects of study – practices, events, participants on the one hand, semiosis, modes and affordances, genres, signmakers and signs on the other. From each of these further questions follow, uncertainties open up. What *is* a mode, how do modes interact, how can we best describe the relationship between events and practices, how do we avoid becoming the agents producing the new constraints of newly described and imposed grammars?

It is a time for going back to quite fundamental questions, asking old questions again, in the light of new givens and the new difficulties they bring. What are the cultural technologies which are at issue here – the technologies of dissemination of meanings (the media), those of representation of meanings (the modes), and those of production of messages (print and paper; digitality and electronics)? How do they interact, what becomes possible for whom, where is power likely to shift, who is likely to gain and who is likely to lose, and what is our role as academics in all that? The authors in this volume are attempting just such a task, starting from their own experience as practitioners and researchers, trying to find ways of speaking across their fields, traditions and the data which they produce. They call on different methodologies – some more semiotic and some more ethnographic in style – reflective and close to the ground, able to see two things more precisely: the specific social, cultural and individual reasons for the uses of particular resources (why speech and gesture for this part of the task, and why writing and image for that?), and the significance of the work of those who make their representations, always in interactions with others.

In this, the book makes its contribution to a growing move, a part of an increasing awareness that the complexity and fluidity of the world – of which the world of representation is but a part – demands the joining of intellectual, theoretical resources, demands the fashioning of new tools from the old. As two people involved in just that kind of work, we welcome the contribution made by those whose work is represented here.

Introduction

KATE PAHL AND JENNIFER ROWSELL

This book sits at the interface between the New Literacy Studies and multimodality. Since their conceptions over a decade ago, there has been an ideological lacunae, of greater or lesser proportions according to where researchers have been situated, between the New Literacy Studies and studies of multimodality. On one side, there is a growing body of work which sees literacy as a social practice (Street, 1984, 2000, 2005; Heath, 1983; Barton & Hamilton, 1998). On the other side, there is multimodality, which opens up meaning-making to a multiplicity of modes (visual linguistic, oral, gestural, etc.) and has been identified with the work of Gunther Kress (Kress, 1997; Kress & van Leeuwen, 1996). We decided to assemble this collection because it is time to merge a social practice account of literacy *with* a description of communicative systems. We need this collection to demonstrate the powerful possibilities of such a synthesis. People in the volume are at the forefront of research in literacy education. Although we are working across theoretical perspectives, we have a common understanding of literacy as a social practice with an eye to the impact of new communicational systems on how we make meaning. We recognize that to move forward, we need to mediate social practice with communicational networks to have an informed perspective on contemporary literacy education.

It is significant that Brian Street, whose work began by describing literacy as a social practice from his ethnographic fieldwork in Iran, should be writing with Gunther Kress, whose work identified the need to look at meaning making as multimodal. Street's fieldwork in Iran considered literacy in different contexts. Street identified a tendency for governments to reify literacy *as a set of skills* which he described as autonomous, and through his seminal research, he showed that literacy is in fact culturally and ideologically situated (Street, 1984, 1993). On the whole, the New Literacy Studies has been associated with: the ethnographic work of Heath (1983) who compared language and literacy practices in three rural communities in the US Carolinas; Barton and Hamilton (1998) who studied one community's literacy practices in the UK; and Gee (1996) whose work has looked at situated meanings in language and education. Gunther Kress opened up meaning making by foregrounding the interest of the literacy learner and their singular use of multiple modalities (i.e. not just linguistic but also visual, gestural, three-dimensional, etc.). Kress's work has sparked a proliferation of other work on multimodality in chidren and youth's meaning making (Kenner, 2004; Jewitt & Kress, 2003; Pahl, 1999, 2001, 2002). The work of Kress has been developed in a number of key texts including *Before Writing* (1997) and *Reading Images* with van Leeuwen (1996), in which the original systems of language were opened up to other media.

Travel Notes From the New Literacy Studies has been written at a moment in time in the continuing development of work in the fields of the New Literacy Studies, multimodal literacy, multiliteracies, and critical literacy. It presents instances of practice as case studies, which freeze moments in time, and open them up for analysis. This work carefully and painstakingly traces the flows of meaning across sites. For example, across the Internet from Web space to classroom, or across domains, from corporations to educational domains. This book harnesses itself to ethnography, the study of meanings in contexts over time, to the study of literacy practices in a multimodal context. Ethnographic methods enable researchers to trace practices in texts. It is not enough to analyse texts as single, isolated entities since such a system does not account for the problematic of meaning and the embodied meanings that lie within texts, which instantiate facets of an author's identity in practice.

To access the underlying meanings of literacy practices, we need to not only account for the materiality of texts, that is, the way they look, sound and feel, but also have an understanding of who made the text, why, where and when. Rowsell in her work looking at publishing practices, traced the way meanings crossed from corporate settings and could be discerned within published texts as traces of that process, and then filtered into school literacy practices (Rowsell, 2000). Pahl watched children in homes and her study recognized how habitus was inscribed into social practices and then sedimented within texts (Pahl, 2002). What we, as editors, value is the bringing together of the ethnographic with a focus on literacy as a social practice and multimodality with its emphasis on the variety of communicative practices. In other words, *we see identity and social practice in the materiality of texts.*

Where We Are Now . . .

Scholars in this collection build on the work of both Street (1984) and Kress (1997), so that their studies are constructed around an engagement with social practices and with texts. They lie in a tradition of more recent work coming from the New Literacy Studies including Leander and Sheehy's (2004) collection, *Spatializing Literacy Research and Practice*. Also noteworthy is the work of Larson and Marsh, in theorizing the New Literacy Studies in relation to education (Larson & Marsh, 2005). Detailed ethnographic studies of communities, homes and schools in multilingual settings are drawn together in a collection of articles edited by Martin-Jones and Jones (2000).

This collection revealed the true value of the ethnographic eye which combined with a focus on literacy events and practices provides a fresh consideration of what we can learn from multilingual communities. The New Literacy Studies has gone forward. It has begun to problematize its own concepts. For example, concepts like 'situated literacies' can no longer be taken for granted. While Barton *et al.*'s (2000) seminal collection *Situated Literacies* developed a nuanced consideration of context, this was then rendered problematic by the work of, for example, Wilson, (2000, 2004) in her study of prison literacies and her use of third space theory. Research on on-line communities, such as Davies' (this volume), shows how space can be created by literacy. Janks and Comber make a material difference to the way space is organized at Ridley Grove Public School by growing a huge garden that not only feeds children at the school, but also teaches them about building community. This process takes us to the idea of space informed by context (Leander & Sheehy, 2004).

Likewise, in a multilingual context, literacy practices become more complex and riven by local and global crossings. Recent work by Kenner (2004) and Gregory *et al.* (2004), have begun to develop a theoretical lens to look at multilingual literacy practices in homes and communities. In Kenner's case, she has used Kress's work on multimodality to consider multilingual writing systems in homes (Kenner, 2004). The field has begun to open up and become richly exciting, moving alongside immense global and technological changes. This is the era of the techno/actual street as both real and imagined – children occupy a techno-local/global streetscape as they surf the Internet and create on-line communities and weblogs (Knobel & Lankshear, this volume; Davies, this volume).

The New Literacy Studies

New Literacy Studies represents a tradition of considering the nature of literacy not as a neutral set of skills that we acquire, in school or in other learning contexts, but instead as how people use literacy in different contexts for different purposes. What this implies is a belief that literacy functions in all contexts in different ways guided by different discursive practices. Initially, the strength of the New Literacy Studies was that it privileged the local. Whether in Lancaster, as in Barton and Hamilton's (1998) *Local Literacies*, or the Carolinas, as in Heath's (1983) *Ways with Words*, or within a specific community, like prisons, as in Wilson's (2000) work on prison literacies, ethnographers of literacy practices paid close attention to local emic meanings (Street & Baker, this volume).

In this volume, Street and Baker call upon the notion of *literacy practices* (Street, 1984, 2000) and transfer its underlying principles onto numeracy and practices used in making meaning with numbers. Consideration of the relation between literacy events and literacy practices provides a useful basis from which to engage in field research on literacy as a social practice (Street & Baker, this volume). At an epistemological level, literacy as a social practice is used in all of the studies in the volume, as a language of description to look at meaning making. Some studies look at literacy or numeracy events, (e.g. Street & Baker, this volume; Kell, this volume; Stein & Slonimsky, this volume) whilst some look more at literacy practices across domains (e.g. Rowsell, this volume; Nichols, this volume; Knobel & Lankshear, this volume). The concept of patterned practices adds texture and depth to an understanding of literacy as a social practice and ethnography works well to elucidate such a concept. Literacy events and literacy practices provide us with a common language to use in field studies.

One of the theoretical concerns of the New Literacy Studies has been the recognition that literacy in local contexts sometimes comes from the outside (Brandt & Clinton, 2002). For example, Marsh describes how globalized practices such as Disney advertising impinges on local contexts in the form of advertising, and children are placed simultaneously in local and global spaces as they go shopping and travel on buses (Marsh, this volume). We are excited by the potential of tracing global practices within local contexts, such as Nichols' compelling account of what the concept of De Bono's thinking caps, taken from the global domain of the Internet, looks like as observed in a classroom (Nichols, this volume).

The New Literacy Studies has flourished in providing the field with rich instances of practices in different domains. Recently, the field has turned more to analysing the global, following the work of Appadurai and Bauman in focusing on global practices (Appadurai, 1996; Bauman, 2000). It is fitting therefore that Deborah Brandt and Katie Clinton conclude the book. They began the process of examining the New Literacy Studies with a new eye, considering how globalization can be fitted within the paradigm of the New Literacy Studies in their influential article, 'The Limits of the Local' (Brandt & Clinton, 2002). Their article argues that it is impossible to describe local literacies without attention to global contexts. Furthermore, they argue that literacy can be seen as a 'thing-like' object in some cases, where it resides in a reified form. One of the most powerful observations is that literacy practices depend on technologies, which can be transformed locally but are nonetheless tied to global communication systems. As they note,

> . . . if reading and writing are means by which people reach – and are reached by – other contexts, then more is going on locally than just local practice.
>
> (Brandt & Clinton, 2002: 338)

In other words, when people use literacy in their everyday life, for example, they write a letter ordering building materials, or fill in a form, this practice is in itself shaped by global as well as local context. Brandt and Clinton urge us to be sensitized to the global as well as the local when analysing literacy events and practices.

This brings us to the purpose of the book that we have edited. We, as authors, want to identify the interface between the local and the global to thoroughly account for literacy practice. We need the ethnographic lens to do so, and equally, we need to bring in multimodality. Ethnography provides the contexts and the tracing process we need to understand texts. Multimodality brings in textual dimensions which are material and which are increasingly shaped by exterior, global forms. In Stein and Slonimsky's work (this volume) this synthesis is achieved through an ethnographic analysis of children's oral and written texts in home contexts with a multimodal perspective.

Researchers in this field need to appreciate the relationship between local and global, they need to account for multimodality, they need a methodology like ethnography, which looks at meanings, and only then can they consider phenomena like crossings. Brandt and Clinton have given us a theoretical lens to look at crossings from local to global sites. We have begun to identify ways of doing this. For example, Street takes the concept of disembedding and embedding mechanisms from Giddens to describe texts moving from local to global contexts, a theoretical lens Kell uses in this volume to describe the movement of particular meanings across sites and across modes (Street, 2003). Similarly, in this volume, Nichols uses the theoretical lens of Actor Network Theory to trace particular concepts across sites. Likewise, Rowsell uses Gee's concept of Discourses to account for their materialization in different sites (Rowsell, this volume). In these accounts, scholars from the New

Literacy Studies have used theoretical concepts from other sources (Giddens' concept of disembedding and embedding; Actor Network Theory, Gee's concept of Discourses) and used them within the context of the New Literacy Studies.

Another lens to look at crossings is that of recontextualisation. That is, the lifting of particular genres, or texts from one context, to another. Recontextualisation has been used by such ethnographic researchers as Dyson when describing how children draw on home and community texts and practices, and 'remix' them for the classroom context, combining a medley of radio songs, jingles, and cartoons to make texts (Dyson, 2003). In this collection, several authors bring this concept into their work, noting how different texts are recontextualised across sites, reappearing in different contexts. For example, Kell describes an informant recontextualising her argument through written text, in order to achieve her goals, as opposed to an oral tradition. In doing so, she calls on global patterns of meaning making, much as Stein and Slonimsky describe the child drawing on global banking practices in her oral talk (Kell, this volume; Stein & Slonimsky, this volume). For us, recontextualisation can be glimpsed within artifacts, which are created. These artifacts are then used and become objectified in practice. When we consider artifacts, we need to see them as material, hence the need to look at and account for multimodality in our meaning making.

Multimodality

When we talk about multimodality in the local/global context we are talking about communication in the widest sense, including gesture, oral performance, artistic, linguistic, digital, electronic, graphic and artifact-related. We use mode, from Kress's words, as being the 'stuff', that is fashioned from quite different materials (Kress, 1997: 7). It is clear that the communicational landscape (Kress & Van Leeuwen, 1996) has changed and with these changes we have witnessed dramatic shifts in the way children make meaning from texts of all kinds (i.e. multimodal texts) in all places (i.e. at home and at school). For instance, Millard's work on the *Literacy of Fusion* argues that children's texts have to be seen as multimodal to acquire their full meaning (Millard, this volume). Millard's argument that children need a far wider range of affordances for meaning making in schooled settings brings us to a realization of the importance of multimodal communication as a lens for understanding meanings. The multimodal offers wider affordances than print-based literacy. It stretches out meaning.

The other, equally important point addressed in the collection by Janks and Comber, Kell, and Stein and Slominsky is how literacy practices taking place in local contexts are a means to gain greater access to global literacy practices. In this way, researchers confront the power issues, which lie behind global and local interfaces. Communities without access to powerful discourses can then be given the tools to cross into global sites of meaning making. One way of accessing global literacies is through extending the *affordances* of meaning making. Multimodality is a powerful access point for children's meaning making.

Crossings from the local to the global emerge out of the creation of multimodal texts in local contexts. Children and adults in studies featured by Janks and Comber, Kell, and Stein and Slominsky cross through their meaning making from local sites to global discourses and back by using and applying multimodal meaning making in their text production. In such instances of practice, there is a move from the local to the global sites of meaning by moving texts and people. Illustrated well in the second section of the collection, these studies show how more access to global discourses and practices is enabled by an engagement with multimodality.

Knobel and Lankshear offer an in-depth picture of blogging in its diverse forms, as associated with market models of communication (Knobel & Lankshear, this volume). Multimodality becomes the terrain on which their analysis is based. They note the presence of particular icons and symbols as being part of the embedded landscape of communication that is blogging. Lankshear and Knobel argue for an understanding of blogging, which explores, describes, and takes account of multimodality. Davies notes how multimodal icons and scapes cohere around certain concepts as she analyses Web communities. Like Alvermann, she focuses on how identities can be created in these new Web-based spaces and upheld in ways that give youth power and status (Davies, this volume; Alvermann, this volume).

Street and Baker offer an account of multimodality in numeracy practices, arguing that numeracy can be understood as a multimodal communicative practice. In their analysis of classroom practice, they show how by accounting for the multimodal, an understanding of crossings between and across modes can aid analysis of mathematical positions that may otherwise be difficult to follow. In her chapter, Millard looks at a transformative pedagogy, founded in a literacy of fusion, which blends school requirements with children's current interests. Her metaphor is drawn from fusion cuisine, which combines disparate elements without homogenizing them, for example, a child's use of trading cards and drawing pictures of the creatures within Pokemon stories and using action figures to tell a story. By invoking all the modes in a meaning making ensemble, the child's social and cultural worlds are brought in.

Rowsell's work locates Discourses within modes (Gee, 1996). She analyses basal readers and shows how particular Discourses reside in images as well as words. Janks and Comber draw on a multimodal analysis of alphabet books as a realization of local Discourses. The reason to consider multimodality in texts is that by doing so, we empower the meaning makers and provide them with more affordances with which to make meaning, based on their own experiences. An area of future research would be an investigation of the ways in which multimodality was tied to global or local identities and practices. We can note how globalized Discourses operate in multimodal ways, but also how locally embedded knowledge is instantiated in images.

Multimodality with the New Literacy Studies

What the New Literacy Studies brings to multimodality is that it avoids the essentializing of visual and linguistic forms. It sees them as in-process. Texts are constantly moving and changing, as we have seen with Knobel and Lankshear and Davies' account of teenagers' use of Websites. They cannot be seen as static forms to be considered in isolation, but they move in a web of significance. We need the multimodal in the New Literacy Studies in order to understand texts as material objects. Multimodality gives an analytic tool to understand artifacts such as children's drawings, and to recognize how literacy sits within a much wider communicational landscape. When we consider children's drawings, we are able to trace these back to local contexts. For example, Janks and Comber's study shows us how children's meaning making, viewed in a multimodal analytic context, is tied to the local, and expresses local concerns and identities (Janks and Comber, this volume).

When we look at a text, whether it is a child's drawing, or a screen on a computer, we have to use a multimodal analysis to decipher it. However, without the New Literacy Studies, meanings are lost. The New Literacy Studies ties the representation to social practice. By bringing in Gee's (1996) concept of Discourses, texts can be linked to Discourses. In our work as theorists within the New Literacy Studies, we recognize that different tools can be used to analyse texts. Rowsell uses Gee's concept of big D Discourses to identify cultural identities within texts, as Alvermann does in her work on the Discourses within email conversation (Gee, 1996; Rowsell, this volume; Alvermann, this volume). Pahl, on the other hand, has used Bourdieu's concept of habitus to develop a model of how habitus, as instantiated within social practice, sediments within texts (Bourdieu, 1990; Pahl, 2002). Texts are increasingly multimodal. Images and words are often welded together on-screen or in children's texts. How can we unravel these concepts except by using both a notion of texts as traces of social practice, and recognizing the visual material quality of texts? This method of analysis gives an ideological quality to multimodality.

Ethnography

We see ethnography in the context of a focus on meaning in context (Geertz, 1993). We recognize that the richness of thick description is invaluable in unpacking how texts are created. We also have learned from the concept of etic and emic perspectives in research. For example, Kell's account of emic notions of space in her article gives us an insider's perspective, which can only be gained from a longitudinal ethnographic study (Kell, this volume). By focusing on context, and by immersing within a field, patterns of meaning over time can be slowly uncovered using ethnography. Street and Baker (this volume), signal how an ethnographic-style approach can make sense of local knowledge and emic meanings in the context of wider social and political forces. They argue that local knowledge, as understood by ethnographers, can inform schooled pedagogy regarding numeracy practices.

Ethnography allows us to view multimodality within a larger, broader context of patterned practices. By using ethnography, authors account for personhood and identities working within spaces, which carry histories and power issues on local and global levels. Kell and Stein and Slonimsky in particular show how longitudinal study of local meanings can also address wider global concerns. Thereby, ethnographic work goes beyond thick description, and as Appadurai suggests,

> ethnographers can no longer simply be content with the thickness they bring to the local.
>
> (Appadurai, 1996: 54)

The global too can become the subject of ethnographic research. To that end, several contributors in this volume apply ethnography to the study of global multimodal texts and practices. Both Davies and Rowsell use ethnographic-style methodologies to interrogate texts across contexts, and bring to their analysis a richly textured account of

Discourses, texts and identities across different spaces and crossings (Rowsell, this volume; Davies, this volume).

How can ethnography account for the global? Returning to Brandt and Clinton, we see this argument as central to this book because we are now moving into an arena whereby ethnography has to consider globalization when studying local contexts. In the studies in this book, this is achieved through attention to literacy within a context of multimodality and a focus on long-term meaning within different contexts.

Appadurai uses the term *scape* to depict the cultural and global flows that occur within communication, and they occur in and through growing disjunctures among what he terms: ethnoscapes, technoscapes, financescapes, mediascapes and ideoscapes (Appadurai, 1996). Appadurai uses the suffix -scape to take account of what he calls 'fluid irregular shapes' of cultural flows (Appadurai, 1996: 33). By *ethnoscape*, Appadurai refers to the shifting world in which we live, as migrants or tourists. In this volume, we can see how different uses of the idea of a scape work within different contexts. For example, Marsh invokes Appadurai's *mediascape* to describe young children's experience of popular culture (Marsh, this volume).

An *ethnoscape* focuses on cultural identity, as in Pahl's analysis of a Turkish child's bird texts, which are mixed with images from PlayStation game culture (Pahl, 2005). A *technoscape* is the fluidity of technology and how it moves at high speeds in different contexts, impervious to boundaries. Knobel and Lankshear and Davies clearly demonstrate this as they open up their analysis of texts to the fluid, shifting technological street-scape that is the Web. *Ideoscapes* are often political, related to the movement of global policy shifts. For example, Nichols analyses the De Bono thinking hat within such a paradigm, while Street and Baker look at schooled numeracy as a policy, which then leaves home numeracy practices unaccounted for (Nichols, this volume; Street and Baker, this volume). These studies look at policy in schools, and provide an example of ideoscapes in action. Rowsell's work in corporate contexts can, on the other hand, be placed within the context of *financescapes* as she analyses the flow of corporate information in discursive practice and how financial markets determine texts in practice (Rowsell, this volume).

The Local and the Global

In this book we consider local contexts as shaped by global forces, and try to illuminate that insight through ethnographic work. By focusing on ethnographic studies of multimodal communicative practices we engage with current thinking on how texts are shaped by practices which themselves are both locally based and globally shaped. What do we see as global? We see the global and the local in *instances of practice*. Stein and Slonimsky demonstrate that a global repository of information stretches the affordances of children's worlds in their multimodal texts. Likewise, the global offers Davies' teenagers access to a Web interface and other communicative media. The global opens out worlds and also closes them down. It means access to a wider community of practice, but it can remain closed to those without economic or social capital. Scholars in this volume also problematize the global, and Janks and Comber in particular, critique the notion of the global as affordance for children who lack economic resources.

We understand this process of the local and global interface as one of instances. We consider the high speed ebbing and flowing of the local and global in and out of itself, within spaces, for example Davies' account of teenage Wiccans moves from Web space to local settings. Global migratory patterns make this process complicated. Ethnographic work begins to unpack these meanings but they remain shot through with contradictory messages. Both Stein and Slonimsky and Kell show how in the political context of South Africa, the harnessing of the global and the 'autonomous' reified literacy, as expressed, for example, in banking practices, is vital as a lever for political and social emancipation.

Returning to Brandt and Clinton, we draw on the notion of the Ariadne's thread of meaning whereby you cannot have local without the global and vice versa. The key point here is proximity to either one (Brandt & Clinton, 2002). Within our collection, there are varying proximities presented, for example, Rowsell's analytic eye is near to the global whereas Janks and Comber's analysis is tied to the local but framed within global power dynamics. Marsh gives an account of children's local communicative landscapes through observation but draws on global meanings when she analyses the data. The key point is *where* authors locate themselves in relation to the local and the global.

The Four Parts

We have divided this book into parts in order to help navigate the reader. These parts are no more than ways into our central theme, which is how the New Literacy Studies together with multimodality can be explored in local and global instances. The first part, *Identity in Multimodal Communicative Practices*, signals how identities are evoked in multimodal spaces. Some of the chapters explore, using Gee's concept of affinity spaces, the complex discursive constructions that the web and other new technologies afford young people (Gee, 2003). In Alvermann's chapter, we see how two individuals develop strong ties through an online affinity space that might otherwise not have been possible given differences between their ages and stages.

The next part explores instances of *Multimodal Literacy Practices in Local and Global Spaces*. All the authors in this section problematize the local and global relationship. As well, all authors use multimodality as an instrument to attribute agency to meaning makers, and explore how multimodal texts and practices empower or distance them. The communities these authors work in are highly politicized: many people are disenfranchised and cut off from global systems of power and agency. These studies bring in a powerful sense of inequity with regard to meaning making. In Kell's chapter, we see how a woman can only find a voice and its attendant power by stepping outside of local practices.

The next part focuses on *Crossings in Literacy Practices*, and draws on a globalized set of Discourses to view instances of discursive crossings in local/global contexts. Nichols' argument that De Bono's thinking hats takes agency away from learners is embedded in a careful analysis of how web sites are used by teachers to impose pedagogical frameworks. She also describes how corporate systems infiltrate the field of schooling, as does Rowsell, whose analysis of how corporate publishing agendas impinge on schooled literacy similarly focuses on crossing as a unit of analysis.

The final part, *Multimodal Communicative Practices in Pedagogical Settings*, gives the field of schooling attention. It looks particularly at what a multimodal perspective brings to learning in schools. Chapters in this part demonstrate that multimodality provides affordances for students within schooling contexts. Baker and Street show that if you put a multimodal lens onto numeracy practices in the classroom, the reason for students' misapprehension of concepts becomes clearer. Millard shows how student agency lies in multimodality. She reveals the transformative power of the multimodal in educational settings as a possible future curriculum. We consider it important for the book that we have concluded on a schooling note, with a clear eye to schooling and policy change in this field (Pahl & Rowsell, 2005).

Implications of Travel Notes in New Literacy Studies

Millard's work asks us to consider what a transformative literacy pedagogy might look like. In doing so, she privileges agency in literacy. Many authors in this collection focus on the meaning maker as being at the centre of the process of doing literacy. Luke and Carrington consider the role of the student when they talk about,

> . . . the potential of literacy education as a curriculum practice for the generation of 'student' dispositions, positions and position-takings for viable and powerful life pathways through new cultures and economies, pathways that wind through globalized and local, virtual and material social fields.
>
> (Luke & Carrington, 2002: 233)

We are committed to giving power to the learners. The instances of practice are a means to evoke power and agency to meaning makers. We need to celebrate these instances and keep a close eye to the shifts of power across domains. As Nichols says in her chapter,

> Missing from the utopian vision of a workforce or a student group that is simultaneously compliant, collaborative, self-regulatory and generative of top-class ideas is a sense of human beings – adults and children – negotiating multiple relationships in specific local contexts. Missing is any notion of subjective investment in one's own ways of thinking, speaking or representing (except as a management problem). Missing also is any sense of the continuity of old ways of thinking, of histories, of practice and their possible impact on social subjects (here, teachers) confronted with the demand to re-orientate themselves to new regimes.
>
> (Nichols, this volume)

Meaning makers are at the heart of this volume of studies. Instances of their practices are placed centre stage. This means that we can focus on what the local or the global provides for meaning makers. Sometimes it can be empancipatory (as in Stein and Slonimsky) in other cases, the global is shut out of meaning making (as in Janks and Comber). This volume is in itself an instance of practice. We hope it will encourage others to research more local and global spaces. In doing so, we continue to be committed to the voice of the learner.

References

Appadurai, A. (1996) *Modernity at Large: Cultural Dimensions of Globalization.* Minneapolis: University of Minneapolis Press.

Barton, D. and Hamilton, M. (1998) *Local Literacies: Reading and Writing in One Community.* London: Routledge.

Barton, D., Hamilton, M. and Ivanic, R. (eds) (2000) *Situated Literacies: Reading and Writing in Context.* London: Routledge.

Bauman, Z. (2000) *Liquid Modernity.* Cambridge: Cambridge University Press.

Bourdieu, P. (1990) *The Logic of Practice.* (R. Nice, trans.). Cambridge: Polity Press.

Brandt, D. and Clinton, K. (2002) The limits of the local: Expanding perspectives of literacy as a social practice. *Journal of Literacy Research* 34 (3), 337–356.

Dyson, A.H. (2003) *The Brothers and Sisters Learn to Write*: New York: Teachers' College Press.

Gee, J.P. (1996) *Social Linguistics and Literacies: Ideology in Discourses.* London: Falmer Press.

Geertz, C. (1993) (Fontana edition, first published 1973) *The Interpretation of Cultures.* London: Fontana.

Gregory, E., Long, S. and Volk, D. (eds) (2004) *Many Pathways to Literacy: Young Children Learning with Siblings, Grandparents, Peers, Communities.* London: Routledge.

Heath, S.B. (1983*) Ways With Words: Language Life and Work in Communities and Classrooms.* Cambridge: Cambridge University Press.

Jewitt, C. and Kress, G. (eds) (2003) *Multimodal Literacy.* New York: Peter Lang.

Kenner, C. (2004) *Becoming Biliterate: Young Children Learning Different Writing Systems.* Stoke on Trent: Trentham Books.

Kress, G. and van Leeuwen, T. (1996) *Reading Images: The Grammar of Visual Design.* London: Routledge.

Kress, G. (1997) *Before Writing: Rethinking the Paths to Literacy.* London: Routledge.

Larson, J. and Marsh, J. (2005) *Making Literacy Real: Theories and Practices for Learning and Teaching.* London: Paul Chapman.

Leander, K. and Sheehy, M. (eds) (2004) *Spatializing Literacy Research and Practice.* New York: Peter Lang Publishers.

Luke, A. and Carrington, V. (2002) Globalisation, literacy, curriculum practice. In R. Fisher, M. Lewis and G. Brooks (eds) *Raising Standards in Literacy.* (pp. 231–50). London: Routledge/Falmer.

Martin-Jones, M. and Jones, K. (eds) (2000) *Multilingual Literacies: Reading and Writing Different Worlds.* Amsterdam: John Benjamins.

Pahl, K. (1999) *Transformations: Children's Meaning Making in a Nursery.* Stoke on Trent: Trentham Books.

Pahl, K. (2001) Texts as artefacts crossing sites: Map making at home and at school. *Reading: Literacy and Language.* 35 (3), 120–25.

Pahl, K. (2002) Ephemera, mess and miscellaneous piles: Texts and practices in families. *Journal of Early Childhood Literacy.* 2 (2), 145–65.

Pahl, K. (2005) Narrative spaces and multiple identities: Children's textual explorations of console games in home settings. In J. Marsh (ed.) *Popular Culture, Media and Digital Literacies in Early Childhood* (pp. 126–145). London: Routledge/Falmer.

Pahl, K. & Rowsell, J. (2005) *Literacy and Education: Understanding New Literacy Studies in the Classroom.* London: Sage.

Rowsell, J. (2000) Publishing practices in printed education: British and Canadian perspectives on educational publishing. PhD thesis, University of London.

Street, B. (1984) *Literacy in Theory and Practice*: Cambridge: Cambridge University Press.

Street, B (ed.) (1993) *Cross-Cultural Approaches to Literacy.* Cambridge: Cambridge University Press.

Street, B. (2000) Literacy events and literacy practices. In K. Jones and M. Martin-Jones (eds) *Multilingual Literacies: Comparative Perspectives on Research and Practice* (pp. 17–29). Amsterdam: John Benjamins.

Street, B. (2003) The limits of the local 'autonomous' or 'disembedding'? *International Journal of Learning* 10, 2825–2830.

Street, B. (ed.) (2005) *Literacy Across Educational Contexts: Mediating Learning and Teaching*. Philadelphia: Caslon Publishing.

Wilson, A. (2000) There is no escape from third space theory: Borderline discourse and the 'in between' literacies of prisons. In D. Barton, M. Hamilton and R. Ivanic (eds) *Situated Literacies: Reading and Writing in Context* (pp. 54–69). London: Routledge.

Wilson A. (2004) Four days and a breakfast: time, space and literacy/ies in the prison community. In K. Leander and M. Sheehy (eds) *Spatializing Literacy Research and Practice*. New York: Peter Lang.

Part 1

Identity in Multimodal Communicative Practices

Chapter 1

Global, Local/Public, Private: Young Children's Engagement in Digital Literacy Practices in the Home

JACKIE MARSH

Since the early 1980s, numerous studies have offered valuable insights into the literacy practices undertaken by young children in the home (Heath, 1983; Cairney & Ruge, 1998; Taylor, 1983; Taylor & Dorsey-Gaines, 1988; Weinberger, 1996). These studies have raised awareness of the way in which children's formative experiences in the family are central to a developing understanding of the role and nature of literacy. However, all of these studies were conducted in the last decades of the 20th century when technological advances were transforming the way in which societies communicated, but the effects on children's communicative practices were less well understood. In this chapter, I focus on examining how popular culture, media and new technologies have impacted on the literacy experiences of young children in the home in the 21st century. I draw on data collected in three different studies which explored the media-related literacy practices of 83 young children, aged two-and-a-half to five years, in the UK. These studies were conducted over a period of four years (2000–2004) and the data from all three studies have been used to inform an analysis of the contemporary communicative practices of the children involved. The purpose of this task is two-fold. First, I intend to trace the *continuities* in family practices across the last three decades, despite rapid technological developments. Secondly, I hope to identify the innovative ways in which children's communicative practices in the home are changing, the *discontinuities* in practice, due primarily to social change engendered by technology. Throughout the chapter, drawing from Street (1997), I use the phrase 'communicative practices' to refer to the range of multimodal meaning-making in which young children engage (Marsh, 2003). Using the term 'literacy' for these practices would be to confuse the issue, as Kress (2003) insists, as the word more accurately describes practices which relate to 'lettered representation' (Kress, 1997).

In this chapter, the classification of literacy practices within homes that was developed by Cairney and Ruge (1998) is revisited in the light of children's changing practices in a digital world, and the categories they identified adapted accordingly. In addition, children's engagement with popular culture, media and new technologies in the home is explored in relation to current debates concerning the polarization of global and local, and public and private. Space, place and time are central to consumption and production of media discourses and are thus embedded in the daily practices of many families who live in highly technologized societies (Pahl, in press). The focus in this chapter is on the way in which the complex web of space and time, within both a local/global, public/private context, frames children's media-related literacy practices in home contexts.

Globalization/Localization and Children's Media

Globalization takes place across economic, political, social and cultural planes (Giddens, 1990) and this multifaceted process is endemic in relation to media texts. Some investigations of the way in which media texts are globalized are predicated on notions of cultural imperialism, such as Ritzer's (1998) concept of 'McDonaldization' or Bryman's (2004) 'Disneyization' thesis. In this analysis, cultural heterogeneity is made problematic because of the way in which American media and cultural discourses saturate the international arena. Others suggest that globalization is not such a one-way process, but involves international exchanges of material resources and human capital (Hannerz, 1990). Hay and Marsh (2000), however, suggest that globalization as an international phenomenon has been misrepresented:

> International flows of capital (such as foreign direct investment, FDI) tend to be extremely concentrated within the core 'triad' (of Europe, North America and Pacific Asia) providing evidence of regionalization, 'triadization' or internationalization but hardly of globalization. (Hay & Marsh, 2000: 5)

Certainly, in terms of young children's media culture, the 'triadization' process can be seen in the worldwide take-up of British television programmes such as the *Teletubbies*, the American-Hollywood influence on children's films and computer games and the appeal of Japanese anime, which has informed countless permutations of computer games and collecting cards. Indeed, a careful tracing of cultural trends would suggest that Japanese culture is currently highly fashionable across a range of artifacts. For example, Japanese cool is encapsulated for young children in the introduction of the Bratz doll, 'Tokoyo a Go-Go', which is packaged complete with mobile phone and digital video camera and comes with additional accessories such as a Sushi Bar, Karaoke Bar and a set of robot pets known as 'Virtual Buddiez'.

Although the process of globalization has often been projected as one of cultural imperialism and the homogenization of societies through market-driven goals, a number of theorists have pointed to the way in which localizing practices ensure that cultural goods are never simply adopted, but are adapted to local contexts (MacDougall, 2003; Murphy & Kraidy, 2003). In addition, the synergy produced by the global–local nexus leads to hybridity, which is indicated in Juluri's (2003) summary of the development of satellite broadcasting in India. Although early programming was dependent on American culture, this gave way to a far more complex culture which was:

> . . . marked by foreign channels localizing furiously: films, music videos and advertisements celebrating a new form of Indian national identity in an explicitly global context; and the rise of curious hybrid cultural forms and products such as "Hinglish" (Hindi and English) and Kellogg's Basmati flakes. (Juluri, 2003: 216)

It is this complex interchange of locally-inflected meanings with global discourses, leading to the production of new and hybrid texts, which informs much of young children's interactions with the media in contemporary society.

However, the adaptation of media products by very young children needs further scrutiny. These often constitute not so much localized practices at a community level (which is often the unit of analysis for the localization process) as familial (micro-local) practices in which children adapt globalized discourses in ways which reinscribe family narratives and collective memories (Pahl, in press). Nevertheless, as Morley and Robins point out, there is a danger in over-emphasizing the extent to which an individual child can adapt global media practices, thus viewing them as 'a kind of semiotic guerilla' (Morley & Robins, 1995: 127) in their ability to transgress or transcend hegemonic discourses; readings are, of course, framed in some way by the texts themselves (Atkinson & Nixon, 2005). In the analysis of the way in which children and their families construct localized practices with regard to media texts, and the interplay of structure and agency within this, I draw on Appadurai's notion of 'mediascapes' (1996). Appadurai (1996) identified a number of global flows, or -scapes, which described the disjunctures created as a result of the globalization process, disjunctures relating to differences in political, economic and social discourses. The -scapes he identified are: ethnoscapes, technoscapes, financescapes, ideoscapes and mediascapes. Of most interest to the analysis in this chapter is the concept of mediascapes. For Appadurai, 'mediascapes' refers both to the global distribution of media and the images/ideologies conveyed through media. These mediascapes are experienced by global audiences as a complex mix of modes through which commodification is linked to the social, cultural and political world. They provide sets of metaphors for daily lives:

> Mediascapes, whether produced by private or state interests, tend to be image-centred, narrative-based accounts of strips of reality, and what they offer to those who experience and transform them is a series of elements (such as characters, plots and textual forms) out of which scripts can be formed of imagined lives, their own as well as those of others living in other places. (Appadurai, 1996: 35)

Although Appadurai moves on in this analysis to present the public in contemporary societies as lacking agency in a way which locates him within a Frankfurtian school of thought in relation to mass consumerism, his development of the concept of mediascapes is highly salient in forming an understanding of how young children incorporate media into their daily lives in the home. Before taking a closer look at this process, however, it is important to explore previous work which has sought to identify the communicative practices children undertake within a family context.

Young Children's Literacy Practices Within the Home

In the last three or four decades, there have been a number of studies that have informed understanding of the range of literacy practices in which young children engage in the home (for a review of these, see Cairney, 2003). In relation to this chapter, I wish to foreground one of these studies, that of Cairney and Ruge (1998). In a study of 27 Australian families, Cairney and Ruge determined four distinct purposes for literacy in homes. The first purpose was literacy for establishing or maintaining relationships. Children, siblings and parents and carers reported a rich range of literacy practices which included reading and writing letters to relatives and friends, reading bedtime stories and making birthday cards. The second purpose was literacy for accessing or displaying information. Families engaged in reading a range of texts such as shopping lists, TV guides, newspaper articles. Literacy for pleasure and/or self-expression was the third purpose identified and this involved reading books, comics and magazines, writing stories and keeping personal diaries. Finally, Cairney and Ruge identified literacy for skills development as an important part of family life and this included activities such as writing the alphabet or 'read aloud' practice. Whilst this study was important in categorizing family literacy practices in this way, it was conducted during a period when children's techno-literacy practices were not identified as being important in terms of their everyday lives. This, however, has been addressed by more recent research (Knobel, in press; Marsh, 2005a; Rideout *et al.*, 2003). It is clear that many young children in the 'developed' world are engaged in a rich range of communicative practices from birth, many of which are deeply embedded within the discourses of popular culture, media and new technologies. In the next part of this chapter, I will review some of these multimodal practices in relation to the framework offered by Cairney and Ruge (1998) and, in the process, explore how they relate to issues of globalization and space.

The Studies

The analysis in this chapter draws on data collected in studies which explored young children's media-related literacy practices in the home. Altogether, the data discussed in this chapter relate to 83 families in the UK. These families took part in three different studies I have conducted over the last five years. Each study focused on tracing the popular cultural, media-related and techno-literacy practices of young children in the home. These studies are outlined in Table 1.1. The data from these studies were compared and contrasted in order to address the following questions: What are the roles and functions of the media-related literacy practices engaged in by young children in the home and how do these relate to the categories determined by Cairney and Ruge (1998)? The following analysis is organized according to the four categories identified by Cairney and Ruge (1998), outlined previously, in addition to a further purpose which was identified in all of the studies: communicative practices in identity formation/performance.

Communicative practices for forming social relationships

The children in all three studies were engaged in a rich range of practices in which family relationships were reinforced and extended. As in the Cairney and Ruge study (1998), shared reading of print-based texts played a major part in family life. This reading related to popular

Table 1.1 Overview of studies

	Study	*Participants*	*Methods*
Study 1	Marsh and Thompson (2001)	18 families from a white, working class area whose 3- and 4-year-old children attended a local nursery.	Families kept a literacy diary of children's activities over a one month period. 15 parents interviewed about children's activities.
Study 2	Marsh (2004a)	44 families from a white, working class area, with children aged 2.5–3.11 years.	Parents/carers completed questionnaires which provided information about children's media-related literacy practices. 26 parents interviewed about children's activities.
Study 3	Marsh (2004b)	21 families with 4-year-olds living in UK. Families varied in terms of cultural heritage and social class, and were volunteer participants in a BBC television series about their children's development.	Parents/carers completed questionnaires which provided information about children's media-related literacy practices. 21 families interviewed about children's activities. Children took photographs of their favourite activities and took part in follow-up interviews.

culture and media in a number of ways, as it involved the sharing of texts related to popular cultural and media interests, such as picture books based on television and popular cultural narratives, TV guides, catalogues and magazines.

However, a wide range of other texts was shared, including television programmes and films. For example, for four-year-old Sameena, watching Hindi films and Indian television programmes on a satellite channel with her family was a way of participating in established family rituals, distinct from her time watching children's programming, as indicated by Sameena's mother:

> ... in the daytime she watch most of the CBeebies or programmes like that and after that 'Spider-man' and evening times she watches our Indian programmes with me and her family.

These daily acts of communal viewing are not simply routines, Steeg Larsen and Tufte (2003) argue, but ritualized acts in which watching television together 'symbolically integrates each member into the family as a social institution, (re-)establishing each member's place and position in it' (Steeg Larsen & Tufte, 2003: 103). In Sameena's case, these ritualized acts also served the purpose of acknowledging and celebrating the cultural heritage of the family, made possible in many homes by the use of satellite television (Kenner, 2005).

As discussed elsewhere (Marsh, 2004a, 2005a), children played out narratives they had encountered in films and television programmes and involved family members in this play, important for both development of narrative understanding and facilitation of intersubjective experiences with family members. This process was an important element in the localization of globalized media practices. Appadurai (1996: 54) argues that although imagination and fantasy have always played a central role in human lives, as can be seen in the plethora of myths, legends and narratives developed within cultures through time, globalized mediascapes have normalized fantasy as a social practice. Certainly, within the families who took part in the studies reported in this chapter, fantasy play was an established part of family practices and the data are rich with examples of global mediascapes providing scripts for the children's own imaginative play, play which drew in members of the family. So, the mother of two-and-a-half-year-old Nathan regularly pretends to be Tommy, a character in *Rugrats*, slipping in and out of the role as he goes through the day, drawing his mum into this particular mediascape:

> ... because of the "Rug Rats" video that he's got, at the beginning of it Chucky's talking like as a narrator. And he says on that "Tommy's the bravest baby I ever knowed", and he gets me to say that. I have to pretend to be Chucky and say that a lot.

Mediascapes inflected daily routines to the extent that they became established practices, shored up by the spending habits of families. Toys and artifacts related to favourite narratives were bought for children and used to create mediascaped worlds which permeated family life. These globalized narratives were, through this process, adapted into localized family practices, a process identified by Robertson (1992, 1995) as 'glocalization'. However, despite the extensive prevalence of the glocalization of texts and practices in out-of-school contexts, this process is rarely acknowledged within educational institutions. Luke and Carrington (2002) suggest that glocalized literacy practices would involve 'material repositioning; critical analysis and repositioning of flows; reflexive analysis of other and local texts' (2002: 246). In the very early years of schooling, this should involve children's critical reflections on the ways in which cultural texts are shaped in their own lives (for an example of this in practice, see Vasquez, 2004).

Other media-related practices also contributed to the development of social relationships. Across the studies, children participated in a range of techno-social practices, which included using mobile phones to talk to family members and watching family members send and receive SMS text-messages. Many children prompted family members when they received text messages:

Interviewer: Do you think he knows about text messages?
Mother: Yes.
Interviewer: Does he ever try and pretend to send one?
Mother: No, because he's supposed to be receiving them at the moment, but he's got Vodafone.... and every time it bleeps with a message he throws it at me and says, "Read it, mummy".

The shared reading of some of these messages took place outside of the family home, of course, on buses, city streets and shopping centres. This is one illustration of the way in which space is changing for contemporary children in relation to the notions of 'public' and 'private'. Much has been written about the way in which mobile telephones privatize public spaces (Katz & Aakhus, 2002), but there has been less extensive reflection on the implications for young children's understanding of public/private spaces. For many children in these three studies, the boundaries between public and private were permeable. Their families engaged in exchanging private messages, both written and oral, in public spaces, using mobile phones; practices which children observed and sometimes participated in. Public spaces also orientated children and family to home, through the use of such technologies as plasma screens in shopping malls, a preferred marketing tool for contemporary businesses. As Bolin (2004) suggests:

> Television screens have the potential to address more effectively the consuming subject in public spaces, as if he or she were at home, as opposed to more traditional media, such as outdoor advertising, or window displays. (Bolin, 2004: 140)

In addition, some shops in shopping malls and town centres now provide toys and games that children can use whilst their parents and carers browse, again creating a blurred distinction between home and the outside world. On any busy shopping day, many young children can be observed in these shops, sprawled across floors, engaged in small-world play and oblivious to the public nature of the environment.

For previous generations, the boundary markers between private and public were much more distinct. However, the possibilities offered by the increasing convergence of media and the processes involved in remediation of narratives across various media platforms (Bolter & Grusin, 1999) mean that the mediascapes which inform children's lives in the home also infuse public spaces. In all of the three studies, parents suggested that taking their child into public spaces opened up the opportunities for recognition of characters related to communicative practices undertaken in the home:

> Sometimes he'll even spot something on the shelf that I haven't even seen because it's so either far away or so small or something. In fact, my mom was amazed the other week: we went into one shop and he noticed a *Postman Pat* book simply from the cover, from the spine, that's what I mean, that was just placed like that in the shelf. And he looked at the spine and he recognised the way the letters were and the colour. There was no *Postman Pat*, obviously, on that, it was just the writing. And he knows because he recognises his own books from the spine as well on his shelf, you know. He knows the way the letters go and the same with other things as well. He said, "I want that *Postman Pat* book", and my mum said, "There isn't a *Postman Pat* book", looking for the figure. And he wasn't there because he'd just seen the writing. So even that, he knows how they look on the screen and in the shops and things so . . .

The consequences of this privatization of public space are, as yet, untraced in much of the literature relating to young children's engagement in communicative practices, but it is clear that the media industry have been quick to exploit this particular third space (Soja, 1996) through marketing strategies which mean that shop windows, buses, bus stops and billboards are awash with images and logos from popular media narratives. Children thus move from an intense engagement with these narratives in the home to an outside world that is rich with semiotic significance in relation to their lived mediascapes. The ultimate means of dissolving the boundaries between public and private in relation to these mediscapes is, of course, a theme park and it is no surprise, therefore, to witness the proliferation of theme parks and other attractions which focus on children's favourite characters, programmes and films.

If children and families in these studies were experiencing the blurring between private and public in public spaces, then the opposite effect was also apparent; that is, the public appropriation of private spaces. For example, the use of the internet opened up closed familial spaces to others, as the mother of four-year-old Hannah indicated:

Mother: She likes going on CBeebies, she likes the Barbie home page, she is just learning how to use MSN.
Interviewer: What?
Mother: The instant chat messages, so she'll tell me what she wants to say to somebody.

As might be expected, the majority of young children taking part in each of these studies were not able to communicate independently using technology such as email, chat rooms and text-messaging, but they were able to participate in these practices with older siblings and parents acting as scribes, in similar ways to the practices of previous generations with regard to adults scribing letters and notes for children. The home was often a site for engaging in communication with the wider world, with some of these interactions taking place with a known interlocutor and others involving an unknown audience, such as chat room messages and the use of interactive satellite and digital television.

There were other notable patterns with regard to space and media in the home. Various moral panics in relation to children and media have given rise to concerns about young children in contemporary society being isolated, so focused on watching television and playing computer games that they are becoming asocial (Holloway & Valentine, 2003). Indeed, there is evidence that teenagers' use of media is generally private (Livingstone & Bovill, 1999). In contrast, data from these studies suggested that these younger children were remarkably social in their use of media. In Marsh (2004b) parents were asked where various activities took place in the family home. It was found that children usually watched television and used computers in the hub of family life, in living rooms, kitchens and other shared rooms. Ironically, it is the act of reading books which appeared to lead to these children being alone in their bedrooms most often. There was some shared reading of books by parents and children in bedrooms, which took place at bedtime, but most reading took place alone in children's bedrooms. This was very different from children's engagement in other communicative practices, which either took place alongside other family members, or actively involved them.

Communicative practices for accessing or displaying information

This particular purpose for literacy was an extensive feature of the Cairney and Ruge (1998) study and this was also the case in the three studies reported here with regard to media texts. Parents reported their children referring to a large range of texts in order to access information about the content of video games and films, for example, reading junk mail/catalogues/computer game covers and magazines, reading teletext on satellite television, reading TV guides and accessing Websites on the internet (e.g. BBC children's site).

In Marsh (2004b) one four-year-old child, Mandy, who lived on a farm, regularly reported on the weather forecast for her family, as it was important to their working lives:

> She will have to watch the weather forecast because obviously our lives depend upon the weather forecast so you know things like that . . . if the forecast comes on she'll shout "Forecast", you know so we all know. She knows that it means a lot to us and so she can . . . she has been doing that for years you know, she can even hear it and say, "Right okay, you've got to come and watch it", because she knows that it is important to us.

In this way, children were becoming acculturated into the 'information economy' (Lanham, 1993) and identifying media sources as providing significant knowledge for daily life. Websites and mobile phones were also becoming increasingly important for some families in accessing data and so children were observing these textual practices playing a central role in retrieving and managing information. In addition, some children, although unable to decode printed text, were able to retrieve Websites themselves through the use of the 'Favourites' option in their Web browser, simply by memorizing its place in the list. Despite this and other evidence of sophisticated navigational and information retrieval skills, many early years settings fail to build on this expertise, assuming that children enter the nursery as 'tabula rasa' in relation to these literacy practices (Arthur, 2005).

Communicative practices for pleasure and/or self-expression

Perhaps unsurprisingly for research which explored the lives of very young children, it was this purpose which permeated much of young children's use of popular culture, media and new technologies in the home. Parents described their children being enthralled by a range of television programmes, films, computer games, console games and books, toys and artifacts relating to popular cultural narratives. Of the 375 photographs of their favourite things taken by four-year-old children in the latest study (Marsh, 2004b), 33% featured toys, television sets, computers and console games. The screen was a dominant icon in many of the photographs, as indicated in Figure 1.1.

Of course, other aspects of children's lives were also important to them. Fifteen percent of the photographs featured siblings and parents, and another 8% related to the garden and garden playthings such as swings and slides. But toys and artifacts related to media and popular culture were the most prominent set of photographs and included items such as X-Box games, artefacts to promote small-world play and dressing-up clothes related to favourite media narratives. It was through these pleasurable practices that globalized media discourses became localized practices that drew from family histories and collective memories (Pahl, 2002, in press).

Communicative practices for development of skills, knowledge and understanding in relation to language and literacy

Children engaged in a range of media-related communicative practices which promoted skills development, often encouraged by their parents. For example, they played phonics games on computers, completed puzzles in comics and played interactive games on satellite television, which required some skills practice. Parents across all of the studies reported

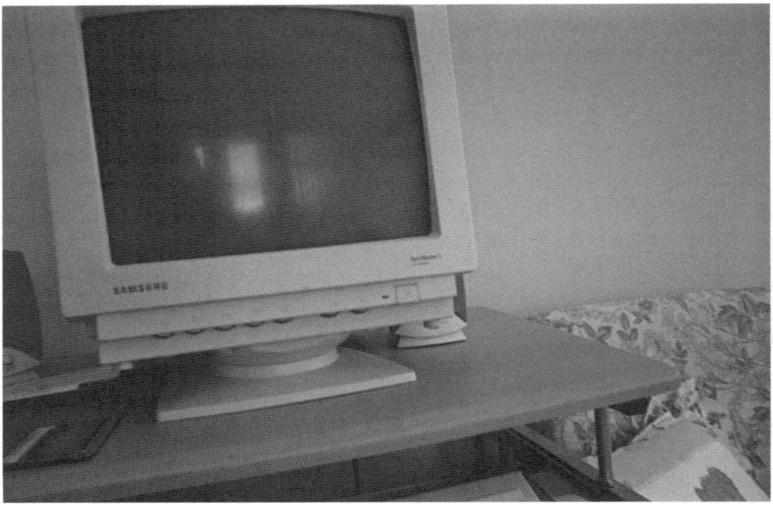

Figure 1.1a

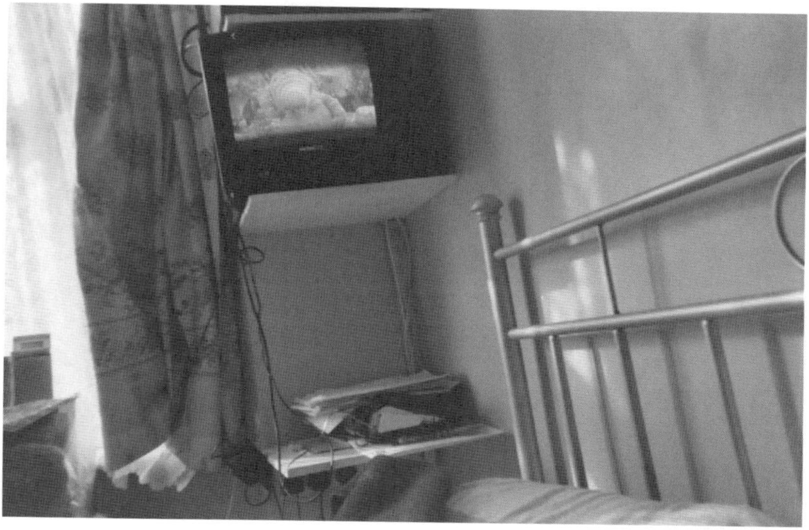

Figure 1.1b

Figure 1.1c

Figure 1.1d

the development of a range of skills, knowledge and understanding they felt had resulted from engagement with a range of popular cultural and media texts. Language was a recurrent theme, with parents keen to point out the perceived effect of media on their children's linguistic repertoire:

> He uses quite a few words that people think, "Where's he got that from?" and I know, mostly, that he's got it from the programmes and things, especially, you know, like big words that you wouldn't really expect him to know at two. I mean, I know he's nearly three, but he's been talking really well since before his second birthday. He was already talking in sentences then. So, you know, and especially long sentences and big words that you wouldn't really expect him to know, quite specific language, especially like on "Bob the Builder" if he's talking about something or on "Thomas the Tank Engine", which he likes. If they're talking about specific engine parts and, you know, fenders and all this kind of thing, he'll ... pick up on it.

Some parents of bilingual children felt that their children had learned English from watching television:

Interviewer: . . . what do you think she learns from watching television?
Mother: She learns most of English from the telly.
Mother: Because she wouldn't be where she is with her English if it wasn't for television.
Interviewer: So how do you know that's television that's helped her in that?
Mother: Because all our family speaks Welsh, [her dad] and I, we only speak Welsh at home, you know we have friends over, most of them are Welsh. You know, she wouldn't have heard a lot of English if it wasn't for television and that sort of thing.
Interviewer: What about nursery?
Mother: It's Welsh.

Other parents reported that their children had developed knowledge of phonemes, graphemes, vocabulary, key words and so on through their engagement with media. Whether or not children had acquired these skills was not a concern of these studies; what was of interest was the positive attitude parents articulated towards their children's engagement with media, a contrast to the negative stance of some educators (Arthur, 2005). Parents regularly turned to media and new technologies in order to facilitate the development of their young children's communicative skills, aware that these resources would be important to their children's futures:

> . . . my decision about buying him [a digital camera] was that I could have bought him a cheap disposable one, but because he is learning how to take photographs and whatever, a lot of it is fingers and you know just the corner of something, so at least with the digital we can get rid of it, we don't have to pay for the printing and whatever. And also because it is modern technology, he is never going to have to use a real camera, you know, we have already got a digital camera, so let's be sensible here and get him something that is actually a commodity, if you like, of his era.

Some parents were aware that their children's schools were less well equipped than they should be, or perhaps had different priorities. For example, Marlene, a parent who lived in an area of socio-economic deprivation, noted that the local school had only just acquired computers:

> Unfortunately, the schools in the poorer areas that don't have the right funding for it or they don't spend it right (I don't know which one it is) – don't seem to have things like computer. I mean [School X],

> has only just got a computer, which I'm pleased about but, I think in today's, today's age and society and all that, you do need one... They need absolute basics: mouse control, keyboard skills. I don't think it's going to be very long before they're not writing with paper and pencil, you know ... I don't think they're going to be writing for many generations. I'd probably give it about three and then I don't think they'll write anymore apart from scraps of notes in the house.

Families across all of the studies were making clear links between acquisition of skills, knowledge and understanding and new technologies and doing what they could to enhance children's experiences in this regard. Of course, this did lead to the educational appropriation of the leisure use of technology as parents led their children to the 'edutainment' Websites related to television characters, with some of these sites offering inappropriate educational content that limits children's technological expertise. For example, Lankshear and Knobel (2003) suggest that sites such as these often ask children to engage in 'print-and-complete' or 'click-and-action' exercises which require some form of adult involvement in order for the children to understand the task. This, Lankshear and Knobel (2003) argue, may inhibit young children becoming independent users of the Internet.

The data shared in this chapter would indicate that there are a number of continuities between the practices outlined in previous studies of children's literacy practices in the home and the techno-literacy practices in which these children engaged. The four categories of purposes for engaging in this range of communicative practices, as identified by Cairney and Ruge (1998), can be mapped onto the more recent data. However, there were differences. In all of these studies, an additional purpose for multimodal communicative practices within family homes was apparent. This was the use of communicative practices for identity construction and performance of self.

Communicative practices for identity construction and performance of self

The synergistic relationship between identity and consumption has been widely acknowledged:

> Following a line of argument that began with the recognition that goods are building blocks of life-worlds, we have suggested, as have others, that they can be further understood as constituents of self-hood, of social identity. From this point of view, the practice of identity encom-

passes a practice of consumption and even production. (Friedman, 1990: 327)

Although production is almost an after-thought here, throughout the three studies reported in this chapter, children's production in relation to popular culture, media and new technology was of central importance in identity construction and performance. Playing with toys and artifacts that were part of the narrativized semiotic system formed by popular cultural and media texts (see Fleming, 1996) was an important means of expressing individual identity. The role of the globalization–localization dialectic was important here in tracing the way in which children adopted and adapted cultural icons, artifacts and narratives in order to articulate aspects of identity (for a more extensive discussion of the role of media in identity construction and performance of self, see Marsh, 2005b).

Conclusion

For many children in contemporary societies, communicative practices in the home focus on popular culture, media and new technologies. No longer is it possible to explore the literacy practices of young children as an isolated set of social practices, embedded as they are within a complex 'inter-media textual web' (Kinder, 1991). However, this discourse has yet to permeate the early years curricula within most countries. It is as if the developments in young children's lives outside of nursery and school are occurring within a self-contained, virtual bubble that has little to do with the stuff of the first years of schooling, which generally continues to focus on phonics, print-based literacy texts and canonical narratives. In contrast, in this chapter, it can be seen that that, at least in the first five years of these children's lives, family spaces are complex spaces in which globalized narratives are localized on a micro-level, public and private boundaries blur and there are no hard-and-fast rules about 'real' and 'virtual'. This is the techno-territory of family life in the 21st century and unless early years educators acknowledge the rapid changes which are taking place, the curriculum offered to many of these 'toddler-netizens' (Luke, 1999) will continue to offer outmoded and irrelevant reflections of their lived realities, rooted as they are in ever-changing mediascapes.

References

Appadurai, A.J. (1996) *Modernity at Large: Cultural Dimensions of Globalization.* Minneapolis: University of Minnesota Press.

Arthur, L. (2005) Popular culture: Views of parents and educators. In J. Marsh (ed.) *Popular Culture, New Media and Digital Technology in Early Childhood* (pp. 165–82). London: RoutledgeFalmer.

Atkinson, S. and Nixon, H. (2005) Locating the subject: Teens online @ ninemsn. *Discourse: Studies in the Cultural Politics of Education* (Special issue: New Literacies: New Texts).

Bolin, G. (2004) Spaces of television: The structuring of consumers in a Swedish shopping mall. In N. Couldry and A. McCarthy (eds) *Mediaspace: Place, Scale and Culture in a Media Age* (pp. 126–44). London: Routledge.

Bolter, J.D. and Grusin, R. (1999) *Remediation: Understanding New Media.* Cambridge, MA: MIT Press.

Bryman, A. (2004) *The Disneyization of Society.* London: Sage.

Cairney, T. (2003) Literacy within family life. In N. Hall, J. Larson and J. Marsh (eds) *Handbook of Early Childhood Literacy* (pp. 85–98). London; New Delhi; Thousand Oaks, CA: Sage.

Cairney, T. and Ruge, J. (1998) *Community Literacy Practices and Schooling: Towards Effective Support for Students.* Canberra: DEET.

Fleming, D. (1996) *Powerplay: Toys as Popular Culture.* Manchester: Manchester University Press.

Friedman, J. (1990) Being in the world: Globalization and localization. In M. Featherstone (ed.) *Global Culture: Nationalism, Globalization and Modernity* (pp. 311–28). London: Sage.

Giddens, A. (1990) *The Consequences of Modernity.* Cambridge: Polity Press.

Hannerz, U. (1990) Cosmopolitans and locals in world culture. *Theory, Culture and Society*, 7 (2), 237–51.

Hay, C. and Marsh, D. (eds) (2000) *Demystifying Globalization.* Basingstoke: Macmillan.

Heath, S.B. (1983) *Ways With Words: Language, Life and Work in Communities and Classrooms.* New York: Cambridge University Press.

Holloway, S.L. and Valentine, G. (2003) *Cyberkids: Children in the Information Age.* London: Sage.

Juluri, V. (2003) "Ask the West, will the dinosaurs come back?" Indian audiences/global audience studies. In P.D. Murphy and M. Kraidy (eds) *Global Media Studies: Ethnographic Perspectives* (pp. 215–33). New York: Routledge.

Katz, J. and Aakhus, M. (eds) (2002) *Perpetual Contact: Mobile Communication, Private Talk, Public Performance.* Cambridge: Cambridge University Press.

Kenner, C. (2005) Bilingual children's uses of popular culture in text-making. In J. Marsh (ed.) *Popular Culture, New Media and Digital Technology in Early Childhood* (pp. 28–50). London: RoutledgeFalmer.

Kinder, M. (1991) *Playing with Power in Movies: Television and Video Games from Muppet Babies to Teenage Mutant Ninja Turtles.* Berkeley, CA: University of Berkeley Press.

Knobel, M. (in press) Technokids, Koala Trouble and Pokémon: Literacy, new technologies and popular culture in children's everyday lives. In J. Marsh and E. Millard (eds) *Popular Literacies, Childhood and Schooling.* London: RoutledgeFalmer.

Kress, G. (1997) *Before Writing: Rethinking the Paths to Literacy.* London: Routledge.

Kress, G. (2003) *Literacy in the New Media Age.* London: Routledge.

Lanham, R.A. (1993) *The Electronic Word: Democracy, Technology, and the Arts.* Chicago: University of Chicago Press.

Lankshear, C. and Knobel, M. (2003) *New Literacies: Changing Knowledge and Classroom Learning.* Milton Keynes: Open University Press.

Livingstone, S. and Bovill, M. (1999) *Young People, New Media: Report of the Research Project: Children, Young People and the Changing Media Environment.* London: London School of Economics and Political Science.

Luke, C. (1999) What next? Toddler netizens, Playstation thumb, techno-literacies. *Contemporary Issues in Early Childhood* 1 (1), 95–100.

Luke, A. and Carrington, V. (2002) Globalisation, literacy, curriculum practice. In R. Fisher, G. Brooks and M. Lewis (eds) *Raising Standards in Literacy* (pp. 231–50). London: RoutledgeFalmer.

MacDougall, J.P. (2003) Transnational commodities as local cultural icons: Barbie dolls in Mexico. *Journal of Popular Culture* 37 (2), 257–75.

Marsh, J. (2003) One-way traffic? Connections between literacy practices at home and in the nursery. *British Educational Research Journal* 29 (3), 369–82.

Marsh, J. (2004a) The techno-literacy practices of young children. *Journal of Early Childhood Research* 2 (1), 51–66.

Marsh, J. (2004b) BBC child of our time: Young children's use of popular culture, media and new technologies. Unpublished report.

Marsh, J. (ed.) (2005a) *Popular Culture, New Media and Digital Technology in Early Childhood.* London: RoutledgeFalmer.

Marsh, J. (2005b) Ritual, performance and identity construction: Young children's engagement with popular cultural and media texts. In J. Marsh (ed.) *Popular Culture, New Media and Digital Technology in Early Childhood* (pp. 28–50). London: RoutledgeFalmer.

Marsh, J. and Thompson, P. (2001) Parental involvement in literacy development: Using media texts. *Journal of Research in Reading* 24 (3), 266–78.

Morley, D. and Robbins, K. (1995) *Spaces of Identity: Global Media, Electronic Landscapes and Cultural Boundaries.* London and New York: Routledge.

Murphy, P.D. and Kraidy, M. (eds) (2003) *Global Media Studies: Ethnographic Perspectives.* New York: Routledge.

Pahl, K. (2002) Ephemera, mess and miscellaneous piles: Texts and practices in families. *Journal of Early Childhood Literacy* 2 (2), 145–65.

Pahl, K. (in press) Children's popular culture in the home: Tracing cultural practices in texts. In J. Marsh and E. Millard (eds) *Popular Literacies, Childhood and Schooling* (pp. 21–45). London: RoutledgeFalmer.

Rideout, V.J., Vandewater, E.A. and Wartella, E.A. (2003) *Zero to Six: Electronic Media in the Lives of Infants, Toddlers and Preschoolers.* Washington: Kaiser Foundation.

Ritzer, G. (1998) *The McDonaldization Thesis: Explorations and Extensions.* London: Sage.

Robertson, R. (1992) *Globalization: Social Theory and Global Culture.* London: Sage.

Robertson, R. (1995) Globalization: Time-space and homogeneity-heterogeneity. In M. Featherstone, S. Lash and R. Robertson (eds) *Global Modernities* (pp. 25–44). London: Sage.

Soja, E. (1996) *Thirdspace: Journeys to Los Angeles and Other Real-and-Imagined Places.* Oxford: Blackwell.

Steeg Larsen, B. and Tufte, T. (2003) Rituals in the modern world: Applying the concept of ritual in media ethnography. In P.D. Murphy and M. Kraidy

(eds) *Global Media Studies: Ethnographic Perspectives* (pp. 90–106). New York: Routledge.
Street, B. (1997) The implications of the New Literacy Studies for education. *English in Education* 31 (3), 45–59.
Taylor, D. (1983) *Family Literacy: Young Children Learning to Read and Write.* Portsmouth, NH: Heinemann.
Taylor, D. and Dorsey-Gaines, C. (1988) *Growing Up Literate: Learning from Inner City Families.* Portsmouth, NH: Heinemann.
Vasquez, V.M. (2004) *Negotiating Critical Literacies with Young Children.* Mahwah, NJ: Lawrence Erlbaum.
Weinberger, J. (1996) *Literacy Goes to School: The Parents' Role in Young Children's Literacy Learning.* London: Paul Chapman.

Chapter 2

Ned and Kevin: An Online Discussion that Challenges the 'Not-Yet Adult' Cultural Model

DONNA E. ALVERMANN

This is a case study of an ongoing e-mail discussion between an eighth-grade student named Ned and a graduate research assistant named Kevin. Both were of African-American heritage and both expressed an abiding interest in a local, socially conscious rap group that became the focal point of their online interactions. It was through being privy to these exchanges and working closely for a semester with Ned and Kevin, who were participants in a study of youth culture and after-school literacy practices, that I began to question the very notion of youth as a subculture.

Adolescence and *adolescents* are no longer the transparent or stable terms they once were thought to be in some corners of the academic world. These signifiers are currently undergoing considerable scrutiny (Lesko, 2001; Vadeboncoeur & Stevens, 2005) as researchers, theorists, and practitioners alike explore ways of seeing and talking about young people that move beyond the dominant discourses of youth. In fact, contemporary research on young people's multiple literacies complicates the very notion of *adolescence* – a term Appleman (2001) once critiqued as a status category, or 'a kind of purgatory between childhood and adulthood' (2001: 1). This research on youth literacies, whether in edited volumes (Alvermann, 2002; Lankshear & Knobel, 2003; Sefton-Green, 1998; Vadeboncoeur & Stevens, 2005) or in refereed journals (Chandler-Olcott & Mahar, 2003; Guzzetti & Gamboa, 2004; Hagood, 2000; Moje, 2000), disrupts certain assumptions about what counts (or should count) as valued literacy practices among people of all ages, while not falling prey to an overly simplistic celebration of youth culture.

Beyond Youth as a Subculture

In this chapter I draw from a theory of youth culture (Amit-Talai & Wulff, 1995) that is critical of the notion that adolescents are incomplete adults. Rather than view young people as 'not-yet' or incomplete adults and thus less competent and less knowledgeable than their elders – a view held by some scholars (e.g. Coleman, 1961; Forcey & Harris, 1999; Hall & Jefferson, 1976; Parsons, 1942/1964) who conceptualize youth as a subculture structured by age and sex roles – I prefer, like Amit-Talai and Wulff (1995), to think of youth not as separate from the adult world but as 'knowing something else that has to do with their particular situation and surroundings' (1995: 11). This situated perspective on youth culture argues for literacy practices that avoid categorizing people in ways which divide us (the adults) from them (the youth). It also argues for exploring how all of us (adults and youth alike) act provisionally at particular times given particular circumstances and within particular discourses (Morgan, 1997).

It is not my intention to imply that subculture theory, the dominant paradigm of the Centre for Contemporary Cultural Studies in Birmingham, England since the 1970s, is without merit. Quite the contrary, for as Tait (2000) has pointed out, subculture theory offered a conceptual advancement over the Chicago School's delinquency model of the 1930s and the reductionist theories of Marxist ideology. A problem inherent in a subculture theory of youth is, according to Tait, the 'unitary understanding of power that translates its exercise solely in terms of social control' (2000: 204). That is, when we conceptualize power as social control, we have no recourse but to view youth as dominated and repressed. In rejecting this view and arguing for a reinterpretation of power – one in which power is productive, resides in relations that are changeable, reversible and unstable, and is dispersed through discourses – Tait aligns his thinking with Foucault (1988) most notably.

For example, in choosing to work within the New Literacy Studies (NLS) framework, I recognize that meanings associated with reading and writing vary across cultural time and space and take root in social practices that involve relationships of power (Kress & Street, this volume; Lankshear & Knobel, 2003). Taking the NLS perspective into account, along with the multiple and complex ways that adolescent and adult discourses interanimate each other, I attempt in this case study to demonstrate through the use of analytic tools such as cultural models, social languages, situated meanings, and Discourses (Gee, 1999, 2004) how age categorization is achieved. Specifically, I am interested in how findings from a larger semester-long, online discussion study worked to challenge the 'not-yet adult' cultural model highlighted in this particular case.

The Larger Online Study

The purpose of the larger study (Alvermann *et al.*, 2002) from which this case is drawn was to explore how youth who struggled when reading school-assigned textbooks approached tasks that required them to do critical readings of popular culture texts of their own choosing (e.g. magazines, comics, TV, video games, music CDs, graffiti, e-mail and other Internet-mediated texts) during an after-school media club. Along with two graduate research assistants (Margaret Hagood and Alison Heron), I met weekly for one and a half hours after school in a public library with each of three different groups of students in Grades 6–9 for an entire semester (14 weeks); two additional graduate students (Preston Hughes and Kevin Williams) assisted in transcribing and interpreting the videotaped club meetings; the remaining graduate student (Jun Yoon) assisted in data management.

Data sources for the case study included the following: transcripts of my initial and follow-up interviews with Ned, his mother, and the librarian in charge of the young adult section of the library; Ned's daily after-school literacy log, which he kept seven days a week for 14 weeks; three videotapes of Ned's participation in club meetings; printed copies of Ned's e-mail interactions with Kevin; and my field notes. For the purpose of focusing on a discourse analysis of Ned's and Kevin's online interactions, I used only two of the data sources just described, namely, the printed copies of their e-mail discussions and my field notes.

Participants and Their Music

Ned, a 14-year-old African-American boy, was in the eighth grade when I first met him. According to school records, he had scored in the lowest quartile on the district's standardized reading test. Less academically inclined than his mother would have liked, Ned's daily efforts in core classes were sufficient for making him eligible to play on his middle school's football team. Ned was popular among his peers and a valued running back, but when his grades began to drop toward the end of the semester, he was cut from the team. From my first interview with Ned, it was clear that he had a passion for sports and envisioned himself going on to play college football.

Ned loved rap music. A self-styled rapper, Ned had formed his own rap group and had created a home page for it on the Web, which he named the M-L-P Boyz (Major League Player Boys). The group consisted of Man (aka Ned), L'il Thug, Tron and G-money. Together, they composed raps that they subsequently committed to memory and performed for special occasions. But Ned's major interest in rap centered on a group from Atlanta, Georgia, known as the *Goodie MOb*, an acronym for 'The Good Die Mostly Over Bull', whose members include Big Gipp, Khujo, T-Mo and Cee-lo. The Atlanta group's first album, *Soul Food* (1995), stands as one of the earliest Southern rap albums to emerge on a major label. Besides being pioneering, *Soul Food* also distinguished itself by addressing serious social issues.

Kevin Williams, currently a doctoral student in the Department of Social Foundations at the University of Georgia, was one of five research assistants who worked with me on the media club study. Early in the study, Kevin learned of Ned's interest in doing a project on the *Goodie MOb*. Quite coincidentally, Kevin had been a high school classmate of Big Gipp, Khujo and T-Mo, and so he volunteered to help Ned learn more about the group. As a high school student in the late 1980s, Kevin had listened to *Public Enemy*, a rap group whose political views and critical lyrics were similar to those of the *Goodie MOb*.

Method of Discourse Analysis

For the purpose of this chapter, I used Gee's (1999) method of discourse analysis. Its central premise is that 'whenever we speak or write, we always and simultaneously construct or build six things or six areas of "reality"' (1999: 12). The six building activities (and some of their 18 corresponding questions) consist of *semiotic building* (e.g. what social languages are relevant and irrelevant), *world building* (e.g. what Discourses are being re/produced), *activity building* (e.g. what actions are going on), *socioculturally-situated identity and relationship building* (e.g. what roles, positions and their accompanying knowledges, beliefs, feelings, values are relevant or irrelevant to a given situation), *political building* (e.g. what status, power, and identities are relevant or irrelevant), and *connection building* (e.g. what sorts of connections – looking to the past and/or future – are made to other people, things, ideas, institutions, and Discourses).

In this chapter, I use these six building activities and their associated questions in conjunction with the four primary tools of inquiry (thinking-devices) that Gee (2004) recommends: social languages, situated meanings, cultural models and Discourses. As thinking-devices, all four of these tools enabled me to analyze a nine-stanza account of Ned's and Kevin's online interactions, but it was cultural models that helped me think most pointedly about youth culture in relation to the adult world. Thus, the last section of the chapter is largely centered on a discussion of the data that used cultural models as an analytic tool.

Gee's (1999) guidelines for discourse analysis are just that: he is very clear in his writing on the topic that there are no 'rules' to be followed 'step-by-step' (Gee, 1996: 96). He does, however, encourage those who use his method to apply the tools of inquiry discussed above to address particular themes or issues present in a given data set. Toward that end, I selected a 750-word excerpt from Ned's and Kevin's online interactions around the *Goodie MOb* that was representative of the data from the larger 14-week media club study. Working within that excerpt, I selected several key words and phrases and asked what situated meanings they presented, especially given what I knew about the larger context in which they occurred. As I thought about certain situated meanings, I looked for linguistic details (e.g. 'I-statements' and patterned repetitions) that seemed important, and for evidence of socially-situated identities that were both enacted and recognized by the participants. To engage more deeply with the data, I asked myself several of the 18 questions alluded to earlier, and of course, I jotted down questions of my own as they came up. Guided by my initial question (how did Ned and Kevin's online interactions work to challenge the 'not-yet-adult' cultural model), I continued to use the four analytic tools as a means of illuminating the final points I wanted to make in relation to that question. The process was one of many starts and half-finishes, followed by more revisions to my thinking, and then a 'final' analysis.

To represent this analytic process, I used several of the transcription conventions that Gee (1999) recommends. For example, I numbered the lines of the printed version of the online conversation between Ned and Kevin (broken down into idea units) and underlined words that represented salient pieces of information in relation to the larger themes or issues they addressed. Then, I organized the lines into nine stanzas for the purpose of connecting relevant pieces of information. The nine stanzas in their entirety revealed both the macrostructure (large pieces of information set off by Roman numerals) and microstructure (numbered lines within stanzas) of the excerpted piece. These summaries will provide points of reference and context in the section on findings.

I. *Making and Accommodating a Request*

Stanza 1 (Ned introduces himself to Kevin, declares his allegiance to a well-known local rap group, the *Goodie MOb*, and requests that Kevin help him with a self-chosen media club project about the group.)

Stanza 2 (Kevin signals his willingness to accommodate Ned's request and offers some background on his personal knowledge of the *Goodie MOb*, whom he refers to as his "home boys". Specifically, Kevin attended high school with members of the group and counted Khujo as his closest friend.)

II. *Reciprocating and Showing Appreciation*

Stanza 3 (Ned provides two Websites on the *Goodie MOb* that he thinks Kevin might find interesting.)

Stanza 4 (Kevin acknowledges his appreciation of the Websites that Ned recommended and offers to answer questions about T-Mo, whom he assumes is one of Ned's favorite members of the *Goodie MOb* group.)

III. *Disagreeing*

Stanza 5 (Ned politely requests information on C-loe, not T-Mo, and he gives reasons for preferring C-loe's style of rapping.)

IV. *Researching*

Stanza 6 (Kevin gives Ned an assignment: "Look at the cover and credits of *Goodie MOb*'s first album and find the names of the people in their dedication".)

Stanza 7 (Ned responds and asks if Brandon Williams, one of the people mentioned in the dedication, is related to Kevin.)

V. *Giving Feedback and Taking Leave*

Stanza 8 (Kevin acknowledges that Ned is correct in assuming that Brandon Williams was related to him; in fact, it was his brother. Kevin then describes how both Brandon's death and the death of Barak Martin, a friend, were the result of two separate drive-by shootings that inspired some of the *Goodie MOb*'s songs, such as "Pall Bearers". After giving Ned one more question to research – namely, finding out who received a treasured shot-out from the *Goodie MOb* in their album "Soul Food" – Kevin suggests that they continue to correspond after the media club study ends.)

Stanza 9 (Ned discovers that Kevin received the "shot-out". He thanks Kevin for sharing a personal story about the *Goodie MOb* and says that he, too, would like to keep in touch after the study ends.)

Findings

This section of the chapter is divided into four subsections: social languages, situated meanings, cultural models and Discourses. It is my hope that each subsection provides sufficient data from the case study of Ned's and Kevin's online discussion for passing judgment on the usefulness of discourse analysis as a means of exploring the validity of the 'not-yet adult' cultural model.

Social languages

My approach to social languages in this chapter is to define them as Gee (2004) has done; that is, they are ways of using language in order to enact particular socially situated identities. Of course, as Gee has cautioned, this definition,

> in no way [implies] that enacting and recognizing *kinds of people* . . . is a matter of people falling into rigid kinds. Enacting and recognizing kinds of people is all about negotiating, guessing, and revising guesses about kinds of people; it is all about contesting and resisting being positioned as a certain kind of person. Thus, there are often no strict boundaries to social languages. (Gee, 2004: 42, emphases included in the original)

To illustrate how Ned used social language to enact his identity in relation to Kevin (at least as situated within their discussion of *Goodie MOb*), consider the following two excerpts from Stanzas 1 and 3:

Stanza 1 (Ned)
1a My favorite rap group is *Goodie Mob*
1b because they talk about life

1c and the sciety in there neighbor[hood]
2a Like for instance
2b the song I think should describe them
2c is Sky High
2d because that's like a fact in life
3a If you would listing to their songs
3b you would know that they rap
3c from the hart

Stanza 3 (Ned)
2a I found two good websites
2b about goodie mob
2c you might want to know about

In both stanzas, Ned makes repeated references to himself ('my', 'I') as an informed knower who is fully competent to discuss the *Goodie MOb*'s place in the world of rap. Ned's two references to knowing as much, if not more, than Kevin can be found in lines 3a–3c in Stanza 1 and in lines 2a–2c in Stanza 3. The absence of any mitigating talk on Ned's part, such as 'I don't know' or 'It seems to me', suggests even further that Ned did not position himself as Kevin's subordinate, at least not when it came to interacting online about a rap group they shared in common.

In fact, it might be argued that if either of the two e-mailers expressed deferential language, it was Kevin (the adult) when he wrote in Stanza 4 (lines 4a–7b) that he'd be willing to 'try' to answer any questions Ned might have about T-Mo. In the same way, Kevin's use of the phrase 'If you would like' (line 6b in Stanza 4) suggests that he does not presume to know a lot about his younger e-mail partner's likes and dislikes regarding the individual members of the *Goodie MOb* group. Even when Kevin could have situated himself as the adult and thus more competent and more knowledgeable about *Goodie MOb*'s first album, *Soul Food*, he did not. Instead, his statement in Stanza 6 ('By the way, the first album was "Soul Food" which I know you probably know') suggests that Kevin was well aware of, and respected, Ned's knowledge of the order in which the rap group's releases had appeared.

Situated meanings

As we just saw in the discussion of how social language is used to situate one's identity in relation to someone else in a particular context, words do not have mere utterance-type meanings. As Gee (2004) explains it, '[words] also have meanings that are specific and situated in the actual contexts of their use' (Gee, 2004: 44). To illustrate how this is clearly the case in Ned's and Kevin's email correspondence, consider the following:

Stanza 1 (Ned)
1a My favorite rap group is *Goodie Mob*
1b because they talk about life
1c and the sciety in there neighbor[hood]

Stanza 2 (Kevin)
1a I hear you like my home boys
1b *Goodie MOb*!

In both of these exchanges, Ned and Kevin rely on each other's shared knowledge (and perhaps experiences) of life, in particular US urban neighborhoods. For example, in Stanza 1, Ned signaled Kevin that he knew *Goodie MOb* was known for its lyrics about society's ills from the perspective of those who live in the neighborhoods known colloquially to the their residents as 'the "hood"'. In responding to Ned's e-mail, Kevin signaled that he not only understood Ned's reference to *Goodie MOb*'s socially conscious raps, but that he also counted himself a part of the urban scene depicted in the group's lyrics. Kevin identified his connection to the *Goodie MOb* in one word: 'home boys'. Although Kevin (as he explains later in Stanza 8) was no longer physically living in 'the "hood"', he once did; thus, in referring to *Goodie MOb* as his 'home boys', he seems to be communicating a sense of solidarity with the brothers. This interpretation seems warranted given that Kevin describes later in Stanza 8 how members of the *Goodie MOb* supported him and his family after his younger brother was shot and killed.

Not all situated meanings are of the kind just described. In the data from the larger study of Ned and Kevin's online discussion, the phrase 'shot and killed' appears repeatedly in Kevin's description of the drive-by shootings at The Beautiful Restaurant in Southwest Atlanta in the early- to mid-1990s. Although this phrase contains words that have general meanings, the patterned sequence in which Kevin used them would suggest he wanted to communicate their special meaning in relation to the drive-by shooting deaths of first his best friend and then his brother in front of The Beautiful Restaurant. My hunch is that Ned interpreted the phrase's situated meaning, in all its graphic imagery, precisely as Kevin intended it.

Not words, but acronyms, the letters M.P.H. (standing for a Masters of Public Health degree) next to Kevin's name in Stanza 4 (line 8), and AKA = MAN next to Ned's name in Stanza 5 (line 5), signal a pair of situated meanings that are ambiguous at best.

Stanza 4
8 Kevin Pee-Wee Williams, M.P.H.

Stanza 5
5 Ned Bluffton, AKA = MAN

Considered in the larger context of the stanzas leading up to Stanza 8, there is evidence to suggest that Kevin got Ned's attention when he placed M.P.H. (signifying his Masters of Public Health degree) after his name for the first time in Stanza 4. Ned reciprocated in the very next stanza by signaling that he, Ned Bluffton, was also known as MAN (the name he used in the rap group that he had formed and for which he had created a home page on the Web). Only this time, Ned had transformed 'Man' (as it appeared on his home page) to 'MAN' – not surprising, perhaps, given that M.P.H. has all uppercase letters. It is also interesting that Kevin's nickname, PEE-WEE, which he introduced in his signature line in Stanza 2, didn't evoke an earlier response from Ned. For reasons unknown, it was only after the appearance of M.P.H. that Ned reciprocated in kind.

Also unknown is why Ned spelled *Goodie Mob* with a lowercase *o* in *Mob* whereas Kevin spelled *MOb* with an uppercase *O*. My own searches on the Web for the 'correct spelling' of the rap group's name proved futile, although I did not find it spelled the way Kevin spelled it on any of the sites I visited. When I asked Kevin about the 'alternative' spelling, he looked puzzled and said that it was the spelling his home boys used. It is of interest here simply because *MOb* appears to have a situated meaning known only to individuals close to the group.

Cultural models

According to Gee (2004), 'cultural models help people determine, often unconsciously, what counts as relevant and irrelevant in given situations' (2004: 45). For example, they 'explain' why words and images have the particular meanings that they do, and they 'fuel their ability to grow more' (Gee, 1999: 81). Thus, in the previous section, it was a shared cultural model of what counts as relevant in the world of socially conscious rap that enabled Ned to declare his allegiance to the *Goodie MOb* 'because they talk about life and the sciety in there neighbor [hood]' (Stanza 1, lines 1b–1c). Similarly, Ned knew he was on firm footing when he observed that if Kevin listened to *Goodie MOb*, he would know that the members of the group rapped from their hearts (Stanza 2, lines 3a–3c).

Citing the work of Hutchins (1995) and Shore (1996) on cognition, culture, and the problem of meaning, Gee (1999) enlarged upon the concept of shared cultural models when he wrote:

> Cultural models are usually not completely stored in any one person's head. Rather, they are distributed across the different sorts of "expertise" and viewpoints found in the group ... much like a plot to a story or pieces of a puzzle that different people have different bits of and which they can potentially share in order to mutually develop the "big picture". (Gee, 1999: 81)

That cultural models typically do not reside in any one person's consciousness (or unconsciousness) makes them an interesting analytic device. For example, a cultural model that seemed to be operating in the e-mail discussion between Ned and Kevin was that of how to do research for a school assignment. Although Ned chose on his own to research the *Goodie MOb* for his media club project – in fact, as my field notes show, it was Ned who devised the name 'freedom activity' as a descriptor for the free-choice project – in the end, it appeared to be the cultural model of how to do school research that determined in part why Ned initially positioned himself as 'student' to Kevin's 'teacher', a position that Kevin readily took up:

Stanza 1 (Ned)
4 Because I'm doing a <u>project</u> on them
5a Could you give me
5b some kind of <u>facts about them</u>?

Stanza 2 (Kevin)
2 I will <u>help</u> you with your project
3a One <u>condition</u> is
3b that you <u>have to</u> e-mail me
3b and <u>keep me informed</u>.

4a Today I will start with a little basic information
4b about the members of the group

- -

9a The next time I write
9b I will tell you a little more about Khujo
9c in terms of when he started rapping

Later, in Stanza 8, after Ned had satisfactorily answered Kevin's question about the names of the people to whom the *Goodie MOb* had dedicated their first album, Kevin praised him for doing a good job. This pattern of question/answer/praise continued when still later, Kevin said, 'Your last bit of homework is to look up which members of the group gave me a shot-out in their personal thank yous in the "Soul Food" album'. As these excerpts demonstrate, the cultural model of 'doing a school assignment' instantiates the 'not-yet' or 'incomplete adult' cultural model to which I alluded earlier in the chapter. What is different in the online interactions between Ned and Kevin, however, is that the two cultural models – doing school research and viewing youth as 'incomplete adults' – were not fully stored in either Ned's or Kevin's head. This is evident in the excerpts from Stanzas 3 and 4 that follow. Note, for example, a reversal of roles in terms of who found some relevant Websites (Ned) and who benefited from them (Kevin); as well, who was invited to ask questions (Ned) and who said he'd try to answer them (Kevin):

Stanza 3 (Ned)
2a I found two good websites
2b about goodie mob
2c you might want to know about

Stanza 4 (Kevin)
1a I appreciate you
1b giving me the web sites.
2 I have enjoyed looking them up
- - - - - - - - - - - - - - - - - - -
7a E-mail me some questions about him [T-Mo]
7b and I will try to answer them

Perhaps most telling of all was the fact that Ned did not act on Kevin's offer to ask any question that he (Ned) might have about T-Mo. Instead,

Ned gave several good reasons why he preferred to know more about C-loe than T-Mo:

Stanza 5 (Ned)
2a I would like to know
2b more about c-loe
2c because I think
2d he knows how to rap better than the rest
3a I ain't trying to put the rest down
3b but I think
3c he has more charicteristics
3d in his raping style
4 His style is creative

This scenario, in terms of how it played out, is hardly a good fit with a cultural model that views young people as being less competent and less knowledgeable than their elders. Of note, too, in Stanza 5 (line 3a) Ned is careful to let Kevin know that he isn't trying to put down T-Mo and the rest of the group in terms of their rapping ability. This sign of maturity, again, is hardly representative of a person who is a 'not-yet' adult.

Discourses

Discourses are ways of speaking, writing, thinking, and behaving in the world. Each Discourse incorporates what Gee (1996) has referred to as 'a usually taken for granted and tacit "theory" of what counts as a "normal" person and the "right" way to think, feel, and behave' (Gee, 1996: ix). Unlike cultural models, which are storylines of how things work in the world, a Discourse is concerned with how a person enacts a certain sort of person (a socially situated identity) through interacting with other people. As Gee (2004) explained, 'Discourses recruit specific social languages (ways with words) and cultural models (taken-for-granted stories), which in turn encourage people to construct certain sorts of situated meanings – that is, encourage them to read context in given ways' (Gee, 2004: 41). Thus, what a person says (or does) and what other people hear (or see) will vary greatly depending on the context in which such communication takes place. Even though the people involved may be speaking the same language, there is room for misinterpretation. Consider, for example, an excerpt from my field notes describing the day I brought a purchased copy of *Goodie MOb's* first album, *Soul Food,* to the media club for Ned.

Shortly after 4:00 p.m., I arrived at the meeting room reserved for the media club's use in the left wing of the public library, a large modern building located adjacent to the middle school that Ned attended. As was typical, the majority of the club members had arrived early and had settled into their favorite activities. Bob, Seymour, and James were seated on the floor around a Nintendo game already in progress, which Ned, who had arrived after me, then joined.... Within 5 minutes of joining his friends, Ned looked up and hollered down to my end of the room: "Miss Donna, did you get *Goodie MOb?*" I had, but it had slipped my mind. When I produced a copy of "Soul Food" from my black canvas bag, Ned left his 3 buddies to finish the video game by themselves. He immediately opened the CD case, read off the list of raps on the back of the case, and put the CD to play in one of the two boom boxes nearby. With headphones on, he was soon engrossed in the group's music. I also noted that he was reading the printed insert that came with the CD as he listened to the group rap.

After some time had passed, Ned came over to where I was working with [another club member] and asked me if I wanted to listen to *Goodie MOb* with him. I said I did and followed him back to the CD player, where he proceeded to turn up the volume on "Soul Food," the song for which the album is named. Although I listened intently, I had trouble distinguishing one word from the next in some of the raps—a fact that didn't escape Ned's attention. Strategically, he reached over to the CD case, withdrew the insert containing the printed lyrics, and began running his finger under the lines of the rap that boomed out into the room. No one else looked up from what they were doing as Ned and I sat on the floor for a good 15 minutes listening to the various tracks on the *Goodie MOb*'s first album.

After listening to the track titled "Cell Therapy," I reached for my book bag to get out the most recent issue of *Blaze,* a magazine that I had purchased for its feature story on the *Goodie MOb*. When Ned showed no visible interest in reading the article, I asked him if he'd like me to read aloud the part on "Cell Therapy." He said he would, but after a couple of paragraphs I could tell he wasn't interested. His attention wandered, and he began to play with the CD case, opening and closing it for no apparent reason. I asked him if he'd rather I read about Cee-lo, his favorite of the rappers. He said he would. This time he remained engaged, following along as I read aloud, for about a page.

When it was time to switch activities so that those who had not had access to the computers in the young adult section of the library could take their turn, Ned headed to a computer with the CD in hand and e-mailed Kevin the names of the individuals who were listed on the insert's dedication page.

As illustrated in this excerpt from my field notes, Ned's enactments as reader and non-reader varied according to how he read the context. Initially eager to locate information on the CD jacket by himself (or to run his finger under the lines of print that I needed in order to understand the rappers' lyrics), Ned enacted the competent reader. But when I introduced a magazine article on the story behind 'Cell Therapy' – a new world order in which Blacks in the 'hood' would be singled out, searched, and seized – Ned showed no visible interest in reading it. Almost immediately our Discourses of competent and incompetent reader recruited specific social languages and cultural models that enabled us to assume certain socially-situated identities and to act on those assumptions. For example, I read the context as one that required a competent reader, and Ned appeared to read it as one that required a passive listener, a socially-situated identity which he only partially enacted. We both constructed certain sorts of situated meanings around 'Cell Theory' as a result of our clashing Discourses, but those constructions only served to highlight the interesting contrasts between a context that required competency in aurally comprehending texts (the CD lyrics as rapped by *Goodie MOb*) and a context that required competency in visually comprehending a printed article about one of *Goodie MOb*'s songs.

Discussion

In the field of literacy studies, issues of power are inseparable from the storylines (cultural models) that help us determine, often unconsciously, who we are in relation to other people with whom we wish to identify or be recognized by. Moreover, according to Gee (2004), 'the situated meanings of words and phrases within specific social languages trigger specific cultural models in terms of which speakers (writers) and listeners (readers) give meaning to texts' (Gee, 2004: 45). For example, in one cultural model of youth culture – one that views youth as a subculture structured by age – adolescents are typically not accorded the 'right' to give meaning to certain texts. That right, so to speak, is reserved for their elders, who are deemed in that particular cultural model to be more competent and more knowledgeable than youth.

However, in another cultural model of youth culture, often referred to as the situated perspective, young people are viewed as integral to the adult world and as knowing certain things that have to do with their particular situation and surroundings. This cultural model, in my estimation, seems a relatively good fit with the data just analyzed. But what warrants such a claim? More specifically, what did my analysis of Ned's and Kevin's semester-long, e-mail discussion reveal that would suggest serious challenges to the 'not-yet adult' view of youth culture?

Challenges to the 'not-yet-adult' cultural model

One challenge to this model can be observed in the way that Ned used social language to enact his identity in relation to Kevin. Rather than enact a subordinate position for himself in the conversation about *Goodie MOb*, Ned demonstrated in his initial e-mail to Kevin that he knew certain things that had to do with his particular situation and surroundings. He appeared to impress Kevin with his knowledge of the characteristics of socially-conscious rap, and later, with his choice of recommended Web sites on the *Goodie MOb* group. Early on, in an unsolicited e-mail sent just to me, Kevin corroborated my impression that Ned had presented himself well. In Kevin's words, 'To have a person [Ned's] age be able to recognize the social relevance of a group like *Goodie MOb* shows that this young person has developed some very needed skills'.

A second challenge to the cultural model that views youth as incomplete adults was noted in the way that both Ned and Kevin accorded relatively 'equal' status to each other's e-mailed contributions. For example, Ned appreciated the personalized 'behind-the-scenes' story of the *Goodie MOb* group, and Kevin appreciated Ned's recommended Web sites. Similarly, Ned appeared to have no qualms about contrasting C-loe's ability to rap with T-Mo's, and Kevin seemed not to be offended by Ned's assessment. In sum, neither participant appeared to pull rank, so to speak, although it was evident from the sheer length of Kevin's e-mails that he dominated the conversation in terms of information shared.

A third challenge to the 'not-yet-adult' view of youth culture can be seen in the way Ned and Kevin enacted their identities as 'student' and 'teacher' in relation to one another. Unlike what the 'not-yet-adult' cultural model would predict, the two participants did not appear to let their age differences stand in the way of their shared interest in (and willingness to comment on) the *Goodie MOb*. Although Ned appeared to be the 'needy' one in that he initially requested Kevin's help on the research project, it could be argued that to some degree, at least, Kevin was also needy: that is, he needed to share the story of his younger brother's death. Evidence that this could have been the case can be seen in Kevin's explicitly stated appreciation of Ned's steadfastness in tracking down who Brandon Williams was (and perhaps not so coincidentally, in his assigning Ned the task of finding out who received a highly treasured 'shot-out' from the *Goodie MOb*). Then, too, both Ned and Kevin expressed a desire to keep in contact once the study had ended.

Not there yet

Lest it be said that too much fuss is being made concerning possible challenges to the 'not-yet-adult' cultural model, I do want to acknowledge that Ned's positioning himself as subordinated reader/being in my presence during our face-to-face discussion of 'Cell Therapy' is not inconsequential. In that particular situation (and when given no opportunity to negotiate his way out of it), Ned resorted to 'doing adolescence' in a Discourse that is quite congruent with an age-sensitive, youth-as-subculture model. Perhaps the lesson to be learned from this is that if models of youth culture are to change, much work needs to be done in the area of situated meanings, especially in relation to comprehending texts of all kinds (print, digital, symbolic, etc.). For whether one's goal is to analyze a piece of data seemingly so small and insignificant as Ned's decision to add AKA = MAN after his name, or to tackle much larger issues, such as spatializing literacy research and practice (Leander & Sheehy, 2004), as a field we cannot ignore the power of situated meanings (negotiated or otherwise) to trigger specific cultural models of youth and their literacies.

That such models will differ for preschool children's engagement in home-based digital literacy practices (Marsh, this volume) and Ned's online discussions with Kevin in an after-school media club is inevitable. However, I would submit that how social language is used in these contexts to situate a young person's identity in relation to an adult's is not that dissimilar. Nor are the Discourses at work in the chapters by Stein and Slonimsky, and Janks and Comber (this volume) all that different from those operating in the present chapter. For while it might seem at first glance that primary-grade youngsters and their parents/teachers, working continents apart on school-related reading projects, provide quite a contrast to the after-school media club in which Ned was free to pursue his interest in a socially conscious rap group, the actual ways in which both younger and older people interacted to produce certain socially situated identities shared much in common. So much so, in fact, that in a few contexts it was difficult to separate student from teacher, young person from adult.

References

Alvermann, D.E. (ed.) (2002) *Adolescents and Literacies in a Digital World.* New York: Peter Lang.

Alvermann, D.E., Hagood, M.C., Heron, A., Hughes, P., Williams, K. and Yoon, J. (2002) After-school media clubs for struggling adolescent readers: A study of youth's critical awareness. Final report submitted to the Spencer Foundation's Major Grants Program.

Amit-Talai, V. and Wulff, H. (eds) (1995) *Youth Cultures: A Cross-Cultural Perspective.* New York: Routledge.

Appleman, D. (2001, April) Unintended betrayal: Dilemmas of representation and power in research with youth. Paper presented at the meeting of the American Educational Research Association, Seattle, WA.

Chandler-Olcott, K. and Mahar, D. (2003) "Tech-savviness" meets multiliteracies: Exploring adolescent girls' technology-mediated literacy practices. *Reading Research Quarterly* 38, 356–85.

Coleman, J.S. (1961) *The Adolescent Society.* New York: Free Press.

Forcey, L.R. and Harris, I.M. (eds) (1999) *Peacebuilding for Adolescents: Strategies for Educators and Community Leaders.* New York: Peter Lang.

Foucault, M. (1988) Technologies of the self. In L.H. Martin, H. Gutman and P.H. Hutton (eds) *Technologies of the Self: A Seminar with Michel Foucault* (pp. 16–49). Amherst: University of Massachusetts Press.

Gee, J.P. (1996) *Social Linguistics and Literacies: Ideology in Discourses* (2nd edn). London: Taylor & Francis.

Gee, J.P. (1999) *An Introduction to Discourse Analysis: Theory and Methods.* London: Routledge.

Gee, J.P. (2004) Discourse analysis: What makes it critical? In R. Rogers (ed.) *An Introduction to Critical Discourse Analysis in Education* (pp. 19–50). Mahwah, NJ: Lawrence Erlbaum.

Guzzetti, B.J. and Gamboa, M. (2004) Zines for social justice: Adolescent girls writing on their own. *Reading Research Quarterly* 39, 408–36.

Hagood, M.C. (2000) New times, new millennium, new literacies. *Reading Research and Instruction* 39, 311–28.

Hall, S. and Jefferson, T. (1976) *Resistance Through Rituals.* London: Hutchinson.

Hutchins, E. (1995) *Cognition in the Wild.* Cambridge, MA: MIT Press.

Lankshear, C. and Knobel, M. (2003) *New Literacies: Changing Knowledge and Classroom Learning.* Buckingham, UK: Open University Press.

Leander, K.M. and Sheehy, M. (eds) (2004) *Spatializing Literacy Research and Practice.* New York: Peter Lang.

Lesko, N. (2001) *Act your Age! A Cultural Construction of Adolescence.* London: Routledge.

Moje, E.B. (2000) "To be part of the story": The literacy practices of gangsta adolescents. *Teachers College Record* 102, 651–90.

Morgan, W. (1997) *Critical Literacy in the Classroom.* London: Routledge.

Parsons, T. (1942/1964) *Essays in Sociological Theory.* Chicago: Free Press.

Sefton-Green, J. (ed.) (1998) *Digital Diversions: Youth Culture in the Age of Multimedia* (pp. 1–20). London: University College London Press.

Shore, B. (1996) *Culture in Mind: Cognition, Culture, and the Problem of Meaning.* New York: Oxford University Press.

Tait, G. (2000) *Youth, Sex, and Government.* New York: Peter Lang.

Vadeboncoeur, J.A. and Stevens, L.P. (eds) (2005) *Re/constructing "The Adolescent": Sign, Symbol, and Body.* New York: Peter Lang.

Chapter 3

Escaping to the Borderlands: An Exploration of the Internet as a Cultural Space for Teenaged Wiccan Girls

JULIA DAVIES

Introduction

In this chapter I use teenaged Wiccan Websites as a case study to help explore the concept of online space. The discussion is based on the premise that spatiality is of significance to literacy researchers since, as the New Literacy Studies (Barton & Hamilton, 1998; Street, 1995), has illustrated, context is a constituent of literacy events and practices. 'Literacy is primarily something people do; it is an activity, located in the space between thought and text', argue Barton and Hamilton (1998: 3), emphasising the social nature of that process, as being 'located in the interaction between people'. The New Literacy Studies have emphasised that literacy practices and events are all situated, that is, that context is meaningful and influential on all literacy events. Moreover, there is a sense in which not only are discursive practices *located* in space, but also that they *produce* space. As Sheehy and Leander (2004) argue, 'space is a product and process of social relations. Space is not static ... Space as a noun, must be reconceived as an active, relational verb' (Sheehy & Leander, 2004: 1). These ideas, of the relationship between text, literacy practices, social processes and spatiality, are ones I wish to explore in this chapter and have also considered elsewhere (Davies, 2005, forthcoming). This chapter considers a particular on-line community and uses Foucault's notion 'Of Other Spaces' (1986) to explore the space created through teenagers' on-line literacy practices.

The work represented here involved a two-year longitudinal analysis of a number of thematically connected Websites. I used an ethnographic style to collect the data (Green & Bloome, 1997), having a careful regard for cultural and social formations of the sites. My analysis is multimodal (Kress & van Leeuwen, 2001), and follows a process which Barton and Hamilton (1998: 69) have characterised as 'cycling' from data to theory, allowing theories to emerge from the research. The ways in which individuals interact with others online, the multimodal affordances of the Web, the topics being dealt with, the identities presented, as well as the literacy events themselves, constitute the online space. The multimodal affordances were seen to be social as well as educational, allowing the scope for interactants to connect with like minded others; to feel the camaraderie of shared interests; to identify and solve problems in collaboration, and to experiment with ideas and ways of communicating.

In considering the cultural space of the Internet environment, as part of an overall determination to understand digital literacy practices, I briefly describe how I have drawn on the theoretical contexts of Communities of Practice (Lave & Wenger, 1991) and Affinity Spaces (Gee, 2004). However, I more fully illustrate the usefulness of Foucault's conceptualisation 'Of Other Spaces' (Foucault, 1986) in relation to online space. Mitchell and Reid-Walsh (2002) highlight the usefulness of Foucault's concept of 'heterotopias' as described in 'Of Other Spaces' (1986), in relation to girls' homepages, and I am particularly indebted to their work for demonstrating the potential of Foucault's concept in relation to this field.

Wiccan Cyberspace

The screenshot shown in Figure 3.1, is of a teenager's homepage from a growing community of sites adopting a Wiccan cultural discourse. Such sites tend to be bonded within an affinity space defined through their professed values of caring for others, the environment, and an affiliation with age-old traditions and rituals. The page shown, taken from a now obsolete site, featured a scrolling text and eerie music in the background. The music remained in the background across all the site's pages providing a common theme or thread, so that it continually evoked nuances from this initial message and linked the pages in a manner which unified the disparate parts of the site. Its powerful opening used the conventions of a scrolling film, evocative of a Star Wars movie, setting a powerful context for a site using the cultural discourses of witchcraft. Like many of its kind, 'The Silver Circle' site described the Wiccan way of life and gave an online diary version of the author's daily activities. It provided a social history of witchcraft; a message board; a discussion

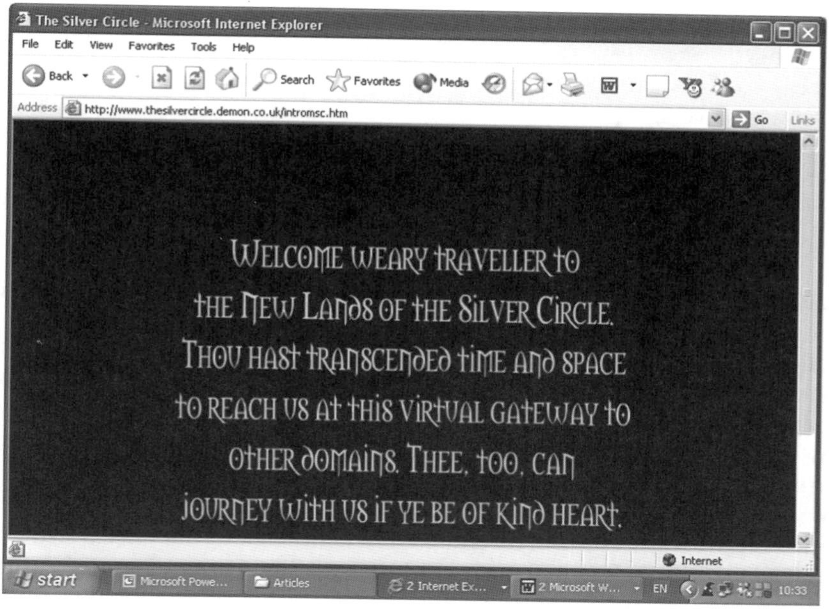

Figure 3.1 www.thesilvercircle.demon.co.uk, accessed September 2003

forum and links to other Wiccan teen sites. When it was live, the site was highly interactive, frequently visited, and often cited by others within the community. There was a sense of activity within the site, as well as references to spaces beyond its boundaries, both online and offline, thus giving a strong sense of community and an affinity with like-minded others. The site thus acted as a kind of repository of knowledge, supplied by the author as well as receiving contributions from other participants in the Wiccan cultural discourse community.

The dramatic prose illustrated above, develops the metaphor of place so often associated with the Internet, mentioning 'domains', a 'gateway' and 'new lands'. Sheehy and Leander (2004) point out the number of spatial metaphors which have been used to describe aspects of the Internet, such as 'chatroom', 'home pages' and 'cafes'. The metaphor extends to the readers of Websites, with words such as 'guests', 'lurkers', 'surfers', 'visitors' and as above, 'travellers', reinforcing a sense of bodily presence within a space. As Lakoff and Johnson (1975) point out, 'the metaphors we live by' are strongly influential in the way we perceive our world, and these metaphors here, reinforce the conceptualisation of the Internet as reified, as social venues even, albeit in some nebulous domain. Fairclough explains,

> . . . when we signify things through one metaphor rather than another, we are constructing our reality one way rather than another. Metaphors structure the way we think and the way we act, and our systems of knowledge and belief, in a pervasive and fundamental way. (Fairclough, 1995: 195)

Nevertheless, while the metaphors in The Silver Circle's homepage illustrated above draw on our understandings of life in so-called 'meatspace', or life 'offline', they seem at the same time to endorse an 'other world' concept. Both ideas reside as a duality; the direct address, 'Welcome weary traveller', works to implicate the reader of the PC screen in an ongoing drama, giving them a specific role, characterised through this form of address. The term 'gateway' drawn from real world architecture, commonly used on the Internet, nevertheless fits the notion of mysticism which is part of the cultural discourse of witchcraft and the Wiccan way of life. The text also refers to the idea of transcending time and space. In this way, this particular teen author reflects a number of spatial themes in her language; the text is powerful, and if her 'travellers' move further through the site, they participate in a drama giving credibility to the authorial construction of a particular kind of space.

The discourses of this site exemplify the way Internet-based texts and the spatiality they produce, can unsettle the binaries of online and offline 'worlds'. The language directs the reader to a specific role, and metaphors of space abound, with such lexicon as 'land', 'gateway', 'traveller' and 'domains' for example. A virtual territory is delineated, but it is not clear where this site begins and ends, since the online links take one to a new part of cyberspace, but which is connected through its link and its discourses with this site (and vice versa). Moreover, the delineation, (through a diary) of a life offline may well be carefully constructed, or at least carefully edited, to appear coherent with espoused Wiccan values and life on-line. It is not clear where, or indeed whether, the boundaries of the online Wiccan cultural discourse begins or ends and it is not clear what the relationship is between the Web writer's online and offline world. The binaries of online and offline are thus destabilised.

The new social and literacy practices which constitute much online activity, afford teenagers opportunities, as Knobel and Lankshear (this volume) argue, to engage in powerful writing. I would also argue, that this powerful writing, partly derives its potency from the immediacy of publication as well as from the 'social alliances' (Blood, 2002: x) that are made in so many online liaisons.

Situated Social Learning

Our sense of space and of spaces is being redefined through new social practices and new technologies, (Ito & Daisuke, 2004). Ito and Daisuke describe the ways in which Japanese teens keep in almost constant mobile phone contact with their close peer group. Meanwhile the Internet allows an even more nomadic existence (Davies, 2005, forthcoming), so that youngsters can interact both within and beyond their immediate peer group, finding newcomers with whom to inhabit an 'affinity space' (Gee, 2004). In affinity spaces, individuals take on different roles within different groups according to their relative expertise and experience within the collective. Like Lave and Wenger (1991), in their description of Communities of Practice, Gee emphasises the importance of social learning within the group. Both theories describe a social model of learning where collaboration, situatedness, or spatiality, are highlighted, within which I also contextualise my work. Lave and Wenger's notion of Communities of Practice stresses the notion of apprenticeship to communities, whereby individuals gradually become enculturated into the ways of a particular group, moving from peripheral to central positions. Wenger talks of a 'sustained pursuit in a shared exercise' (1998: 45) emphasising collectivity overall. I have found it useful to draw from Lave and Wengers' ideas about Communities of Practice which enculturate newcomers, allowing them to join a group through participation. I have also seen how a shared history frequently develops in online groups, sometimes becoming a repository of knowledge from which members draw. Communities of Practice 'evolve as shared histories of learning' (Wenger 1998: 87). As can be seen from this model, the way the apprenticeship works, is that cultural and social values are acquired alongside new skills over a period of time and through collaborative activities. Lave and Wenger describe a process of enculturation where learners are not formally instructed but learn through being part of a group where learning is managed through participation in social formations and practices.

Gee's concept differs somewhat from Lave and Wenger's, seeing affinity spaces as more flexible and open than Communities of Practice, with individuals in possession of more agency and a complex range of ways through which different types of knowledge are acquired. Certainly Gee's recent work looking at the development of digital literacy skills, has focused greatly on digital game playing (Gee, 2003) and is thus transferable to looking at a range of online domains in its more flexible conceptualisation of participants and its interrogation of the term 'community'. Meanwhile 'The Silver Circle' described above, could support an online Community of Practice, and had produced its own affinity space. It had a role in helping individuals to learn, but also provided gateways, or portals through which participants could bring new knowledge to the site. Knowledge, collaboration and community were all important elements within the affinity space I looked at.

Collaborative play has long been established as a process enabling learning. I have discussed elsewhere, ways in which the Internet provides a platform for teenage play, rather like a cyber bedroom, especially for those who may not be allowed to meet on the street or in the homes of others (Davies, 2004) and shown ways in which girls can play out resistant discourses in such spaces without having to leave the home. 'The graphics and images on girls' homepages often resemble or represent the kinds of material culture stored in their bedrooms', explain Mitchell and Reid-Walsh (2002: 153), and these become part of the text through which new discourses are created online. There is a blurring of traditional notions of space here, where the dualisms of outside and inside, or offline and online, are challenged. Similarly, Valentine *et al.* found,

> ... adult moral panics appear to assume a binary distinction between the on-line and off-line worlds, children implicitly recognise that these spaces are not separate but are mutually constituted ... children who use Internet-connected PCs are not socially isolated indoor children, but rather that they use on-line spaces to develop their off-line hobbies, use of space and friendships. (Valentine *et al.*, 2000: 170)

As I shall show below, the online and offline worlds of many young people are seamlessly connected; the Internet is located in a space both within, and without, the 'real world'. Whilst in cyberspace, aspects of lives, and pictures of artifacts, become part of a new digital, textual landscape and gain new meanings within those texts, at the same time the boundaries between this textual space and others are fluid. Foucault's work is useful in elucidating this complexity. In the next section I clarify the research field, before moving to a description of heterotopias.

The Research Focus: The Magic Web

I focus on teenaged girls' sites which are set within the cultural discourses of Wiccan beliefs. This choice of study responds to the burgeoning interest, amongst some teenagers, mostly girls, in experimenting with these discourses, but looking in particular at their use of the Internet rather than having a focus on content. This interest, although being tied up with popular culture (Buffy the Vampire Slayer; Charmed), is nevertheless not quite mainstream and enjoys a kind of 'alternative' branding. In my analyses, I identify how the teenagers make connections and develop collaborative knowledge bases, through the multimodal affordances of the Internet and the discourses of Wiccan beliefs.

Heterotopias

Foucault's concept states that heterotopias are real places, but he also emphasises they are 'countersites', 'placeless places', existing outside of other spaces (Foucault, 1986: 23). Using mirrors as examples, he explains heterotopias are 'virtual spaces' where 'I see myself where I am not' (Foucault, 1986: 23). Similarly the elusive properties of cyberspace allow it to straddle borders of the public and private, the past and present – a challenge to such binaries.

Foucault discussed this concept of heterotopias in his 1967 paper, 'Des espaces autres' long before the Internet became so pervasive in everyday lives; yet the concept illuminates the spatial qualities of the Internet, its contradictions and functions. 'Of Other Spaces' (1986), as the work was later published, described a heterotopia as being governed by six principles, given below.

First, Foucault argued, all cultures contain heterotopias; their forms may be varied, but share commonalities. In the past, heterotopias may have been populated by individuals in crisis – perhaps adolescents, or the elderly. Nowadays, argued Foucault, crisis heterotopias have been superseded by heterotopias of deviation, such as rest homes or psychiatric hospitals. In the context of this study, looking at sites expressing Wiccan cultural discourses, I interpret the space as a heterotopia of deviation, where cyberspace facilitates meetings of teens beyond the family gaze, with the potential to host expressions of feelings or experiences which may be unacceptable elsewhere (Mitra & Watts, 2002; Turkle, 1996). Moreover, in the creation of a new community, with specific beliefs, words and rules, the space in this sense can be viewed as different to, deviant from, the other culture in some way. Moreover, whilst individuals may respond to each other as if they were there bodily (e.g. through avatars, emoticons or linguistic expressions of bodily movements), they are not in fact 'present'. In this sense, the space is deviant.

Secondly, Foucault describes heterotopias as periodically changing their relationship to society; he exemplifies cemeteries, once geographically and socially central, but later spatially and functionally peripheral, reflecting society's changing attitude to death. Similarly, the Internet has functionally transformed; originally designed for privileged individuals to communicate about war, it is contemporaneously and mundanely used for capitalist exchange, socialising and much more. It is accessible to ordinary people, even being used to subvert hegemonic notions (Rheingold, 2003) which, ironically, it was originally designed to protect and sustain. Moreover, the Web changes its function for users according to their task; thus at times it can be used as a place where confidences are disclosed (as in online diaries), but also where the most public of campaigning notices can be placed, such as petitions, or calls to political action.

Thirdly, a single real space can accommodate other spaces normally incompatible; Foucault describes the way theatres host a series of diverse, small worlds or episodes. The Internet provides a range of opportunities for a range of communities; it serves multifarious purposes for all kinds of people. The Internet accommodates sites which contradict each other's content; some sites promote the Wiccan religion, while others might defame witchcraft, for example. Moreover, on a Website, texts can be contained within texts, so that, for example, a link can allow a video clip to become part of a text, but could remain simply as an unopened link. A link can take the reader to a new site, or to a picture. Thus there are 'worlds within worlds', multiple routes and multiple openings. Internet users can commentate on other sites, perhaps leaving hyper links themselves. They can provide intertextual references and even provide links to each other. Several sites can be visited simultaneously through different windows within the same screen. Inconsistencies can co-exist within the discourses across the various windows, or even within the domains of single sites.

Heterotopias, Foucault fourthly argues, are linked to particular slices of time, seeming to enclose it, as in museums, where epochs co-exist. Accumulating time through displayed artifacts, the museum embraces centuries within the present, as it were. Conversely heterotopias can be temporal, like a funfair, which may come and go. I would argue the virtual world embraces both temporal *and* cumulative aspects of the fourth principal. Websites have the capacity to act as records of information, archiving obsolete discussions or press releases, whilst activities such as Instant Messaging System interactions or role play simulations, generate texts which disappear without trace once the interaction ends. Additionally, websites can disappear from the Internet – making reports of research such as this, often difficult to substantiate or validate. Information can be made temporarily or permanently available.

Fifthly, heterotopias 'presuppose a system of opening and closing that both isolates them and makes them penetrable' (Foucault, 1986: 26). Perhaps the metaphor of permeable borders would work well here; life online allows continual movement to and fro, and surfers can occupy, or be interacting in, a number of spaces at once by keeping a range of 'windows' open. Since the borders of sites are permeable, 'members' can stray and return. Yet at the same time, these are restricted access spaces; only particular individuals can enter, as in prisons, barracks or asylums. Otherwise, Foucault explains, 'the individual has to submit to rites and purifications' (ibid) in order to enter. Similarly, whilst theoretically anyone can use the Internet, access is exclusive to those who can pay for the equipment, are part of a culture where access may be provided, e.g. a school. Equipment is frequently password protected and sites within the Internet may be restricted again; conversely however, online diaries and other 'private' texts are available for public scrutiny.

Foucault's last heterotopic principle has two manifestations; being either a heterotopia of illusion, or of compensation. In the former, whilst lacking authenticity, involving itself in some sort of mimicry, the space reveals something about other spaces, perhaps making them seem less credible. Foucault gives the example of brothels, where activities within them enlighten understandings of other institutions. The heterotopia of compensation however, presents itself as idealised; it attempts a perfect form of a lifestyle, such as in Puritan societies or Jesuit colonies. While some argue that the Internet world is a real world (Rheingold, 2003), others see it as a fantasy domain which can provide real insights into the way we should live (Turkle, 1996) and microcosmic cyber communities are used in fantasy role plays and so on. In this next section, I specifically detail the content of the teenaged Wiccan Websites with respect to the notion of heterotopias.

Inside the Web Pages

The heterotopic constituents of the Internet, with its fragile boundaries, its uncertain positionality and its ability to metamorphose from confession box to public platform, render it apt for those exploring ways of being. These characteristics are accounted for by Foucault's first, second and fifth principles, with the Web as a space where deviations can be enacted and discussed; where the function of the Internet is flexible; where participants can acquire a strong sense of belonging through the use of ritualised language and codes of behaviour, a place where membership is restricted to those prepared to display these behaviours. I begin by exemplifying these areas of Foucault's concept.

Foucault talked about heterotopias as if they were mirrors, where 'I see myself where I am not'. Home pages in particular work as if they were fairground mirrors where the impressions given are crafted with care; biographical details are selected, and audiences are addressed in a strange mix of public/confidential tones. In her home page, the author of the text below provides an attractive photograph adjacent to her words. It looks like the editorial page of a teen magazine. The photograph is carefully posed, with a smile straight to camera and presents a conventionally attractive image of western female beauty. Meanwhile, the style of the text reflects the social awkwardness felt by the author and the whole piece combines to illustrate the fuzziness of the public/private boundaries of the Internet. This teenager's use of the discourses of a teenaged girl, of a Wiccan follower, of a host to the site as well as a self consciously overweight person, are all somewhat discontinuous and contradictory allowing the reader to see the 'chinks' in all these roles. Like the teenagers Alvermann (this volume) describes she is not comfortable within such predefined teenage discourses and here seems to struggle:

> I want to start off by saying thank you. Every visitor means a lot to us. As most of you know being a teenager is difficult, but being a teenager following a religion that nobody understands is even more difficult. With one another to talk to I hope that not only do we make our own lives easier but let the general public become aware of our beliefs . . .
>
> . . . I'm slightly overweight but I am working on that problem! . . . I'm just a nice person and usually make "friends" pretty easy . . . Some don't always turn out to really be friends of mine though. (http://magikalteen.diaryland.com)

The author moves between two voices, wavering between the formal, 'I want to start off by' and 'means a lot to us', moving into the colloquial, 'just a', 'pretty easy', and the use of exclamation marks indicating light-heartedness. She seems unsure as to what distance she wants to keep her audience, moving from orator to confiding peer. The semantics focus on the difficulties in teenagers' lives and her references to weight and friendship problems illustrate this. This text shows how the Internet provides a means to distribute one's voice, whilst also providing a sense of closed privacy. This writer appears to be addressing those who are NOT about to betray her as others have, and she assumes understanding, 'as most of you know'. The unevenness in her style and inconsistency in her positionality mark out the insecurities she articulates about her life generally. She is unsure about herself and her friends and seeks through this homepage, to connect with similar others, using the inclusive 'we' in 'we make our own lives easier' to emphasise their communal opposition to some notion of 'the others'. The use of the inclusive pronoun simultaneously defines outsiders. The unsettling of binaries within the space is reflected through this girl's style. Moreover she sees the space as a refuge for what she regards as her non-conformist (deviant) self; someone with a weight problem and few friends.

Ritual language provides the community with identity and territory markers; to use the language betrays insider knowledge. The frequently used greeting 'Merry Meet' and the parting salutation 'Blessed Be' are part of a phatic communication system, which in non-Wiccan situations would just be formed as 'Hi', or 'hello' and 'goodbye' for example. Here the chosen terms denote membership of the community and help define the affinity space. They frame the content of the exchanges in ritualised greetings so that any content is imbued with Wiccan connotations. The Internet can be a space to evade parental gaze and in one discussion group, I found a contribution which mentioned, 'but I am not allowed to light candles in my bedroom, which is not great for a practicing witch' (http://www.the-cauldronnet/viewtopic/). The strange way in which so many of these interactants see the Internet as both an intimate area for exchange, as well as a place for public display, challenges our perceptions of these boundaries. Yet it is all these qualities which are exploited here, so that the space allows contact with others, presenting specific aspects of their identity (whether earnest or playful), whilst also hiding aspects of their identity if they wish.

Often the discourses of the sites are traditional, reflecting the heritage of a long extant Wiccan community; embracing past centuries within the present.

> So ever mind the Rule of Three.
> Follow this with mind and heart.
> Merry ye meet and merry ye part. (WiccanTeen/wiccanre.msnw, accessed March 2005)

As with Foucault's fourth principle, it brings with it a history, which links these youngsters not just to unseen others across space, but also across time. This Wiccan code is ubiquitous; its repetition and spiritual status define it as an incantation. Also referred to is the 'Rule of Three' ('whatever you cast out comes back to thee, so ever mind the rule of three') or 'The Craft' – terms which describe in a short hand way the binding value systems and practices of the community. This is a way in which the community remains closed to outsiders but open to those who wish to follow the code; the fifth heterotopic principle.

Online diaries, like message board interaction, allow a common, though asynchronic experience and, there is the strange illusion of the present. There is a replication of real time, with the linguistic style simulating present time action. Usually these are colloquial and leave many typographical errors uncorrected. This gives a sense of immediacy, of hurriedness, of teeming activity in 'real space'. There is thus the appearance of synchronicity, of synchronic communication, while in fact these texts are archived and non-synchronic. In this way online teenagers can be experimental with time, can play with aspects of their identity, not only presenting themselves to others in a particular way, but also able to view themselves in specific ways too.

> Well, back to school and year 10. No coursework as yet, so im pleased about that:) Its kinda cool because most of the lessons are ones i chose, although i picked music and regretted it within the first week but art was really full up so i cant swap and now i am been forced to sing a solo (like, by myself) in this stupid school concert INFRONT OF PEOPLE. she also said if i rang in ill on the night she would fail me for the assignment, so im pretty much screwed in that department. ... Im planning a samhain ritual, wish there were more pagans in lincolnshire. :(If there are please let me know! BB. (bluemoon/october.html, accessed October 2003)

Other research confirms, as here, the constant reporting of mundane as well as key events which are not merely an exchange of information; the act of repetitive communication can 'open another world of experience beside, or instead of, the one inhabited at the moment' (Mäenpäa, 2001, cited by Rheingold, 2003: 16). Teenagers use technology to share their lives, to demonstrate that they are 'living in the same rhythm or wave with one's closest friends' (Mäenpäa, 2001, cited by Rheingold, 2003: 16). This piece moves across a series of the selves which make up aspects of this girl's life. The life is represented through the pages of her diary, but there is also a sense of her living her life on the diary, looking for online contacts to meet offline. She moves through a range of discourses, some of which seem incompatible – such as the 'Samhain ritual' and her inability to perform solo 'INFRONT OF PEOPLE'. The hetereotopia here supports the incompatible discourses; the teenager has created a space where she can express frustrations, taken from a kind of 'backstage talk' frame, yet knowing she has found an audience.

The Internet as an Empowering Arena

The Internet allows youngsters to remain physically within the home yet reside with friends experimenting with a sense of independence. It is in this kind of arena where the young can challenge others' positioning of them as children; they can use the 'cloak' of the Internet to undermine age as a determining factor. The qualities of heterotopia provide a comfortable borderland which teenagers can escape to; a place joined to, but separate from the real world, with windows through which they can even see themselves.

It is clear that online activities provide a forum for many teenagers to express their anxieties to each other and that whilst the public nature of the Web means that these exchanges have many witnesses, nevertheless it is possible for users to create for themselves a comfortable space, which is both part of, but separate from 'reality'. I have argued that online practices do not occur in a clear and separate space, away from 'offline' activities, but that this is a false dichotomy. The Internet unsettles straightforward definitions of spatiality, and it is partly this, which makes Internet literacy practices exciting and unique. There is a dynamic in process, where, argue Leander and Sheehy (2004: 1) as cited above, space becomes a 'relational verb'. This is where multimodal digital literacy practices create a sense of space for those who are involved in those activities and which allow users to benefit from both drawing on their 'offline experiences' and to bring those into their 'online' activities. Often operating from within communities, I have a sense of learners operating in co-constructed 'other' spaces and benefiting from these interactions.

References

Barton, D. and Hamilton, M. (1998) *Local Literacies: Reading and Writing in One Community.* London: Routledge.

Blood, R. (2002) *We've Got Blog: How Weblogs are Changing Culture.* Cambridge, MA: Perseus Publishing.

Bluemoon (2006) on WWW at http://www.dreamwater.net/bluemoon/october.html. Accessed October 2003.

Davies, J. (2004) Negotiating femininities on-line. *Gender and Education* 16 (1), 35–49.

Davies, J. (2005 forthcoming) Nomads and tribes: On line meaning-making and the development of New Literacies. In J. Marsh and E. Millard (eds) *Popular Literacies, Childhood and Schooling*. London: Routledge/Falmer.
Fairclough, N. (1995) *Critical Discourse Analysis*. London: Longman.
Foucault, M. (1986) Of other spaces. In *Diacritics* (J. Miskowiec, trans.). Spring: 22–27.
Gee, J.P. (2003) *What Video Games have to Teach us about Learning and Literacy*. New York: Palgrave Macmillan.
Gee, J.P. (2004) *Situated Language and Learning: A Critique of Traditional Schooling*. London: Routledge.
Green, J. and Bloome, D. (1997) Ethnography and ethnographers of and in education: A situated perspective. In J. Flood, S. Heath and D. Lapp (eds) *A Handbook of Research on Teaching Literacy Through the Communicative and Visual Arts* (pp. 181–202). New York: Simon and Shuster Macmillan.
Ito, M. and Daisuke, O. (2004) Intimate connections: Contextualising Japanese youth and mobile messaging. In R. Harper, L. Palen and A. Taylor (eds) *Inside the Text: Social Perspectives on SMS in the Mobile Age*. On WWW at http://www.itofisher.-com/mito/archives/itookabe.texting.pdf. Accessed November 2004.
Kress, G. and van Leeuven, T. (2001) *Multimodal Discourse: The Modes and Media of Contemporary Communication*. London: Arnold; co-published in the United States of America by Oxford University Press Inc., New York.
Lakoff, R. and Johnson, M. (1975) *Metaphors We Live By*. Chicago: University of Chicago Press.
Lave, J. and Wenger, E. (1991) *Situated Learning*. Cambridge: Cambridge University Press.
Leander, K. and Sheehy, M. (eds) (2004) *Spatializing Literacy Research and Practice*. New York: Peter Lang.
Magikalteen.diaryland.com. On WWW at: http://magikalteen.diaryland.com. Accessed November 2003.
Mäenpäa, P. (2001) Mobile comunication as a way of urban life. In J. Gronow and A. Warde (eds) *Ordinary Consumption* (pp. 107–24). London: Routledge.
Mitchell, C. and Reid-Walsh, J. (2002) *Researching Children's Popular Culture: The Cultural Spaces of Childhood*. London: Routledge.
Mitra, A. and Watts, E. (2002) Theorizing cyberspace: The idea of voice applied to internet discourse. *New Media and Society* 14 (4), 479–98.
Rheingold, H. (2003) *Smartmobs: The Next Social Revolution*. Cambridge: Perseus Publishing.
Sheehy, M. and Leander, K. (2004) Introduction. In K. Leander and M. Sheehy (eds) *Spatialising Literacy Research and Practice* (pp. 1–14). New York: Peter Lang.
Street, B. (1995) *Social Literacies: Critical Approaches to Literacy in Education, Development and Ethnography*. London: Longman.
Thecauldronnet. On WWW at: http://www.thecauldronnet/viewtopic/. Accessed July 2004.
Thesilvercircle.demon.co.uk/. On WWW at: http://www.thesilvercircle.demon.co.uk/intromsc.htm. Accessed September 2003.
Turkle, S. (1996) Parallel lives: Working on identity in virtual space. In D. Grodin and L.R. Thomas (eds) *Constructing the Self in a Mediated World* (pp. 156–75). London: Sage.

Valentine, G., Holloway, S. and Ningham, N. (2000) Transforming cyberspace: Children's interventions in the new public sphere. In S. Holloway and G. Valentine (eds) *Children's Geographies: Playing, Living and Learning* (pp. 156–73). London: Routledge.

Wenger, E. (1998) *Communities of Practice.* Cambridge: Cambridge University Press.

Wiccanteen. On WWW at: http://www.groups.msn.com/wiccanteen/wiccanre.msnw. Accessed March 2005.

Chapter 4

Weblog Worlds and Constructions of Effective and Powerful Writing: Cross with Care, and Only Where Signs Permit

MICHELE KNOBEL AND COLIN LANKSHEAR

Introduction

Interest in the extent to which texts (and the larger practices in which they are embedded) can and do cross sites is by now quite well established within literacy studies. This is particularly true in relation to schooling, where a raft of concerns ranging from issues of equity to the current preoccupation with student (dis)engagement in classroom learning, have focused on the extent to which it is possible and proper to try to port elements of out of school cultures across to classroom learning in pursuit of expansive educational purposes and ends.

This chapter explores a single characteristically contemporary 'moment' in this ongoing narrative. It brings together the pedagogical aim of helping students become effective and powerful writers with the latest classroom appropriation from online environments – namely, the weblog. We begin with a brief overview of the emergence of weblogging as a cultural practice that has attained global proportions during the past five years. We next consider a thesis about power dynamics in the 'blogosphere' and how these dynamics are associated with different *forms* of blogging and varying constructions of *effective and powerful writing*. Three exemplars of highly effective and influential blogging that reflect our range of forms of blogging are briefly described and from these we derive some key features of effective/powerful blogging as practiced by 'experts'. The chapter concludes with a consideration of school blogging at an early stage in its evolution and considers the prospects of expert-like effective blogging 'crossing' to school practices.

Weblogs: A Short Overview

A weblog – or 'blog' for short – is most easily described as 'a website that is updated frequently, with new material posted at the top of the page' along with the date when it was posted (Blood, 2002: 12). In the early 1990s, blogs generally comprised webpage-based lists of annotated hyperlinks that the webpage builder found useful or interesting. These early weblog publishers – 'bloggers' – tended to be working or studying in the computer field and were comfortable with coding webpages and hyperlinks, and their blogs acted as internet content filters or thematic indices to internet content.

In 1999, however, two dotcom companies, Pitas.com and Blogger.com, made weblog publishing much more accessible for a much wider range of people by making freely available weblog templates and hosting services for anyone who wanted to create a blog. This made it relatively easy for Internet users who were not so familiar or comfortable with using hypertext markup language (HTML) codes or with the principles of effective webpage design to publish their own weblogs. Almost like a virtual Big Bang, the blogosphere exploded outwards seemingly overnight. One conservative estimate from 8 June 2004 cited more than 1.2 million *active* English language blogs operating worldwide, with a further 700,000 blogs in other languages (www.idlewords.com/crawler/crawl_report.pl). Other estimates are much higher.

Technorati.com, a blog index and search engine, claimed to be tracking almost 2.7 million blogs in June 2004, and over 4.65 million on 8 October 2004. LiveJournal.com, another popular free blog hosting service, cited almost 3.2 million accounts on its books alone in June 2004 and well over 4.7 million by 8 October 2004 (www.livejournal.com/stats.bml, accessed 8 June and 8 October 2004). In October 2004, LiveJournal was also registering over 19 thousand new posts each hour (which translates into over 300 new posts to LiveJournal blogs per minute).

The new generation of bloggers ushered in by Do-It-Yourself blogware services was much more diverse than the original blogging generation. Many began using weblogs as a medium more closely akin to regularly updated journals than indices of hyperlinks, and postings could document anything and everything from what the blogger had for lunch that day, to movie and music reviews, to highly personal introspection, through to the latest illustrations or projects completed by the blogger for offline texts, and the like. Many weblogs now are hybrids of both, or a mix of musings or anecdotes with embedded hyperlinks to related websites. Rebecca Blood, an early blog adopter, describes this new use of weblogs as being concerned with creating 'social alliances' (Blood, 2002: x). In other words, weblogs are largely interest-driven and intended to attract readers who have (or would like to have) similar, if not the same, interests and affinities.

Structure and appearance

There are no hard and fast rules for what a blog should look like. In general, however, there are a number of generic features that most blogs seem to share. Most blog front pages, for example, are divided into two main content columns (see Figure 4.1).

One column houses the weblog posts (referring to the right hand column of text in Figure 4.1), with each post ordered chronologically from the most recent to the least recent entry. Each blog post is automatically dated and entries are archived after a certain period (e.g. a few days, a week, a month). Blog posts can be accompanied by a number of reader-focused features in the form of a comments function where readers can

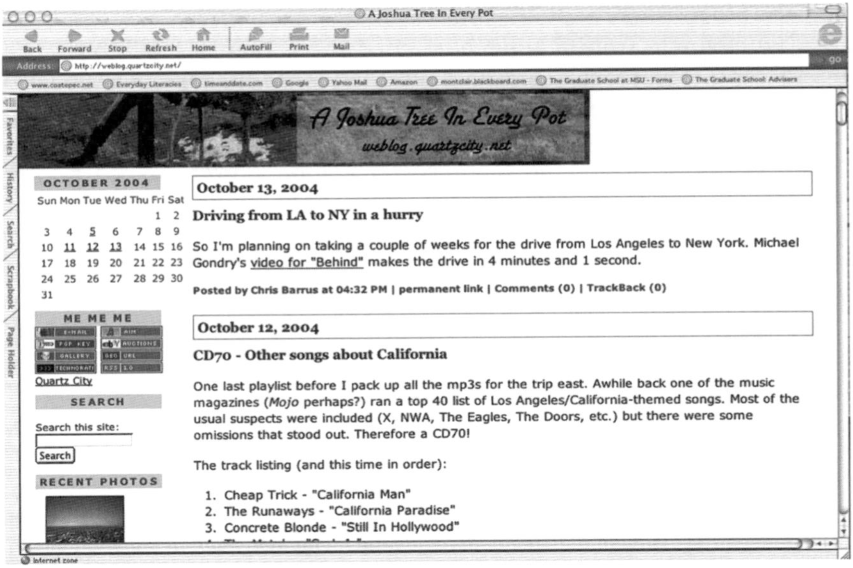

Figure 4.1 A typical blog (weblog.quartzcity.net)

comment on each post; a trackback service that enables readers to 'audit' the newsworthiness or popularity of a post by seeing which blogs have hyperlinked to it; and so on.

The second column plays more of a menu or index role on a blog. For example, this column often includes a calendar that can be used to access archives of previous posts on a given day. This column can also include hyperlinks to the blogger's contact details, their eBay auction page, a service where readers can donate money to the blogger, their instant messaging aliases, their online photo gallery, lists of music currently being listened to, their Amazon.com wishlist and the like, along with hyperlink lists of the blogger's favourite blogs and Websites.

Blog posts themselves are usually quite short – often no more than a few lines of text in length. In the early days of blogging, blog posts tended to be one of two kinds: posts that included hyperlinks to other Websites and those that did not. Recent technical developments across a range of blog hosting service providers mean that blog posts can now include images and voice files, with some blogs comprising solely pictures or mostly voice audio files (with many of the files sent directly to the blog from mobile phones) and little written text at all.

Typology

Blogging has evolved into diverse forms and serves a range of social purposes. Some of this diversity is captured in Figure 4.2 below, which offers a provisional typology of blogs.

Blogs and Powerful Writing

During the past three decades various ideas have been advanced in a range of contexts concerned with literacy in theory and in practice about the conditions under which people can read and write more or less *powerfully*. Within Latin America, variations around Paulo Freire's construction of literacy as 'reading the word and the world' within a praxis of transformation have been well known since the 1960s and, within some specific contexts, have been highly influential. Within North American settings concepts of 'critical literacy' and 'critical pedagogy' have had some influence, although the best established conceptions of effective writing have tended to be associated with approaches embedded in Rhetoric and Composition Studies as well as in versions of 'whole language' and 'process writing'. In Britain and Australasia, work on critical language awareness and initiatives based on appropriations of systemic functional linguistics have been prominent during the past 20 years. Blogs offer some interesting

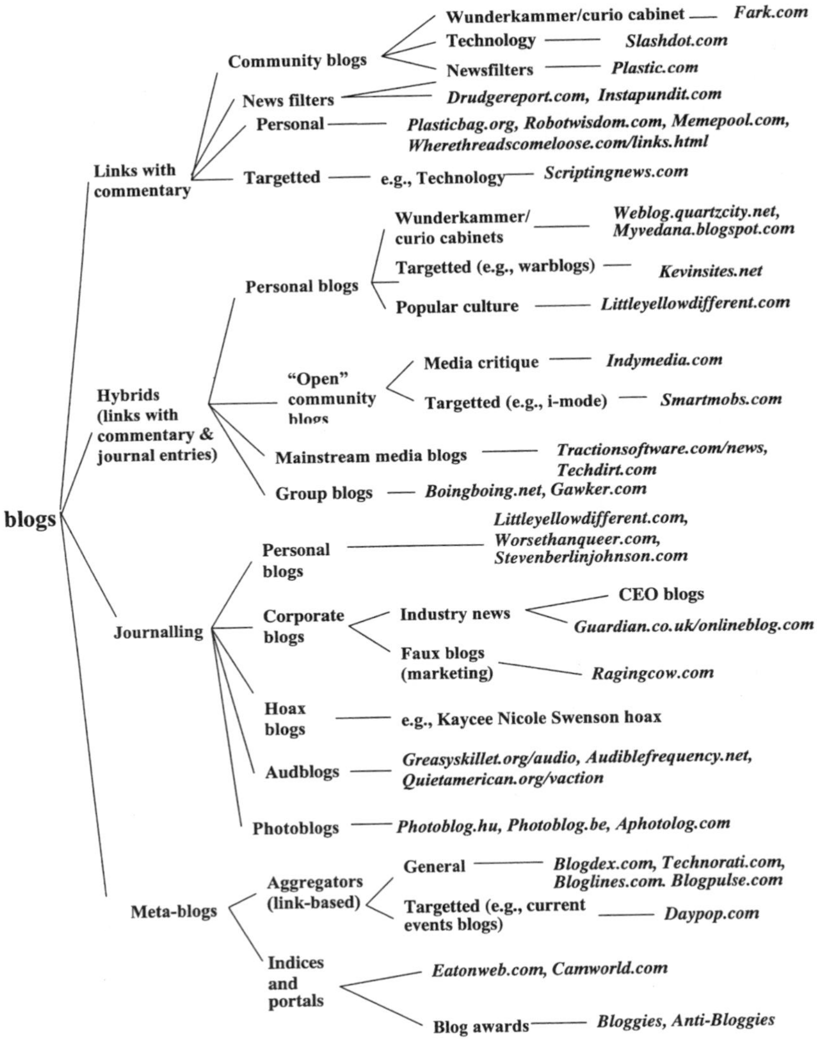

Figure 4.2

angles on questions about literacy in relation to power generally, and about the conditions under which practices of literacy might plausibly be spoken of as 'powerful' within the context of 'information' or 'knowledge' societies. This, of course, is a context where *potentially* our use of 'written' language (broadly conceived) can reach larger audiences than were imaginable just 10 years ago.

A recent paper by Clay Shirky (2003), drawing on original work by N.Z. Bear (2003) (www.myelin.co.nz/ecosystem), explores patterns of power distribution among weblogs and offers a line of explanation for the well known tendency in cyberspace for a relatively small number of sites to account for the great majority of viewer traffic or 'hits'. N.Z. Bear sampled more than 400 weblogs and arranged them in rank order according to the number of inbound links they have (based on the number of other weblogs that hyperlink to them). (Lists and counts of inbound links are available via aggregation services, like blogdex.com, popdex.com, daypop.com.)

The findings reported in the first quarter of 2003 indicated that from the population of the 433 blogs sampled, the two top ranked blogs on their own accounted for 5% of inbound links. As reflected in Figure 4.3, the

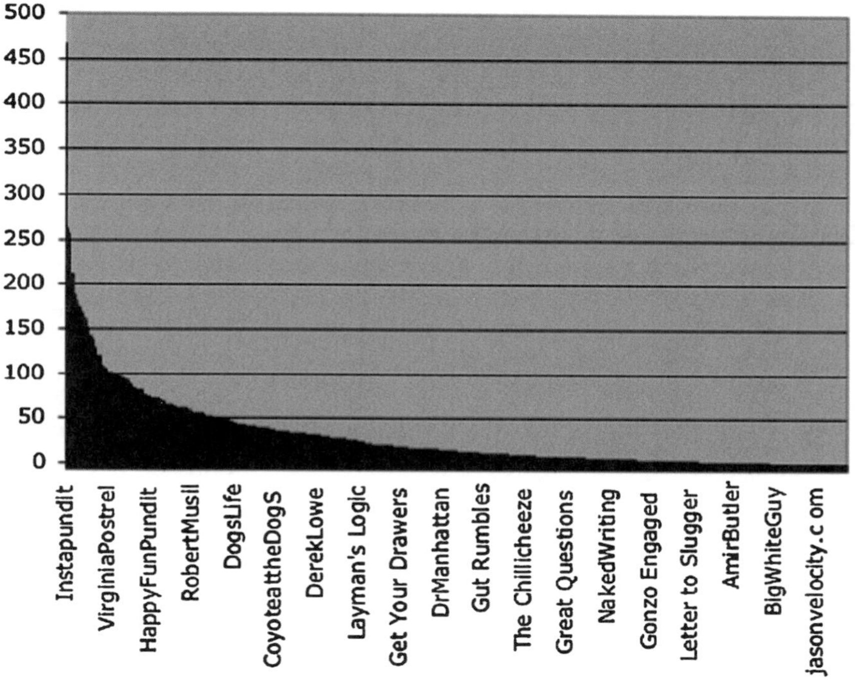

Figure 4.3 Weblogs and power law distribution (Shirky, 2003: 2)

top 12 blogs accounted for 20% of all inbound links, and the top 50 blogs (or just 12% of the total sample) accounted fully for 50% of the inbound links.

While N.Z. Bear's project has ended and does not provide recent data, up to date listings – such as are available on the Technorati.com site – are entirely consistent with the original data and, indeed, several of the top-placed blogs in the original study continue to maintain leading places in Technorati's most recent 'top 100 list' (www.technorati.com, accessed 7 June 2004).

Shirky explains the graph by means of the concept of 'power law distributions'. Based on developments in the mathematics of markets, the idea behind power law distributions is that in any system where many people are free to choose between many options, a small subset of providers will attract a disproportionately large amount of the choices exercised. According to Shirky, 'the very act of choosing, spread widely enough and freely enough, creates a power law distribution' (Shirky, 2003: 1). The greater the diversity of options the steeper the curve. This is because any option chosen by one chooser is more likely – even if only by a tiny amount – to be chosen by another chooser, Choices are influenced by choices previously made by others, or what Shirky (2003: 4) calls 'a preference premium' shaped by positive feedback. Within free and diverse systems, 'any tendency toward agreement, however small and for whatever reason can create power law distributions' (2003: 4).

Distributions, Power and Writing

The wider arguments and concepts associated with the thesis that power law distributions are operating in the 'blogosphere' have important implications for how we might think of powerful writing in relation to blogs and similar kinds of online text production, distribution and exchange.

Shirky's (2003) arguments and, indeed, the very practice of calculating the 'powerfulness' of blogs by reference to their numbers of inbound links, echo ideas advanced by Jean-Francois Lyotard's (1984) account of the postmodern condition. They remind us of the extent to which we are currently living under the dual 'signs' of *information* and *markets.* Information is a market *par excellence.* Within the mainstream of contemporary thinking, to be influential means gaining purchase or edge in the market of ideas. From this standpoint powerful writing will be a function, in the first instance, of achieving success in some market or other. This is why blogs are especially significant so far as offering a contemporary window on powerful writing is concerned. Blogs are most emphatically operating under market conditions and are widely being written about and thought about in these terms. In the burgeoning and over-saturated information market inhabited by blogs, power laws are readily apparent if we equate 'power' with such indicators as attracting many hits, inbound links, comments from readers, and gaining a lot of attention (as indicated by numbers of mentions, and 'near-the-top-of-the-list' positions in key word searches and aggregator tallies), and so on. Consequently, within the information market, being a powerful writer might be equated quite simply with scoring well on such indicators. In the case of blogs specifically, the association between writing and power is most easily rendered in terms of inbound links, which can be understood as transfers of attention to the blogger by other people (cf. Goldhaber, 1997, 1998).

From this perspective, Shirky makes some interesting observations so far as powerful writing and being or becoming a powerful writer within the blogosphere are concerned. And, as cases like andrewsullivan.com or instapundit.com remind us, it is important to recognise that the blogosphere is a context in which very considerable power is wielded so far as influencing thinking and advancing points of view are concerned. We will consider just three key ideas here.

First, Shirky (2003) observes that it is *relatively* more difficult for latecomers than earlycomers to become 'stars'. This is because in addition to being noticed and 'picked up' by others they actually have to *work against* preference premiums that are already in place. In other words, they do not come into a genuinely free and open market, or onto a truly level playing field, because there are already 'tendencies toward agreement' operating within the 'blogosphere'.

Second, Shirky acknowledges that there are 'doubtless [many bloggers] who are as talented and deserving as the current stars, but who are not getting anything like the traffic [the stars do]' (2003: 5). Moreover, he says, this trend will only intensify in the future, as the number and diversity of weblogs increase.

Third, Shirky describes a 'social order' of bloggers and argues that the 'top' and 'tail' of this social order will correlate very closely with different types of blogs and blogging activity. According to Shirky, 'weblog technology will be seen as a platform for so many forms of publishing, filtering, aggregation, and syndication that blogging will stop referring to any particular coherent activity' and the 'head and tail of the power law distribution [will] become so different that we can't think of J. Random Blogger and Glenn Reynolds of Instapundit as doing the same thing'

(2003: 5). This coheres well with the typology of blogs we have provided earlier in this paper.

From the standpoint of power understood in classical market terms, different kinds of blogging activity are not all equal. Shirky says that those bloggers who are at the 'head' of the social order of webloggers will, in effect, be mainstream media types: that is, 'broadcasters'. They will be generating so much traffic they will have no time to correspond/converse/communicate. They will simply be 'putting out'. By contrast, the long 'tail' of webloggers will be the personal journal/conversational types writing for a few friends and engaging with them via their blogs. Between these poles will be blogs intended to involve their creators in 'relatively engaged relationships' with 'moderate sized audiences' (2003: 5). These might be blogs that, say, professionals working within their respective specialist areas create in order to galvanise an affinity group in which they will play key or leading roles.

Two Implications for 'Powerful Writing'

Without underestimating the sheer importance of the kind of power associated with the market model of the blogosphere, it is important to note that the different forms of blogging distinguished by Shirky (2003) as corresponding to the top, middle and tail of the social order of bloggers may be associated with quite different concepts of powerful writing, and of experiencing oneself as a powerful writer. Within the blogosphere 'powerful writing' becomes highly ambiguous. If we take the 'top' as representing what it is to be a powerful writer – i.e. the full-blown *market* model – then powerful writing consists in attracting disproportionately large numbers of inbound links. At the other extreme, however, if we construct a concept of powerful writing based on the 'tail' of the blogger order, then experiencing power as a writer might come from 'publishing an account of your Saturday night and having your three closest friends read it [so that] it feels like a conversation' (Shirky, 2003: 5). This would be particularly so if these friends posted comments on your blog and/or followed up on their blogs with accounts of their own Saturday nights (Shirky, 2003: 5).

Shirky's 'middle' of the blogging order, based on involvement in relatively engaged relationships with a moderately substantial audience suggests the important role that might be played by membership in an affinity spaces or identity group in achieving power as a writer. If one's blog can be established as representing or serving some identifiable constituency or affinity group, one is likely to generate many more 'hits' and inbound links, and/or mobilise more attention and influence than one could by saying the same thing the same way as a 'free-standing' individual. Alternatively, a blogger operating in this middle range might achieve powerful effects by providing what Richard Lanham (1994) calls effective 'attention structures', or by hitting on a useful 'service' that meets the needs of significant numbers of individuals who have a common need or interest. For example, one might operate a blog that specialises in updating annotated bibliographies on a particular theme or themes, or one might mobilise links to online literature reviews, or to 'cheats' for video-computer games.

Two Exemplary Blogs: stevenberlinjohnson.com and Little.Yellow.Different

stevenberlinjohnson.com

Steven Johnson is a leading internet commentator and author who co-founded and edited the legendary online magazine Feed.com in the late 1990s. He might fairly be described as an internet public intellectual. A semiotics major from Brown University and author of books on interface culture and brain theory, Johnson's weblog (stevenberlinjohnson.com) began on 11 November 2002 (Figure 4.4) and has become a popular source of opinion on matters relating to internet culture, politics (from a 'centrist liberal' perspective), pop science, urban development in New York, hi tech news and design in general, among other areas.

Carefully archived back to its inception, Johnson's blog emphasizes economy and clarity in its design, is rich in hyperlinks on topics covered in his regular posts (currently two to three per week), and keeps Johnson's work and personal profile strongly in the foreground. At the time of writing, the right hand column featured a small colour photo of Johnson, a brief descriptive promotional statement for his latest book, a short list of links to some of his recent published essays, a list of topics covered in his recent postings, small cover photos of his first two books with hyperlinks to their listings on Amazon.com, a calendar of his appearances in US towns to promote his latest book, a list of sites and publications (with hyperlinks) he has written for, a relatively short (18 items) list of links to other people's blogs, a search tool for trawling Johnson's blog, and hyperlinks to his blog archives.

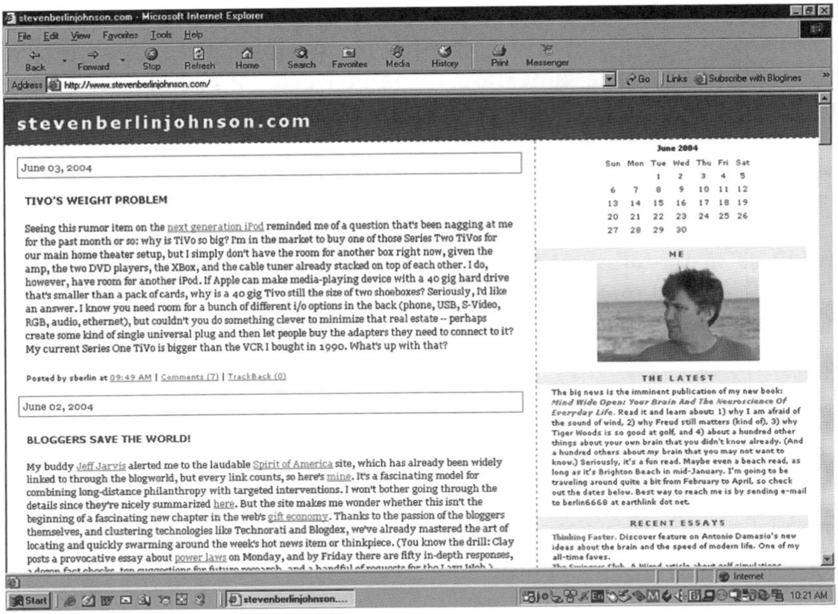

Figure 4.4 Screen shot of Steven Johnson's weblog (www.stevenberlinjohnson.com)

After just a short time exploring Johnson's blog a 'savvy' reader will have a good sense of

- how Johnson wants to be seen publicly – the blog does important identity construction and portrayal work;
- why Johnson operates a blog – and reasons range from self promotion and advertising to enhancing his presence in the money and attention economies (in his inaugural blog posting in November 2002 Johnson referred to blogs as vanity sites), to taking a position on current issues he sees as important (e.g. he fell in behind the invasion of Iraq after initially appearing to be opposed to it), and supporting the current 'Spirit of America' initiative (donate 'life-enhancing' – from a characteristically US consumerist perspective – things to Iraqis to help them make an optimal transition to 'democracy');
- some potentially powerful 'affinity maps' – e.g. constellations of influential people in the blogosphere who take centre/centre right/right wing positions on global political issues;
- a particular perspective on a range of technological innovations.

Readers will find they can glean information quickly and easily because of the blog's 'clean' and 'lean' layout, and the coherence of its hyperlinks. Moreover, it will be apparent that Johnson's sources are ones that many people regard as credible – even if one personally disagrees with their perspectives. The chances are very good that the reader will come away with something of genuine use to their own purposes. Our own initial forays into stevenberlinjohnson.com netted the link to Clay Shirky's (2003) argument on power distributions in the blogosphere (Lankshear & Knobel, 2004).

Little.Yellow.Different

The weblog *Little.Yellow.Different* (www.littleyellowdifferent.com) won the overall Bloggies award for excellence in 2003. It began in June 2000 and is authored by Ernie Hsiung, a 27-year-old, self-described overweight, short, gay, Chinese-American web designer and developer who works for Yahoo! *Little.Yellow.Different* is a regularly-updated, journal-like space that Hsiung uses to inform his readers about such things as renovations he is making to a recently purchased apartment, events going on in his life (e.g. appearing on a television game show, making a trip to Disney World, subscribing to cable television, starting his new job with Yahoo!), aspects of his relationships and interactions with his parents and relatives, and his ideas and views on elements of popular culture. While many journal-type weblogs (which tend to be heavy on accounts drawn from the author's life and light on annotated hyperlinks) have been criticised on the grounds of being somewhat banal celebrations of the microinformation of everyday life, *Little.Yellow.Different* has attracted a strong following of readers who are keen to read Hsiung's semi-regular, often hilarious accounts of what has been happening to him lately.

The design for Hsiung's weblog is polished and elegant (see Figure 4.5). In its default mode, the main body of the blog is white, set against a two-tone green background (which he refers to as a 'dull puke olive color'). The font used throughout the blog is clean and easily read. The main title banner for the page shows an artful 'ghosted' image of Ernie, and holds most of the navigational links for the blog.

Comments on posts are accessed by clicking on a link at the end of each post and are displayed in chronological order. Running down the side of the main blog section is what Hsiung refers to as a 'mini-blog'. This is where every few days he lists hyperlinks to websites he finds noteworthy.

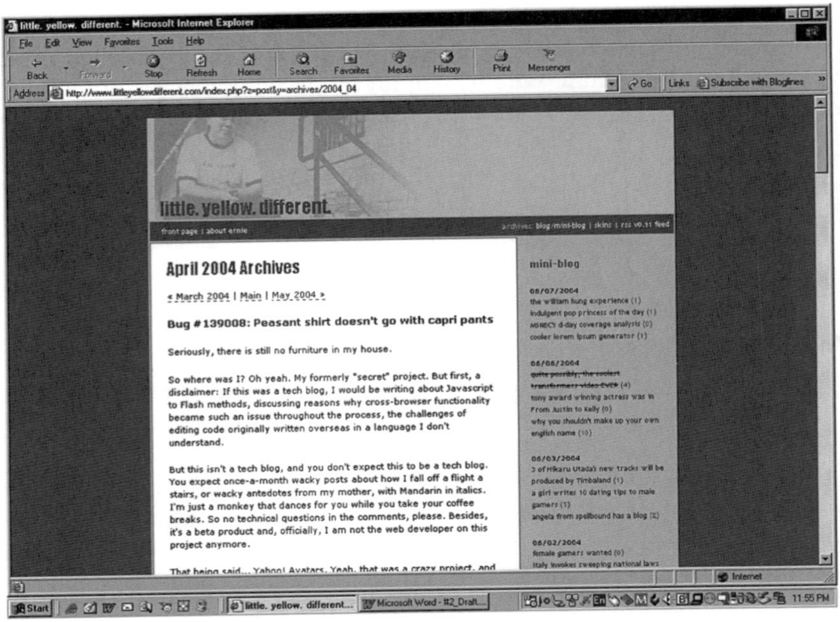

Figure 4.5 A screen shot of Little.Yellow.Different (www.littleyellowdifferent.com)

Reading *Little.Yellow.Different* over even a short period of days is enough to reveal important recurring themes in the posts. These include:

- Different challenges and benefits to be had from growing up Chinese-American.
- Gay cultural practices (including spoofing his own gay identity by confessing certain musical tastes, romantic attractions, interior decorating motifs, etc.).
- Comments on popular culture trends and events.
- Finding the humour in almost everything that happens to him.
- Keen-eyed observations on a range of social relationships, including those he has with work colleagues, friends, family and relatives, etc.

Hsiung's accounts of navigating American and Chinese cultures are often deeply ironic (and infinitely patient) and regularly offer insights into what it means to be on the receiving end of mainstream America's tendency to homogenise all 'Asians'. His practice of recounting word-for-word dialogue in his blog posts becomes the perfect medium for both unveiling cultural ignorance on the part of others and for making pointed social commentary without resorting to blunt-edged, heavy-handed criticism. For example, he recounts an exchange at work as follows:

Engineering lead:	We don't have a lot of time to finish this project. It's a good thing another country has implemented an avatar system already.
Ernie:	(looks through code) Uhm, this is a lot of code. And these javascript comments are in Korean.
Engineer:	But aren't . . .
Ernie:	. . . I'm *Chinese.*
Engineer:	Oh. This project is still due next Tuesday.

Little.Yellow.Different is less overtly political and 'global' than blogs like Steven Johnson's. Nonetheless, it is common for Hsiung's posts to attract 30 or more comments from readers. Comparisons across weblogs show that this is a high level of traffic per post. The link statistics generated for this weblog amply support claims regarding its popularity. In October 2004 Technorati.com calculates there are almost 1300 in-bound links from other weblogs to *Little.Yellow.Different.* Other evidence attests to its popularity. For example, when Hsiung lost his Silicon Valley job in 2001, *Little.Yellow.Different* devotees mobilised to create an online 'ErnieAid' project and raised money to help tide him over until he could find another job.

Purpose, Presentation and Point of View: Key Characteristics of Effective Weblogs

The exemplary weblogs discussed above were purposefully selected to span some of the range of weblog 'types' on the internet (cf. Lankshear & Knobel, 2003). For all their differences, however, they share some important features in common. These indicate what we identify as necessary criteria to be met for producing effective blogs. Three criteria stand out in particular, all of which seem to us relevant for considering the educational significance and potential of weblogs.

The first is a strong and clear sense of *purpose* for the blog. This is integral to having a sustaining reason or motivation for producing and updating it on a regular basis. Unless its creator has an authentic purpose – however whimsical this might be – a blog is unlikely to survive the demands on time, energy, and resourcefulness involved in maintaining an enduring and effective blog. While purposes can be of any kind, they need to be sufficiently well-defined and contained for the author to be able to generate posts and links that keep readers interested and believing in the blogger's credibility. For example, it is clear that Steven Johnson's personal investment in maintaining and promoting his own online presence and credibility within techno-culture affinity groups helps drive his weblog. Johnson is not bashful about including a list of links to online essays he has written. This carries the implication that readers who are interested in the commentaries he posts on his blog are likely to find these essays useful, interesting and/or compelling as well.

The second criterion for an effective blog is having a recognisable and well-informed *point of view.* Indeed, a blog without point of view is practically a contradiction in terms (cf. Dibbell, 2002). Exemplary blogs show very clearly the role and importance of a coherent and identifiable point of view against which readers can 'rub' and even 'test' their own values, beliefs, experiences, worldviews, and so on. Johnson's blog provides a classic 'three click entrée' to point of view within the blogosphere. In his post for 2 June 2004, under the heading 'Bloggers save the world', Johnson informs his readers that (original hyperlinks are underlined in the following text): 'My buddy Jeff Jarvis alerted me to the laudable Spirit of America site'. Clicking on the first hyperlink takes one to Jarvis's site, where the entry for 1 June contains information on the Spirit of America initiative. One click from there takes readers to the 'Spirit' site. Meanwhile, if one scrolls to the bottom of Jarvis' posting, at the end of his tributes to everyone who has supported the initiative, we find an opportunity for a third click: 'Surprise, surprise, surprise: Dave Winer dissents'. Making the third click on this last hyperlink brings us full circle on point of view: Winer's posting for 1 June, on his outstanding *Scripting News* blog (www.scripting.com). Winer's post concludes as follows:

> Jeff Jarvis is promoting a site called Spirit of America. I don't know much about it, and I don't sign up for political causes I don't know much about. I see other bloggers singing glowing praises for it, but sheez, how could they know? I don't think bloggerdom should be used like TV talk shows. I said I don't stand up for causes I don't understand. I guess that's a polite way of saying that I don't even *like* what they're doing. I think we need to get over ourselves in America, our time is just about over, unless we stop guzzling so much gas and

start electing leaders with brains, morals and courage. I feel I have to say I like Jeff, I really do, he's come through for me twice at BloggerCon, and I appreciate that. But his politics are 180 degrees opposite mine, even on tactics. I think the best thing the US can do for the world is get our own house in order and stop trying to fix the world, something we're exceedingly bad at.

Finally, purpose and point of view being equal, differences in blog effectiveness will largely reflect differences in *quality of presentation.* Many of the best known bloggers adopt clean and lean formats, and use crisp prose and draw on existing resources (via hyperlinks) to convey information rather than going over the ground again. Effective blogs are easy to navigate and follow long established navigation practices (e.g. underlined blue text signals a hyperlink). In addition, of course, blogs must be accessible in order to be effective. This translates into practices like avoiding unnecessary use of images and other media (like animations) that are heavy on bandwidth, in order to facilitate fast loading times, and ensuring that one uses template layouts and the like that can be read by a range of Internet browsers.

Blogs at School: Overview

Powerful writing and literacy pedagogy: Impediments to 'crossing'

The kinds of points we have made here do not cohere well with typical approaches to pedagogy aimed at powerful writing. For example, powerful writing tends to get 'individuated' in writing pedagogy. It is generally assumed that the individual is the bearer of a powerful writing capacity, and that the power in their writing is a function of his or her own understandings, as well as his or her command of the language, genre, creativity, style, and so on. Our engagement with Shirky's (2003) ideas suggests, however, that much of the power in powerful writing may lie in affiliation with some larger collective.

Moreover, the three variants of power associated with Shirky's top, middle and tail of the blogging order are not well reflected in mainstream approaches to powerful writing. So far as the top is concerned, the kind of attention-sustaining qualities manifested by stars and elites within the blogosphere are not accounted for in pedagogical strategies like 'scaffolding' effective revision and editing of written work, maintaining fluent fidelity to genre, and the like. As often as not, commanding attention is a function of breaking generic conventions, of hybridising, and so on. And in terms of power or effectiveness, in any significant sense, 'revision' is icing on the cake. If there is no cake to begin with, the icing has no point. Success lies in 'being there' in the first place, yet this emphasis – let alone modelling how it might be achieved in substance – is notoriously absent in most writing pedagogy, with its technicist emphases on aspects of formal style, grammatical rectitude, generic purity and the like.

The same holds for the middle and the tail. In fact, most powerful writing pedagogy actually impugns the principle lying at the heart of the kind of practices Shirky identifies with the long tail of the blogging order: the wish to communicate intimately with a few friends. This is not a space where the grammatically correct sentence rules supreme, or where critical literacy is the order of the day. It is not even a space where having something *significant* to say holds sway. Indeed, parading one's trivial interests and ordinariness may often be of the essence. And the idea that there is – or could possibly be – some identifiable 'personal journal' weblog genre able to be reduced to a concise and definite set of criteria and norms that could be taught in classrooms as applied meta knowledge is defied by the actual forms and practices engaged by bloggers.

Similarly, while writing pedagogy often emphasises the need to attend to audience and, perhaps, to have a conception of 'the ideal reader', the fact remains that students in school-based writing classes typically have no authentic, tangible audience. Moreover, there is little or nothing in writing pedagogy that invites students to begin from their concrete membership of affinity groups, or to go about establishing a constituency for real life (non-artificial) purposes (cf. Millard, this volume). On the contrary, much of the authentic writing students do in school settings for real audiences is *ultra vires* and discounted, if not actively surveilled and punished.

Effective blogging and literacy pedagogy: No crossing here

The school blogs we have surveyed on sites like the Schoolblogs.com hosting service provide little evidence of students and teachers working from a base of authentic purposefulness. Many student posts to school-endorsed blogs look more like being compulsory requirements and/or linked to student grades for the course rather than artifacts born of intrinsic interest. Missing in the vast majority of school blogs are the lively wit of blogger posts found elsewhere and the written comments they often attract from readers. (Indeed, many school blogs do not even have the comments function enabled.) In many cases the nature and quality of writing posted to school blogs invite a 'why bother?' response. Quite simply, it is often difficult to fathom why one would go to the trouble of setting up a blog in order to record the kind of content posted.

A typical example is provided by a sixth-grade blog (URL removed for purposes of anonymity) where it is evident that a single person has the authority to make the posts and other participants (students) send copy to be blogged. The 3 June post offers the following 'report' from the social studies subject area.

> Our math class is working on converting fractions to decimals then to percents, mixed number and improper fractions. We had an extra credit challenge of cooking something at home, bringing it to class and dividing it equally among our classmates. We were learning about how we double and/or triple recipes that use fractions (or parts of wholes). In our next Investigation, we will be designing a layout of a 100 square meter garden. This will teach us how to apply what we know about fractions and decimals in a real life situation.

There is typically little evidence of ideas development in school blogs. Evidence of well-defined and strongly advocated points of view is rare. A typical case in point is where students were required to post assignment work to the class blog (URL removed for purposes of anonymity). Representative examples of posts include:

- A student posting 'his' biography of Francis Drake. This involved entering the statement 'Here is my biography on Sir Francis Drake' and providing a link that takes the reader to a relatively short chronological listing of key events in Drake's life.
- A second student posting a web address that was found in the course of researching Drake's biography. The student writes: 'When I was doing my Biography of Sir Francis Drake I ran into this good site. I got most of my information from it and it has a good picture of Sir Francis Drake!'
- A third student posting the address of a website containing Drake's diary from one voyage. The student found the website via a Google.com search.

Some students in the same class from which the above examples are drawn have created personal weblogs. These, however, are uniformly underdeveloped and none of them indicates any evidence of significant personal investment. For example,

> hellooooooooooooooooooooooooooooooooooooooooooooooooooooo-oooooooooo i just dropped in to say a gigantic enormous hellooooo-oooooo. Good bye to you and you and you.

A significant number of school blogs are operated solely by teachers and act as a kind of 'school-home' course content interface for students (and their parents) to keep abreast of assignment due dates and assessment criteria, textbook pages to be read, and online resources recommended by the teacher. For example, a seventh-grade science teacher uses his blog for posting assignment descriptions and assessment criteria and related websites (e.g. 'You will create an essay on Evolution and explain why it was and still is such a controversial theory'). The same blog is also used to link to Quicktime videos of science quiz contests, to post an advance notice of a forthcoming slide show documenting the school's participation in the Martin Luther King march for peace and justice, to display textbook ordering information, and so on. Each post is linked to a comments section, but no comments had been posted when we visited the blog. Moreover, it is difficult to conceive what kinds of comments a reader could sensibly make. There is no evidence of student participation in this blog, although students (and possibly parents as well) seem to be the target readers.

Where Now? Some Implications for Pedagogy

Blogging provides an interesting contemporary angle on the theme of 'crossing' with reference to literacy education and which underpins this book. Blogging invites us to consider the extent to which the 'units' that cross or do not cross settings are *practices* as constituted within kinds of interactive spaces. When 'blogs' and 'blogging' cross from affinity spaces (i.e. participation in networks of shared interests, purposes and perspectives etc.) (Gee, 2004) in the blogosphere to the kinds of learning spaces constituted by school classrooms, the 'crossing' may be more apparent than real. Certainly we find little or nothing in school blogs that resembles the exemplars of effective blogging we have described earlier. This is not to deny that surface similarities can be found between many 'non-school' blogs and school blogs – particularly among blogs of the live journal variety, which can be heavy on the 'cheese sandwich' effect (where a blog has little to say beyond the level of what its author had for lunch that day), and many of which quickly become inactive.

A key point here, of course, concerns the extent to which it is educationally appropriate to want blogging to cross over to schools in its non-school varieties. This is not a straightforward matter (cf. Gee *et al.*, 1996: chap. 1). What we *can* say, however, is that if we want to introduce blogging into classroom activity with a view to encouraging the qualities of effective and powerful writing evinced by, say, news bloggers, or fan fiction writers, gadget or media review bloggers, and so on, then a first task for teachers and learners will be to try to create conditions in which genuine affinity spaces can emerge and be supported.

This might be as basic as giving students extensive scope for writing about their interests as a way of making spaces within the classroom for affinities to play out. Blogs, developed individually or collaboratively, might be devoted to gaming tips, music, fan fiction, manga drawing techniques, and so on. It might be a matter of giving students a great deal of time to explore the blogosphere, and other cyber spaces to find (examples of) where they want to be. (This type of activity aims at travelling as far as possible from vacuous daily 'free writing' exercises in journals that use writing prompts like 'You wake up and find you are 3-inches tall. Describe your day', or 'You are a flower. Explain what type of flower you are and why'.) This is hardly rocket science. Young people with online lives outside of school establish and inhabit affinity spaces as 'second nature'.

Where more structured approaches are required, the emphasis might be less on the free ranging pursuit of affinities and more on guided, semi-structured opportunities to experience and emulate expertise. This might, for example, be done by having learners search and explore a range of news blogs to identify multiple perspectives on a story/event and work toward blogging a position of their own. It is important to remember here that blogging does not necessarily entail operating one's own blog. It might be enough for some to post a comment to other people's blogs and flex their writing efficacy in that way. Alternatively, students could work collaboratively to trace the development of a broadcast media critique circulating in the blogosphere (news and media commentary bloggers are renown for their ability to pick up on and mercilessly dissect under-reporting, factual errors, or misrepresentations in commercial broadcast news services). A timeline or graphic organiser – with time-points measured in hours – can be constructed to show how the critique was first announced and then subsequently built upon in order to better understand how blogs can operate as distributed networks of expertise and insight.

Conclusion

Weblogging is a local writing practice that can have global reach. Equally, it is a global writing practice that has local reach. This allows individuals who have the interest and wherewithal to do so to access and participate in affinity spaces where expertise, stimulation, and point of view come free. Within such contexts, possibilities for acquiring the capacity to write effectively and powerfully are greatly enhanced by comparison with enduring the kinds of models schools typically make available. Certainly, there is no limit to the opportunities available for emulating effective practice.

References

Blood, R. (2002) Weblogs: A history and perspective. In Editors of Perseus Publishing (eds) *We've Got Blog: How Weblogs are Changing Culture* (pp. 7–16). Cambridge, MA: Perseus Publishing.

Dibbell, J. (2002) Portrait of the blogger as a young man. In Editors of Perseus Publishing (eds) *We've Got Blog: How Weblogs are Changing Culture* (pp. 69–77). Cambridge, MA: Perseus Publishing.

Gee, J. (2004) *Situated Language and Learning: A Critique of Traditional Schooling.* New York: Routledge.

Gee, J., Hull, G. and Lankshear, C. (1996) *New Work Order: Behind the Language of the New Capitalism.* Sydney: Allen & Unwin.

Goldhaber, M. (1997) The attention economy and the net. *First Monday.* On WWW at http://www.firstmonday.dk/issues/issue2_4/goldhaber. Accessed 2.7.00.

Goldhaber, M. (1998) The attention economy will change everything. *Telepolis* (Archive 1998). On WWW at http://www.heise.de/tp/english/inhalt/te/1419/1.html. Accessed 30.7.00.

Lanham, R. (1994) The economics of attention. *Proceedings of 124th Annual Meeting, Association of Research Libraries.* On WWW at http://sunsite.berkeley.edu/ARL/Proceedings/124/ps2econ.html. Accessed 2.7.00.

Lankshear, C. and Knobel, M. (2003) *New Literacies: Changing Knowledge and Classroom Learning.* Buckingham and Philadelphia: Open University Press.

Lankshear, C. and Knobel, M. (2004) Mapping the blogosphere #1: Function and power in weblogging. *Invited Plenary Address to the 11th International Literacy and Education Research Network Conference on Learning,* Havana, Cuba, 28 June.

Lyotard, J.-F. (1984) *The Postmodern Condition: A Report on Knowledge* (G. Bennington and B. Massumi, trans.). Minneapolis: University of Minnesota Press.

N.Z. Bear (2003). On WWW at http://www.myelin.co.nz/ecosystem. Accessed 4.4.03.

Shirky, C. (2003) Power laws, weblogs and inequality. On WWW at http://www.shirky.com/writings/powerlaw_weblog.html. Accessed 7.6.04.

Part 2

Multimodal Literacy Practices in Local and Global Spaces

Chapter 5

Critical Literacy Across Continents

HILARY JANKS AND BARBARA COMBER

Two Universities, Two Schools, Two Continents

The northern suburbs of Johannesburg, South Africa, are home to middle class, predominantly white, families.[1] Their large tree-filled gardens give

> Johannesburg the distinction of being the largest man-made urban forest, with six million trees in public parks, private gardens, and on pavements. On satellite pictures, the suburbs are a green splodge of colour, closely resembling a rain forest. (http://www.joburg.org.za/2003/aug/aug25_trees.stm)

It is no wonder that many of these suburbs are called *Park*town, *Park*wood, *Park*view, *Park*hurst, Craighall *Park, Green*side. A similar Website for Adelaide, South Australia, states that:

> Light's vision for Adelaide was a fully planned place with wide roads, squares and gardens. He designed a grid layout of wide streets and surrounding parklands, which gives the City an easy to understand and relaxed feel. (http://www.capcity.adelaide.sa.gov.au/html/adelaide.html)

The understanding that the number of trees and parks in a neighbourhood is a significant marker of social class is not an astonishing discovery, except perhaps when it is made by children in Grades 2/3 (Comber *et al.*, 2001). In 1996, Marg Wells' seven- and eight-year-old students, walking through Ferryden Park, South Australia, 10,082 kilometres from Johannesburg as the crow flies (6265 miles, 5444 nautical miles) (http://www.indo.com/cgibin/dist?place), were counting trees in their neighbourhood, assessing their condition and plotting them on maps. Their tree research project started as part of a 'literacy and social power' curriculum unit, in which the children were asked to identify aspects of their 'school, neighbourhood and world' that they were concerned about and imagine how they might be changed for the better. The focus on neighbourhood grew out of Wells' realisation that the urban renewal project was likely to directly impact on the children and their families, both by improving the physical conditions in the local neighbourhood, but also, by demolishing many of the old housing trust dwellings in which they lived, ultimately forcing relocations for a significant proportion of that neighbourhood. Wells made the neighbourhood the object of study to demonstrate to children how they might positively engage in aspects of the change process and benefit from it, whilst always being aware that there were some aspects well beyond the control of the local community. These seven- and eight-year-old children had numerous concerns about their local area as they currently experienced it – such as robberies, noise, rubbish and the lack of healthy trees. Wells encouraged the children to select a concern they would like to research further where perhaps they could make a positive difference. Their priority was trees. They wanted to know why some streets, houses and suburbs had more trees than others. With Wells' help, they collected data to make a case to the local council and the redevelopment authority, Westwood, for the greening of their neighbourhood. The economically depressed area where Wells teaches is known as *The Parks.* The suburbs are called Angle *Park*, Mansfield *Park*, Ferryden *Park* as well as Ridley *Grove* and Challa *Gardens* – a 'grim joke' because 'The Parks is a bleak grid of bleached fibro and brick bungalows' where public housing came to be seen as 'housing for the poor' (Comber *et al.*, 2002: 1).

Paulina Sethole, is the principal of Phepo Primary School[2] in Atteridgeville, a African township,[3] 50 kilometres from Johannesburg and 10,082 kilometres from Adelaide as the crow flies (6265 miles, 5444 nautical miles). Her school, like Wells', is also situated in a neighbourhood where there are few trees and fewer gardens. As part of her *Feed the Child, Feed the Nation Project*, Sethole developed an extensive organic vegetable garden on the school grounds that provides children with a hot meal every day (Janks, 2003). Environmental awareness, together with practices that teach children how to conserve natural resources, are fundamental to the school's ethos. To extend its green consciousness in a township characterised by red dust, the school planted an indigenous garden and donated a tree to each of its neighbours. In sharing its knowledge and its limited resources with the community, the school is modelling *ubuntu*, the African philosophy based on the belief that 'a person is a person through other people'. In teaching its students the importance of reaching out to one's neighbours, Phepo school has also contributed to upgrading its surrounding locale. Educators in both schools independently identified trees and gardens as a social issue; both schools worked in different ways towards engaging children in material change that might improve their everyday living conditions and at the same time used the research as a catalyst to introduce them to new representational resources that would give them the opportunity to communicate with young people beyond the local.

The Research Project

The research project on which we report here, is based on an ongoing collaboration between two universities and two schools on two continents. It began as a small scale literacy study funded by the University of South Australia (UniSA) in 2001: *Critical literacy, social action and children's representations of 'place'*. Barbara Comber and Pat Thomson, in researching literacy teaching and learning in disadvantaged schools in South Australia, had become increasingly intrigued by Wells' ongoing innovative work with children investigating neighbourhoods undergoing urban renewal. They were particularly interested in the ways in which the literacy work crossed over into local social and material action (Comber *et al.*, 2001). By this time Wells had moved to a school one suburb away, also within the perimeter of *The Parks*, also high poverty and also listed for urban renewal as part of the Westwood Redevelopment Project. Wells was now teaching a Grade 3/4 class and working closely with her school principal, Frank Cairns, to incorporate neighbourhood studies into the curriculum across the school. The neighbourhood is one of the poorest areas of metropolitan Adelaide and indeed in the nation, and includes a highly culturally diverse community, including many Indigenous, Chinese, Vietnamese, Laotian and Cambodian families. Eighty percent of students at Ridley Grove Primary School are on school card. School cards are given to families whose socio-economic circumstances means that they are allocated health cards. It is a recognised indicator of poverty in South Australian schools.

Thomson and Comber worked with Wells and Cairns to theorise how children engage with their 'place' in the world and how 'critical literacy' might make new resources available for neighbourhood as a social practice (de Certeau *et al.*, 1998). They invited Hilary Janks from the University of the Witwatersrand in Johannesburg to join them, in the belief that a comparative study across different contexts of poverty would produce a better understanding of the relationship between 'habitus' and 'habitat'

(Bourdieu, 1999) that might open the way for thinking about the local in relation to the global.

Janks elected to work with Sethole and teachers at Phepo school. Many of the children in this school live in informal shack settlements[4] and come from families living below the breadline; for some the hot meal at school is their only meal. In addition, prior to Sethole's appointment, the school lacked basic necessities such as paper, crayons and books; classes of up to 116 children were squashed into small classrooms with children sharing chairs. Janks deliberately chose a school that countered the discourses of deficit often associated with African education in South Africa. Phepo is a place of both vision and heart; in touch with the needs of the community it serves, with an environmental programme that helps students think positively about who they are and where they come from.

In earlier papers (Comber *et al.*, 2002; Janks, 2002), we examined the different articulations of the project in the two different contexts by a consideration of how the children's lived realities led to the production of substantially different artifacts.[5] The children's texts, produced in different modalities, using different materials and different media, drawing on different funds of knowledge (Moll, 1992) and confronting different social issues, demonstrated the inseparability of text and context (Halliday, 1985; Fairclough, 1989) and confirmed our sense of the value of the local in children's textual production. In neighbourhoods where children are witness to change that is sometimes frightening – in *The Parks* some children's homes are being bulldozed to make way for upmarket housing, partly demolished houses are targets for fires and the neighbourhood endures escalating crime rates; in Atteridgeville people are dying of AIDS and neighbours are living in shacks, without electricity, running water or sewerage – the local is never parochial. In South Africa, school children's protests about the imposition of Afrikaans in their classrooms was the spark that ignited the 1976 Soweto uprising. Local action is political and it teaches children about agency, and the power they have to change 'their world' as they understand it. We agree with Haraway that 'the only way to find a vision is to be somewhere in particular' (Haraway, 1991: 196).

Mobilising Educators

In the early stage of the project we were not sure how to bring the two schools together. We could compare and contrast their histories, their material realities, their 'funds of knowledge' (Moll, 1992), their pedagogies and classroom processes, and the children's textual representations, in order to make sense of the different conditions of possibility in these two research sites. But this inclined to mere juxtaposition; we had no way of making these schools 'talk' to each other. Furthermore, it worried us that we were piggybacking on the work of Wells and Sethole. We were conscious that our own social locations as university researchers gave us privileged access to both local schools and global communities of practice. The artifacts produced by the students and their teachers were mobile and so were we, but the teachers and the students were left in the local. Often those who live and work in poverty are least able to move beyond the local (except of course as refugees or as cheap labour somewhere else).

Analyses of globalization take for granted the ways in which digital communication technologies and 21st century modes of transportation have shrunk the world, enabling flows of information and people. What is generally omitted is the question of access to mobility. For teachers and students living and working in poor communities, the rest of the world is as far away as ever. The 10,082 kilometres as the crow flies separating Johannesburg and Atteridgeville from Adelaide makes these destinations infinitely unreachable for people with no money. Even cyber space is out of bounds, unless both schools are wired and the children and teachers are computer and Internet literate. We needed to find ways of moving people, not just ideas and texts.

How researchers turn their intellectual and cultural capital into resources for communities that they work with is both a political and an ethical issue for research. It would be simple to say that Thomson, Comber and Janks found the funding that would enable Wells and her school principal to visit Atteridegville in 2002, and Sethole and two teachers to visit Adelaide in 2003. However enabling the school principal and two teachers from Phepo and the school principal and a teacher from Ridley Grove to visit each other involved extensive lobbying and networking with professional associations and the state educational bureaucracy in South Australia. In short, the researchers' cultural capital, networks and time were critical in making the travel happen for the school-based educators. And these visits proved to be crucial. It was these visits that connected the schools across the 10,082 kilometres as the crow files that separated them. In our work overall, when we discuss the ideas which have been taken up across the schools, why they were taken up and how they translate in different sites, we consider the importance of the 'going to be there', the 'being there' and the 'having been there'. In this chapter the emphasis is on the 'going to be there'. In other words, we consider what difference the fact that their teachers and principal were visiting each other in South Africa and South Australia made to the students' production of texts in each site. What did they need to take into account to write and draw for young people in different locales from their own?

'Going To Be There'

In 2001, Pat Thomson suggested *A is for Aunty,* a picture alphabet book authored and illustrated by Elaine Russell (2000) an Australian Aboriginal woman, as a resource for the project. In *A is for Aunty,* Elaine Russell, re-imagines her childhood memories and importantly the places where these occurred, through her art and storytelling. Interestingly, her choice of the alphabet book genre – an old western technology for teaching reading – in a sense, allows her to tell a different story of childhood – a counter-story of 'the stolen generation'[6] – in a way that is accessible to many readers, including children (Russell, 2000). Her bold paintings of the Mission at Murrin Bridge, near Lake Cargelligo, on the Lachlan River where she grew up, and her engaging vignettes capture the quality of life in her community. This children's book is written in simple English and the drawings are bright with a clarity and simplicity of style that children could emulate. In addition, Russell's aboriginality provided a possible point of connection for African children in South Africa and Aboriginal children at Ridley Grove Primary School.

Teachers at Phepo had been attracted to the alphabet book from the beginning, but felt it to be quite a challenging task. Seeing the professionalism of Wells' books they were filled with admiration, and despite feeling quite daunted, thought that, with the support of Janks, they should attempt such work with their students. There was general agreement that because Phepo children spoke African languages, writing a book in English was a task for students in Grade 7. Only once they knew that the teachers and the books were going to Australia, did Janks, the Grade 7 teachers and the students push themselves to produce *A is for Atteridgeville.*

Alphabet Books and Place: Telling the Here to Others Who are There

The alphabet book project, *A is for Arndale* and *A is for Atteridgeville,* produced on two different continents is the cross continental project that we want to explore in this chapter. In both places this project was energised by the physical reality of the teachers carrying the books across the world to an audience of children somewhere far away: energised by the 'going to be there'. 'Reading and writing have always been tools that take us across borders [and] build bridges across cultures and communities' (Luke, 2003: 20).

A is for Arndale

With her class, Wells spent time discussing what each letter of the alphabet would stand for. They needed to decide what they wanted to say about their place and how they lived their lives to the young people in Atteridgeville. They chose a range of places to describe, from malls, to delicatessens, video hire shops, fast food outlets and restaurants, to outdoor places (beach, catchment, parks) to places of activity at home (playing Game Boys, watching TV) and away from home (bike-tracks, judo, football, netball, ice-cream vans) and institutions (hospital, school, kindy, library). Two pages were devoted to more abstract concepts (Q is for Quiet, Z is for Busy Roads, with the z as a sound effect for speeding cars). The cover and title page *A is for Arndale* represent the local shopping centre, Arndale, in some ways the hub of the community in that it provides a large collection of retail, eating places, services and entertainment in a covered mall. In planning the book it became clear that several children wanted to write about a letter (e.g. B is for beach, B is for bike track, K is for kindy and K is for Karate), hence the simple solution to include multiple entries for selected letters. The children, like Elaine Russell the author who they were emulating, wrote simple but interesting accounts to accompany their vibrantly coloured paintings depicting their chosen place. Ultimately Wells' class produced a 30-page A3 colour illustrated alphabet book (with the 30 pages allowing each member of the class to make at least one contribution and necessitating two entries for several letters). It was a class-negotiated and collectively produced text with individuals taking responsibility for producing at least one page each to a standard ready for publication. We turn now to several examples of the children's texts to illustrate the kinds of knowledges and experiences children brought to this task. These examples give a sense of the children's relationships with the neighbourhood, both as problematic and pleasurable, and their engagement with popular culture.

Most of the children's entries focus on pleasurable associations with places, perhaps no coincidence given the similar stance of the Elaine Russell book. However there are also texts which allude to the complexities of everyday life. There are brief references to deliberate vandalism:

> One day someone ruined the track on the mound. They dug a shallow trench with their tyre. This is hard to ride over and has caused accidents. I hope it will get fixed soon. (Excerpt from B is for Biketrack)

There are also references to some of the more demanding aspects of life in this busy inner suburb:

> Z is for Busy Roads
>
> Hanson Road is a busy road with lots of traffic.
> When I was trying to ride my bike across Hanson Road in the traffic, it was very difficult.
> When no cars were coming I went riding across the road fast, but then a red car came around the corner. I rode back quickly and waited until the red car went past. Then I rode into the middle of the road.
> Lots of cars drove past and I waited a long time. When the cars were gone, I finally crossed the road and went to the petrol station. I had to fill up a can with petrol for my dad's car.
> Crossing the road this time was worse. I rode up and down, and up and down, waiting for a break in the traffic. I got to the middle and then went very fast and made it across. Then I went home.

Another student also starts with Hanson Road (see Figure 5.1) before going on to suggest that it is not only cars that make life noisy.

> Q is for Quiet
>
> Around our neighbourhood it is usually noisy.
> Hanson Road is a very busy and noisy road. Lots of traffic goes up and down every day.
> There are lots of workers who work on the lights and snapped pipes.
> Some houses in our area are being knocked down and new ones being built. There are big bulldozers and cranes working all day.
> Some houses are very noisy and some are quiet. Neighbours sometimes have parties and they are very noisy. Sometimes it is hard to do your homework and get to sleep. It is best when it is really quiet.

The accompanying painting for this text includes a car that appears as though might be going off the road and into a house from which a white-faced figure looks out. The picture is constructed in bold colours – a bright red house with small green windows, a dark blue sky, a huge yellow sun, a black road with clearly marked yellow lines and the offending purple car with blue windows. The overall effect of the painting is to produce a clash of over-crowded images. It definitely does not look quiet. Indeed the image manages to capture the anxiety expressed by the young writer.

Figure 5.1 Q is for Quiet

The texts in *A is for Arndale* go beyond the typical recounts often produced by children of this age, because they are writing not only to tell about a specific event, but to explain how their life usually is to someone else who may live differently. The children needed to become aware of what they could not take for granted about their readers.

In other curriculum work Wells' class had focussed on where it was safe to go in their neighbourhood at different times of the day and night and where and whether they were allowed to move through the neighbourhood alone. In that work many children had written about dangers and perceived threats on particular streets and places in the neighbourhood (including crime, dangerous driving, 'scary people'). Their book, written for students in Atteridgeville, however, is less revealing about these aspects of their lives. Indeed these young people mostly take this opportunity to present the pleasure and order in their everyday lives, whether it is regular sport, aspects of school and neighbourhood life, or particular treats and personal preferences. One child writes enthusiastically about the school crossing, obviously deciding that this might be of interest to her Atteridgeville peers and clearly proud of her older sibling.

> X is for school crossing
>
> Outside our school is a school crossing. We have school crossing monitors who watch the crossing before and after school.
> My sister is in year 7 and she is a monitor. One of the monitors uses a whistle and the other monitors have broomsticks with hexagons with the word "stop" painted on it.
> When the sticks are held up the cars and trucks stop and the signs are down the cars and trucks go. This makes it safe for us to cross the road.

The illustration which accompanies this text depicts an ordered world and the older school building which is actually set back from the road and only partially visible from the crossing is brought into the foreground where a monitor with outstretched hands maintains control along with the traffic lights. Birds fly overhead. In sharp contrast to the accounts of busy roads and noisy neighbours, and the implied sense of threat these children sometimes experience, the letter X portrays a safe world, a world where older sisters, stop signs and school crossings are in control.

The original impetus for Wells' designing the curriculum about the neighbourhood was, as we explained earlier, the changes being wrought by the urban renewal project. As a result of Wells' intervention and ongoing communication with the council and the developers, the students in Wells' class became involved in designing and advising on a local reserve. One student gives an account of the 'catchment' as they understand it.

> C is for Catchment
>
> Near our school, the Westwood people are making a park but it is not made yet. The park will have an Aboriginal theme with native plants and animals.

> We have been making tiles for the new park. These are going to be stuck on the seats.
> It will be very deep for the rain water to be caught in the catchment area. There will be a small creek. The creek runs through the middle of the park.
> On the sides are lots of small stones and rocks. Some will have animals carved into them. Over the creek there will be a bridge made of wood for people to cross. The water will stay for a little while in the creek. When the rain comes the water stays there until it dries up.

The catchment project has clearly captured this student's imagination. Wells' class had become involved in researching the native flora and fauna of the region and also by making suggestions to the developers for the design of the park and artifacts that would become part of it. While this student writes about what the 'Westwood people' are doing, s/he also writes with agency on behalf of the class and knowledgeably about what's going to happen there.[7] The accompanying illustration shows a bridge crossing a creek with clusters of trees and two smiling children on opposite sides of the bridge with their outstretched arms suggesting that they are inviting readers/visitors into the park.

Mostly though, these nine- and ten-year-old children wrote about their pleasures (eating at McDonalds, the Vietnam Palace Restaurant or the Ice Cream Van), going shopping (at Westfield Shopping Mall or the local deli), going to the beach, playing netball, soccer, football, watching movies and TV, playing computer games.

> U is for Greater Union
>
> Sometimes when I am really, really bored, I go to Greater Union and watch a movie with my cousin, Minh and my little brother Kim.
> My favourite movies are Monsters Inc. and Scooby-Doo. My favourite characters in Scooby-Doo are Daphne and Scooby-Doo and my favourite characters in Monsters Inc. are Boo and Mike.
> My cousin always has to sit in the middle because me and my brother always fight over the popcorn.
> Greater Union is near Arndale.

The alphabet entries capture a sense of everyday life and the ordinary places that are meaningful to them in the context of their lived experiences. Many similar entries give snapshots of what children regularly enjoy in their lives and many give a sense of special and contingent treats that happen when parents can afford them. Some give a sense of

Figure 5.2 I is for Ice Cream Van

their investments in routine events, particular activities and places (I is for Icecream Van, N is for Netball, B is for Beach) (Figure 5.2). In writing for and to the young people at Atteridgeville, these children convey a sense of optimism, enthusiasm and realism in the ways they represent their lives at this time in this place.

Interestingly, shared pleasures in Atteridgeville and Ridley Grove include ice-dream, netball, football, parks and gardens and food. Shared fears included violence, ill-health, robberies and poverty.

A is for Atteridgeville

Teachers and students at Phepo had never before written and illustrated a book. Teachers Shikwambane and Matolong were willing to 'have a go' at it, with help from Janks. What is crucial about the collaboration is that neither the teachers nor Janks could have produced *A is for Atteridgeville* with the children on their own. They needed to pool their linguistic, pedagogical, local and global expertise. Work began in earnest in April 2003 and was completed three months later just in time for the trip to Australia.

At Phepo we worked with the following constraints

- The teachers had no experience or previous training for this kind of work.
- Janks could not visit the school more than once a week, she has very little primary school experience, and she does not speak any of the African languages.
- Shikwambane's Grade 7 class had 44 students.
- Material resources were limited.
- Neither the teachers nor the students were computer literate and the school did not have computers that students or staff could use.
- Children had to produce a book in English, with limited skills in the language. While we were able to use multilingual classroom practices[8] during the production process, the move from the local to the global necessitated the use of English, the only language that could be understood in both schools, for the final product.

Crucially important was the motivation and excitement created by the students' knowledge that *their* teacher would take *their* book to Australia. Writing for a peer audience, who had no knowledge of Atteridgeville became an important pedagogic tool. The students had to think about what this audience needed to know and which of their own taken-for-granted 'funds of knowledge' (Moll, 1992) would need to be spelt out for this audience 10,082 kilometres away.

In most cases the drawings were done after the writing. As the writing was a communal activity undertaken by students in groups, the drawings were not necessarily done by the writer, as was the case with *A is for Arndale*. The students who were interested in producing the visual texts for *A is for Atteridgeville* worked together around a large table, sharing the limited supply of pens and crayons. At times children would collaborate, with one drawing and another colouring. Children worked on topics that interested them. Some of the visuals support or enhance the verbal text, providing a coherent representation across the different modalities; others work against the verbal, providing a counter discourse. The use of the different modalities provided opportunities for different students to contribute and to excel, and the combination is crucial to engaging the reader.

Shikwambane and Matolong relied on Janks to model aspects of the writing pedagogy, which she did by actually taking them through some of the classroom processes themselves. For example, Janks and Matolong worked out their preferred topics for the letters of the alphabet together, learning to choose topics in relation to other topic choices. In other instances, Janks did some of the work. She typed out the students' drafts and replied with questions designed to elicit more detail relating to the students' extensive knowledge of their community. The teachers worked with the feedback in class and learnt the technique in the process, adding additional questions of their own. Janks' use of reply, rather than evaluation (Barnes, 1976), proved to be extremely generative. It established the writing as an interactive communication with a less knowledgeable audience, rather than as a school writing task to be judged by a teacher. When students know a lot, they often are not sure what to include and exclude and the questions provided them with some guidance, as the drafts before and after Janks' questions illustrate.

First draft: H is for HIV/AIDS

HIV is a virus that kills. HIV/AIDS is cause by sleeping around without protection. HIV is spread by someone who is HIV positive who sleeps with others without using a condom. People think that you can get AIDS by using the same toilets or by shaking hands with people who are HIV positive. When a person is HIV positive that person can lose weight, lose appetite. A person with HIV can look after their bodies by eating food that builds their body and give energy and by doing exercise. People with HIV can live a normal life. They don't have to think that they are going to die because they don't have AIDS yet.

Janks asked the following questions:
Is what people think about toilets and shaking hands true?
Can women and men spread HIV/AIDS?
Are lots of people in Atteridgeville dying from AIDS?

Are people worried?
Do people like to talk about it? Do you only talk about it at school?

Second draft: H is for HIV/AIDS

HIV/AIDS is a disease that cannot be cured. Many people in Atteridgeville, specially the young ones, are dying of AIDS. People who are suffering from this disease don't want people to know that they are infected and they don't want to talk about it. Some of those who are HIV positive are spreading this disease by infecting others. HIV/AIDS is caused by sleeping around without protection. HIV is spread by someone who is HIV positive who sleeps with others without using a condom. Many people don't have information about AIDS. They still believe in myths. They don't want to shake hands with people who are HIV positive or even touch them. Another myth is that if you (sleep with) rape a child you will be cured of AIDS. This is one of the reasons why child abuse and rape is high in Atteridgeville. When a person is HIV positive that person can lose weight, lose appetite. A person with HIV can look after their body by eating food that builds their body and gives energy, and by doing exercise.

The drawing that accompanies this text is a neutral image of the AIDS ribbon, worn as a sign of solidarity with AIDS patients. This image is surrounded by positive verbal messages of support: 'I care for people with HIV/AIDS', 'I care for you care for me' and 'My friend with AIDS is still my friend'. The latter is a large sign painted on the outside of the classroom walls at Phepo school. It is as if the abstract symbolisation of the disease, offered by the AIDS ribbon, provides a distancing from the material realities of the disease that children know and have written about.

In facilitating the choice of topics for each of the letters in the alphabet Janks and the teachers were perhaps too directive. In the end though, the students took control. Shikwambane tried to steer the students away from their preoccupation with crime and violence. In brainstorming the letters of the alphabet this had been a recurrent theme. The brainstorm included 'blood', 'crime', 'gangster', 'gun', 'improve crime', 'police'. It was agreed by a process of negotiation with the whole class that 'P is for Police' would be the place to talk about crime. When the students wrote the book they elected to use 'P' for poverty instead, thus displacing crime. Crime had no place to go so it erupted at the end of the book in X is for Xenophobia, Y is for Youth, Z is for Zaka.[9]

The verbal and visual representations of foreigners in X is for Xenophobia are interesting because of the way in which they work against each other. The verbal text attempts to counter negative discourses about foreigners and to deny xenophobia.

X is for Xenophobia

In Atteridgeville we don't have problems with foreigners. Many foreigners have business in Mshengu informal settlement. In some areas, like Soweto, Thembisa and Mamelodi they don't want foreigners because they accuse them of taking their jobs and being involved in crime. In some areas foreigners are involved in selling drugs. Some foreigners married South African wives and some of their children attend school at Phepo Primary school. We play with them and see

Figure 5.3 X is for Xenophobia

> them as children, not foreigners. We in Atteridgeville don't hate foreigners. We don't suffer from xenophobia.

The visual image (see Figure 5.3) offers a contradictory perspective. Here foreigners are depicted with strangely shaped heads, yellow faces, threatened by storm clouds and furtively covered. They are surrounded by African figures with sticks in their hands saying 'you scare me' and 'your frighten me'. Here the visual and verbal texts undercut one another.

The violence is most explicit in their representations of youth (see Figure 5.4).

> Y is for Youth
>
> Many youths in Atteridgeville after passing matric (Grade 12) can't find employment. Some youths cannot afford to pay school fees because their parents are unemployed. There are many youths on the street. Most of them are involved in crime. Some do drugs and commit crime. Many youths are in prison for car-hijacking, robbery and burglary. The Atteridgeville police station is full of youths who have been arrested. Many youths are dying of HIV/Aids. Some youths are involved with youth choirs and organisations that help others.

Figure 5.4 Y is for Youth

The only positive representation of youth appears in the last sentence, 'Some youths are involved with youth choirs and organisations that help others', was proffered only in response to one of Janks' questions.

The picture of 'Y is for Youth' depicts a drive-by shooting, a man lying on the ground with blood spurting out of his chest, another man running with blood pouring from his eye, an oversized gangster holding a man up with a knife to take his money, and a police vehicle with its siren blaring and a policeman firing a gun. It is an unrelenting portrayal of uncontrolled violent crime.

To provide students with an alternative view of youth, Janks produced a handout with information about Hector Pieterson, the primary school child who died in the Soweto 1976 student protests, when the police opened fire on unarmed children. Pieterson has become a symbol of the contribution made by the black youth in South Africa to the freedom struggle. Shikwambane, himself one of the youths involved in the 1976 uprising, spent time with his students re-imagining possibilities for them as youths about to leave primary school in 2003, nine years after independence. Each student then wrote a new version of 'Y is for Youth'. These paragraphs show very little change, suggesting that the daily realities of these children's lives are experienced by them as brutal. This suggest to us that it is not enough to help students reconstruct their texts, if what the texts are representing remains unchanged. Social action that changes the material conditions of these children's lives is crucial.

The garden project discussed fully in Janks (2003), like Wells' project to involve her students in shaping the urban renewal project in their neighbourhood, provided students with opportunities to contribute to changing their material world. The positive effects of the garden project, developed by the principal with the support of BMW, a global motor industry company, inform several pages of *A is for Atteridgeville,* in which students see themselves as agentive subjects (see Figure 5.5).

> BMW[10] made us famous. It helped our school start food gardens. We sell vegetables to the community. Visitors donate money to the school so that we can buy seeds. There are 734 learners at Phepo. Last year there were 630 and in 2001 there were 520 learners. More and more learners want to come to Phepo because the school fees are cheap and the school is beautiful. (B is for Phepo[11])

> At our school we have the Nelson Mandela garden. In the middle is a tall tree, the Mandela tree. The tree is surrounded by four flower gardens – the blacks, the whites, the Indians, the coloureds. After

Figure 5.5 Mondi recycling

the rain the flowers make the rainbow nation. They are in a circle to make one rainbow nation – *simunye* – we are one. (D is for Democracy)

Our school has an environmental project called *Feed the Child, Feed the Nation.* This project consists of the vegetable garden, the herb garden and the indigenous garden. Feed the child feed the nation provides food for learners. They eat. They eat vegetables with bogobe – porridge. The other vegetables are sold to the community. (Extract from F is for Feed the Child, Feed the Nation)

At our school we recycle waste. Learners bring old wheelbarrows, kitchen units, old tyres to school for re-use. We repaint them and plant flowers in them and decorate them. We also recycle paper. The learners bring newspapers on Wednesdays ... Grey water is the water that is used by learners when they wash themselves. This water is used in our gardens to kill insects and for watering the plants. (Extract from R is for Recycle, Reduce, Re-use)

The images associated with these texts show children running with paper to the Mondi recycling bin, food being prepared for lunch with vegetables from the garden, a vegetable plot, water from a tap being carried in the traditional way in a bucket balanced on the head, and an image of Mandela looking at the new South African flag. The most amusing of these is the picture representing a BMW motor car with the words, '**B**e **M**y **W**ife', township slang for the car. All these drawings are representations that highlight an aspect of the verbal texts they accompany.

While many of the texts deal with socially loaded topics, some positive and some negative, like the texts in *A is for Arndale*, many of the letters are devoted to things that children love to do. The children write about the annual fun day at Maroe Park under 'A' is for Atteridgeville; 'I' is for the icecream centre; 'L' is for the languages the students speak. Here they say 'Hello. We hope you like our book' in all the African languages that they 'are proud of'; 'N' is for netball and 'S' is for soccer; 'O' is for Olesang, Atteridgeville's famous, local gospel singer who has many fans in the class; 'T' is for transport and provides plenty of scope for the boys to draw lots and lots of vehicles which they clearly enjoy doing. The children's pleasure is echoed in the visuals. And under 'P' for poverty the children remind us that:

> Poverty does not stop people from enjoying life. The boys are playing with wire cars and the girls are playing with skipping ropes.

Having Been There

Here we have focused on the alphabet books that crossed continents and the impetus that the teachers' travelling with the books gave to this work. How the project is developing, as a result of the principals and teachers having been embodied in each other's place, is a further chapter in this ongoing international research project on place. Allan Luke has recently questioned whether curriculum that works with students' local interests and knowledge 'intellectually or textually or critically ... goes anywhere' (Luke, 2003: 21). We believe that the local is a good training ground for the kind of political action that teaches students that they can assume agency.

While we have been actively committed to working with teachers and young people to develop critical literacy pedagogies for some time, this shared cross-continent project took us in new directions. Here our focus shifted from deconstructive critical analysis of texts produced elsewhere for consumption anywhere (that is, food packaging, advertising, media reports, etc.) to the very specific production of texts for very specific readers elsewhere. With the teachers we exploited the energy that comes from 'going to be there' to generate with young people forms of writing and visual representation that would travel. In the process young people in both places collectively thought about what was significant about the ways in which they live their lives. Such an approach emphasises the reconstructive elements of critical literacy, the need for students to learn to design texts that represent their interests in powerful ways (Janks, 2000). Importantly this project simultaneously expanded the teachers' worlds along with their students.

Our project is far from over. As researchers we have come into the lives of particular schools and specific communities at different points and connected in various ways with the potentials and the problems faced there. We have tried to make available the cultural capital, resources and privileges that come with university positioning. At the same time we have learnt from the inventive and committed practices of the principals and teachers. While small discreet parts of the project are complete – the production of the artifacts for the children in the other place, the reciprocal visits of the school-based educators to each other's schools – in many ways we are just beginning.[12] We face some real challenges as we try to increase the communication and learning between these school communities so that the project is more than a one-off exotic experience for all. We still need to 'connect' these schools electronically and to invite others in. We need to ensure that such schools and learning communities are not shut out of the 'network society' (Castells, 1996) by building an infrastructure that makes such practices part of the normal, as indeed they are in privileged schools. This is important because the learning that is accomplished by seeing someone else's poverty, school, pedagogies, has the power to disrupt the taken-for-granted knowledges that might otherwise fence us in. Developing transnational communities of networked critical educators (school, community and university-based) investigating and analysing the effects of their practices and learning from and with each other and their students is where we want to go next.

Notes

1. Prior to 1994, these suburbs were designated as a whites only area, in terms of the Group Areas Act, a cornerstone of apartheid legislation.
2. 'Phepo', which means 'feeding' in Setswana, is a pseudonym.
3. Ten years after independence in South Africa, townships that were set up as ghettoes for Africans as part of the apartheid policy of separate development, continue to exist. While Africans are no longer restricted to living in these

townships, many cannot afford to move to more affluent areas and many choose to remain with their communities.

4. The politically correct term is 'informal settlement'. The teachers and the children who live in them call these settlements 'squatter camps'. Janks uses the word 'shack settlement' to convey a sense of the material conditions of poverty in which the children live. It is however, important to note that these informal settlements do represent new freedom for people to live where they choose, without the restrictions imposed by pass laws and the Group Areas Act, and people are now able to move to the cities where they stand a slightly better chance of finding work.
5. In Wells' class these included digitised photographs of local houses which the children 'redecorated' using *Kidpix*™, large maps of local streets depicting their residences on sheets of brown paper, individual coloured maps of children's routes to school and many surveys about how they saw their lives and homes now and how and where they imagined themselves in the future. At Phepo the children produced cardboard models of their houses, drawings in crayon on paper, and a photographic map of the school, writing and simple role play 'dramas'.
6. 'The stolen generation' refers to large numbers of Indigenous children who were forcibly removed from their families and taken 'into care' by the authority of the Australian Government. See *National Inquiry into the Separation of Aboriginal and Torres Strait Islander Children from their Families (Australia)* (1997).
7. At the time of writing this chapter the Mikawomma Reserve is complete. The children who had been involved continued to be proud of their role in its design and see it as their park as the principal found out when he showed it to visitors after school hours to be asked by the children who appeared, what he was doing in *their* park.
8. We used codeswitching wherever it was needed to ensure understanding and to enable students to contribute to discussions.
9. *Zaka* is township slang for money and the visual representation of zaka depicts a bank robbery.
10. Janks has written of BMW's association with the school elsewhere (Janks, 2003).
11. We have substituted Phepo for the name of the school.
12. The Phepo teachers returned from their visit to Australia aspiring to emulate the pedagogies that they had seen at Ridley Grove, the organisation of the media centre and the development of children's facility with new technologies. The Ridley Grove principal and teacher were inspired to initiate a garden project that would draw its community into the school. Each took from the other ideas that met their current needs.

References

Barnes, D. (1976) *From Communication to Curriculum.* Harmondsworth: Penguin.

Bourdieu, P. (1999) *The Weight of the World: Social Suffering in Contemporary Society* (P.P. Ferguson, trans.). Stanford, California: Stanford University Press.

Castells, M. (1996) The rise of the network society. *The Information Age: Economy, Society and Culture* (Vol. 1). Massachusetts & Oxford: Blackwell Publishers.

Comber, B., Thomson, P. and Wells, M. (2002) Critical literacy, social action and children's representations of "place". Paper presented at the American Educational Research Association Annual Meeting, 1–5 April, 2002, New Orleans, Louisiana.
Comber, B., Thomson, P. and Wells, M. (2001) Critical literacy finds a "place": Writing and social action in a neighborhood school. *Elementary School Journal* 101 (4), 451–64.
de Certeau, M., Giard, L. and Mayol, P. (1998) *The Practice of Everyday Life. Volume 2. Living and Cooking* (T. Tomasik, trans.). Minneapolis, London: University of Minnesota Press.
Fairclough, N. (1989) *Language and Power.* London: Longman.
Halliday, M. (1985) *Introduction to Functional Grammar.* London: Arnold.
Haraway, D. (1991) *Simians, Cyborgs & Women: The Reinvention of Nature*. London: Free Association Books.
Janks. H. (2003) Seeding change in South Africa: New literacies, new subjectivities, new futures. In B. Doecke, D. Homer and H. Nixon (eds) *English Teachers at Work: Narratives, Counter Narratives and Arguments* (pp. 183–205). Adelaide: Australian Association of Teachers of English and Wakefield Press.
Janks, H. (2002) The politics and history of the places children inhabit. Paper presented at the American Educational Research Association Annual Meeting, 1–5 April, 2002, New Orleans, Louisiana.
Janks, H. (2000) Domination, access, diversity and design: A synthesis for critical literacy education. *Educational Review* 52 (2), 175–86.
Luke, A. (2003) Literacy for a new ethics of global community. *Language Arts* 81 (1), 20–22.
Moll, L. (1992) Literacy research in community and classrooms: A sociocultural approach. In R. Beach, J. Green, M. Kamil and T. Shanahan (eds) *Multidisciplinary Perspectives on Literacy Research.* Urbana, Illinois: National Council of Teachers of English.
National Inquiry into the Separation of Aboriginal and Torres Strait Islander Children from their Families (Australia) (1997) Bringing them home: Report of the National Inquiry into the Separation of Aboriginal and Torres Strait Islander Children from their Families. Commissioner, Ronald Wilson Sydney: Human Rights and Equal Opportunity Commission.
Russell, E. (2000) *A is for Aunty.* Sydney: Australian Broadcasting Corporation.

Chapter 6

An Eye on the Text and an Eye on the Future: Multimodal Literacy in Three Johannesburg Families

PIPPA STEIN AND LYNNE SLONIMSKY

Introduction

In this chapter we present data from an ethnographic study of multimodal literacies involving adult family members and girl children, all of whom are high achievers in school literacy. The study was conducted in and around Johannesburg. We investigate the micro-cultures in each family in relation to what kinds of textual practices count, by whom and for what ends. In this sense we attempt to understand the ideological nature of literacy practices (Street, 1984, 1993, 1995) in each household in relation to how different roles and identities for the child both *as reader* and *as subject* are constituted and projected. Through an analysis of particular literacy events in these households, we show how a father, a grandmother and an aunt consciously scaffold for each child what counts for them as 'good reading practices'. These are not the same in each family. At the same time, we are interested in how each adult family member uses the practice of literacy to project and orientate the child towards certain forms of *worldliness.* Drawing on Appadurai's (2002) work on culture as a capacity worth strengthening in contexts of development, we pay attention to how each adult uses the practice of literacy to develop each girl's 'navigational capacities', their capacities to self-regulate, to map nodes and pathways of access in relation to aspirations and possible futures. These pathways include how to get access to various forms of linguistic, educational, cultural and economic resources. We show how these pathways are both real and imaginary – the dusty roads which lead out of the 'shacks' and the 'townships' to the city of Johannesburg and beyond. We argue that the different ways in which adult family members shape and reshape the 'stuff' of literacy (Kress, 2003) with and for their children has deep effects on children's orientations to the future both as readers and as subjects.

Background to the Study

The data we present forms part of an ethnographic-style study of Children's Early Literacy Learning (CELL) carried out in the Cape, Gauteng and Limpopo Province between 2000–2001. The study draws on ethnographies of literacy in the New Literacy Studies tradition (Heath, 1983; Street, 1984; Prinsloo & Breier, 1996; Barton & Hamilton, 1998), focusing on children's literacy learning in homes, communities and schools in order to establish why some children, and not others, are successful acquirers of literacy. Language issues are a central concern, as there are 11 official languages in South Africa. The legacy of apartheid, with its history of inequitable distribution of educational and economic resources, has had a profound impact on the quality of education and the training of teachers. At a more macro level, poverty and hunger in many areas of the country make the conditions of possibility for successful early childhood education very difficult.

New Literacy Studies and Multimodal Semiotics

Our chapter reflects some of the semantic and conceptual confusion around definitions of literacy in relation to new theorizations of literacy as fundamentally multimodal (Kress, 1997; Kress & van Leeuwen, 2001). We work with the New Literacy Studies and multimodal semiotics as complementary frameworks for thinking about the social practice of literacy. We use the concept of 'literacy events' and 'literacy practices' from the New Literacy Studies to pinpoint specific events involving different literacies, in which adults and girl children are co-participants in activities which involve the use of multiple modes of communication: writing, speech, image and the body in performance. Each 'literacy event' is a multimodal communicative event. We hope to show how these different modes are at work in each event and how the participants draw on different modes as resources in the making and transforming of meaning.

Whilst we focus on the micro-level of a specific episode involving multimodal texts, we draw on ethnographic data to situate these events within the ecology of the family, within the 'web of family life' (Barton, 1994: 149). We have found that the ethnographic data adds important ethical and interpretive dimensions to the micro-analysis of each literacy event: it has enabled us to situate the practice within a larger frame of meaning which makes sense to the participants themselves. We approach our analysis from the vantage point of the adults and claim that each event can be read semiotically, as a complex sign of how individuals within family groupings use the 'stuff' of literacy to shape and reshape their lives, according to their 'interests' in the moment of interaction. This interest arises out of their own social histories, their social locations in that interaction, and their awareness of the social environment in which the interaction takes place (Kress, 2003). These interests are dynamic, in process and changing: what appears to be the focus of concern in these families at the time of the data collection may not be the same now.

Classification and Framing

We work with Bernstein's concepts of classification and framing (Bernstein, 1996) to analyse the shaping of textual practices in the course of each family's joint activity with texts, and also to explore how principles for shaping texts were communicated in each literacy event. We also use these concepts to theoretically describe the specificity of each literacy event. Bernstein proposes that the selection of knowledge and the principles of communication invoked and enacted in any social practice actualize a range of messages. These messages communicate the 'regulative rules' or codes generative in, and of that practice. In turn such codes reflect power and control relations between social groups or agents and create the conditions of possibility for forms of practice, consciousness and identity.

In order to describe the selection of knowledge by experienced practitioners and the principles of communication within pedagogic practices, Bernstein introduces two analytic concepts: classification and framing. Classification refers to the *degree* of insulation or boundary strength between agents and practices, discourses and contexts. The strength of classification that is evoked and maintained between these categories (through a range of evaluative criteria and procedures) expresses the experienced practitioner's sense of the value and identity of the practice. It also enables acquirers to recognize the specialization of practice or what counts as knowledge in that practice or context. In general, the stronger the classification, the more specialized the discourses or practices are and the less socially distributed, but this is always *relational* and works in subtle ways.

The concept of classification allows us to describe the apparent outer limits or boundaries of a practice or context. However to analyse a social practice it is also necessary to develop an account of the form and content of interaction within a practice through the concept of framing. Framing refers to the degree of control that subjects (in this chapter, adults and children) have over the selection and regulation of contents; and over what counts as appropriate interpretations, methods or techniques, and forms and styles of communication. The strength of framing provides the realization rules for the production of a practice. Experienced practitioners' realization rules or sense of relevant meanings are made manifest in their habitual ways of being, doing and saying in interaction in that context. In this process, they model the realization rules of the practice to novices. When framing is strong, there is a visible pedagogy and the transmitter (the teacher, parent, etc.) has explicit control over the regulation of communication, selection of contents and evaluation criteria. Where framing is weak, an invisible pedagogy is operative. In such a case the acquirer has more apparent control over the selection of contents, and the regulation of communication and the rules for realizing appropriate practices are more implicit. Once again, this relationship works in subtle ways. Weak framing or invisible pedagogy may thwart the acquisition of particular discourses or practices, yet it may also create the conditions of possibility for strong socialization into the order of things or high levels of innovation and creativity.

Case Study 1: Dineo and Her Father

> You see, the generation of now are not like us, the generation of the 70s. I did not finish school because I was naughty. I don't want to blame my parents. But at least I was groomed. I want my children to be like me. I want to groom them not by thrashing, but by talking. (Interview with Mr Kapa, Dineo's father)

Dineo Kapa is a nine-year-old girl who lives with her mother, father, brother and sister in a two roomed government–subsidized house in Thokosa township, on the outskirts of Johannesburg. They live next to an informal 'shack' settlement and the Khumalo Hostel, a site of bloody clashes during the 1980s and 1990s between hostel dwellers, who were migrant workers, and Thokosa township residents. Dineo is the middle child and is in Grade 3 at the local state primary school. The school caters mainly for Sesotho speaking children from the surrounding 'shack' settlements.

Both Dineo's parents are unemployed. The only state support they receive is a child grant of R140.00 per month per child ($20). Her mother has a matriculation certificate (Grade 12) and her father left school in Grade 10. Both parents are highly ambitious for their children, as Dineo's mother explains:

> Dineo wishes to become a social worker when she grows. I pray to God that the closed doors can be opened so that I can take her to the level of her desire. That is my dream. I'm sure that this dream will become a reality one day because her father and I are positive.

This support is also manifest in a strong commitment to their children's education. They spend several hours each afternoon assisting their children with their homework. This takes place regularly around the small table in a one-roomed 'shack' in the yard used as a kitchen. Often Dineo is assisted by her older brother. In the communal family bedroom where the children sleep on the floor, there is a small TV and the children watch the 'soapies' each evening with their parents.

The church plays a central role in the life of this family. Dineo accompanies her mother, brother and sister every Thursday evening to a local church meeting held at the back of a small four roomed house nearby. Mrs Kapa sings in the choir. The church is Pentecostal in orientation and the congregation worship in tongues, as well as in Sesotho and Isizulu. Mrs Kapa follows a combination of traditional African religious practices, mixed with forms of Christianity. When her children are sick, she first takes them to see the local sangoma (traditional healer) before taking them to a 'Western' medical doctor.

> I do not mind doing everything there is to be done both along Christian and African traditional lifestyles... This does not give me a problem because my children are exposed to both worlds and they are the ones to make their own choices about this matter. I cannot say one is wrong, the other is good, it is only a matter of belief.

This exposure to 'both worlds' also functions at the level of the family language practices. The children are exposed to the languages and cultures of both parents – Sesotho and Isizulu – but the father's language, Sesotho, has more status as Dineo has been sent to a school where Sesotho is the main African language spoken and taught. In the parents' eyes, these languages and cultures are part of the local, African world. It is English, the language and culture of the world beyond, which the parents are desperate for their children to have access to, as part of their 'grooming' for the future (Granville *et al.*, 1998). This 'world beyond' is the world of 'white schools' in town, literally and metaphorically places which give children access to exclusive, wealthy and powerful networks. Mrs Kapa talks bitterly about these differences.

> I think the schools should have good teachers who can teach our children English. I am very proud that my children are doing well at school but my problem is, how can they compete with children from the white schools? There are many people who believe there cannot be equality in South Africa... If there is going to be any difference, it should be that the schools should have equal education for all the children.

Along with English, literacy is a highly valued asset in this family, shaped by the parents' past experiences as literacy learners. Both of them describe their encounter with literacy as a kind of religious experience. As Mr Kapa recalled:

> When I came to Std 3 [Grade 5], a light dawned on me. I was taught by a very great teacher, her name was Mrs Mofokeng. At the time I couldn't read or write, I could only count numbers, write my name and surname. By that time learning was difficult because I was always classified as a 'fool'... For the first time in my life with the help of Mrs Mofokeng I really understood what the mixture of vowels and consonants represented. She had patience for the 'fools'. I started to love my studies and I moved from the 'fools' to the 'clevers'.

This sense of literacy learning as a form of revelation is revealed again in Dineo's mother's story of her first encounter with literacy:

> When I got to read Isizulu, I think I was in Grade 3, the feeling of knowing how to read was phenomenal, I can't describe it, it was like magic... Knowing how to read and write is very interesting because you remember the time you could not do it and suddenly your eyes are open.

The literacy event which we explore below took place one afternoon around the communal kitchen table. This kind of activity took place on a regular basis, although it was usually the mother, not the father, who played the major pedagogical role. The event, which is recorded on video, is multimodal in its complex, multi-layered combination of the use of spoken and written language, sound, image, gesture, body and space. It is constructed as a *whole family performance* involving the father, the daughter, the mother and the brother who all see themselves as co-participants in the development of Dineo's literacy. What is enacted is a form of ritual, almost religious in its reverence for the book, and for the spoken and written word. Like the weekly religious meeting where people as a group support one physically and emotionally through prayer, song and talk, Dineo's family group themselves closely around her like a blanket. The mother stands behind her daughter with her hand resting reassuringly on her shoulder, while the father and Dineo sit at the table, the father holding the text for Dineo, guiding her patiently and carefully through each text – one in Sesotho, the other in English.

The father's focus here is overtly pedagogical: he is training Dineo in the practice of how to read aloud, how to *perform the text* with skill and accuracy. This event is not constructed as a pleasurable bedtime story reading activity, but as a form of work, of labour. He chooses the two books she is to read from – they are school books and, apart from the Bible, the only books in the house. The first book is a Sesotho school primer, 'Motheo' containing the story of Thabang who is going to town to sell his cow. It is an African version of 'Jack and the Beanstalk'. The second book is a Geography textbook with a unit entitled 'Is Life a Rocky Road?' which Dineo reads in English.

The father is very concerned with how the written text *sounds*. He pays a great deal of attention to Dineo's inflection and intonation patterns in her reading aloud of the Sesotho text. He is acutely sensitive to her pitch and volume, asking her to project and enunciate the words carefully, to 'speak up'. He stops her repeatedly in the flow of her reading to model exactly, and somewhat pedantically, how the Sesotho language should sound, how she should be inflecting her Sesotho phrasing. She repeats his inflection patterns, as the following example shows:

Father: (showing the reader to the camera)Ya, ha re ye he, tswela pele.
[Yes, let's continue.]
Dineo: Nna le Mme ha re ne letho le re ka le jang? ka—
[Me and my mother don't have anything to eat?]
Father: Aa
[No]
Dineo: ka ho (She pronounces the words incorrectly) reolo—
Father: (correcting her pronunciation) ho realo Thabang.
Dineo: Ho realo Thabang.
[Said Thabang.]
Father: Thabang a kere ke ena a tjong jwalo ho ntho, ho monna ya mokgutswane.
[Thabang said that to the short man.]

On one level, the father's focus on inflection and intonation is developing Dineo's coding competence. Effective literacy draws on a range of practices including the skill of breaking the code of written texts by recognizing and using the alphabet, sounds in words, spelling, and structural conventions and patterns (Kress, 2003; Street, 1995). However,

Sesotho as a spoken language is a tonal language which depends on subtle variations of pitch and tone to inflect different meanings. Thus, on another level the father's focus on phonological features shows his appreciation of the relation between coding competence and semantic competence in reading aloud Sesotho texts. Pitch and tone *are* meaning. He is demonstrating and modelling that *the meaning of this story is in the performance.* Reading aloud is akin to oral storytelling: it requires shifts and intonations, an awareness of audience and an attention to poetics associated with oral performance (Scheub, 1975; Hofmeyr, 1994; Gunner, 2003).

This attention to the performance is evident in the next sequence in which he models how greetings should be inflected when telling a story:

Dineo: Kgotso monna e—
[My greetings to you Mr—]

Father: Ee butle, butle (emphasizing the pitch, tone) kgotso___
[No, wait, wait. My greetings___]

Dineo: 'Kgotso monna e mokgutswane,ho dumedisa Thabang ka thabo e kgolo. O ya kae?
['Greetings to you short man,' said Thabang with excitement. 'Where are you going?']

Father: Butle he, ho tsamaiwa ho thwa (emphasis on tone, pitch) Kgotso monna e mokgutswane, ho dumedisa Thabang ka thabo e kgolo. O ya kae? (pointing to the picture in the book) o tloha mona monna ya mokgutswane. Ha re eme moo, tswela pele.
[Wait, this is how you should read. 'Greetings to you short man,' said Thabang with excitement. 'Where are you going?' The short man comes from here. Read.]

The father's insistence on the 'correct' pronunciation signals his interests in relation to a form of linguistic purity as well as ethnic pride in relation to the Sesotho language. Implicit in his pedagogy is a dissatisfaction with Dineo's school teachers, whom he criticizes for their 'incorrect' pronunciation of his language:

> I want them [my children] to follow our culture, I tell them that they are Sothos and must speak Sesotho... You know with their homework, I find that some of the teachers do not know Sesotho, not that I am angry about it, they say that this is so-and-so and I say it is not correct.

The father's interest in performance is further shown when he indicates to her how the written text contains clues, like punctuation marks, which guide the reader in how the text is to be read. He is consciously developing her meta-linguistic awareness. Here he introduces her to the concept of a 'fullstop':

Father: Ho. (emphasis on pronunciation) Ho realo monna eo, kgutlo. Ke eng kgutlo?
['No. Said the man.' Fullstop. What is a fullstop?]

Dineo: Ke fullstop.
[It's a fullstop.]

Father: Fullstop, wa bona he. (pointing at the section to be read) Ha re qhale he, ke mona he.
[Fullstop. Let's start afresh.]

After the reading of the Sesotho story, the father turns his attention to teaching Dineo how to read English correctly. When Dineo is reading the Geography book, he also draws her attention to the 'correct' pronunciation and inflection of sentences and phrases in English, modelling how she should be saying them. As he did with Sesotho, he is demonstrating his criteria of appropriateness in relation to standard spoken English and communicates normative criteria for reading English. As they read this book, the father continues to emphasize inflection, pitch and tone but then stops at the end of a sentence to query the meaning of the word 'rock'. Here he calls on Dineo's mother for help:

Father: (asking the wife) Kana ke eng rock? Rock e jwang mm, ba bua ka eng mo?
[What is a rock? How is a rock? What are they referring to here?] (Turning to the mother)

Mother: Ke ntho eo o tholang Geography?
[It's something that you get in Geography?]

Father: mm...

Dineo: (points to the picture of the rock)

This is a significant moment in which, for the first time, Dineo takes the initiative, asserting her visual literacy skills as she helps her parents to understand 'rock' by pointing to the visual text on the page. It is a clear example of the insertion of the discourse of school in the home, where the child uses her knowledge to support her parents' understandings. But it is also significant because even though the father does not initially know what 'a rock' means, he still reads the sentence aloud with perfect inflections, caesuras and emphases in a manner that communicates that 'a rock' refers to some kind of object. Through this partitioning, he is demonstrating that text consists of units of meaning which are integrated into a textual whole.

Dineo's father is constituting and projecting Dineo as a certain kind of reader, invoking strong classification over the meaning of the text in both the Sesotho and English texts. His emphasis on ostensive meanings, inflection and tone, and reading as performance together communicate the message that while texts are meaningful, this meaning is closed. The meaning is given, and the duty or task of the reader is to extract 'the' meaning in the text, from the text. Taken together, these practices signify that there is a 'right' way to read the text – which he authorizes – and that learning is achieved by adhering to the 'right' way. These are the practices around language which count, and not others.

The activity is also strongly framed. The father constructs Dineo as a learner who must learn to decode the meaning of the text and relay it appropriately through linguistic resources. His practices do not communicate to Dineo that she is a participant reader who has a relation to the text beyond the world inscribed in the text. She is not asked what she believes or thinks, nor recruited to participate in meaning making beyond the level of the linguistic inflection and translation. The father's practices realize his taken-for-granted or implicit constructs of the relation between the reader and the text and communicates the message that the text 'exists': she must receive and reproduce it, not transform it.

Through all these textual practices Dineo learns how to read, what counts as reading and what it means to be a reader all of which transform her consciousness, experience and identity. As long as she continues to reads textual meanings as closed, she may become strongly socialized into the order of things represented in the text because she takes them as 'truth', as the way things are and ought to be and lives them. Alternately, precisely because she does not invest her 'self' in interpreting it, she may be relatively inured to messages about social relations and identity communicated in and through texts. However, if the boundaries of texts do not become more permeable, more open to interpretation, it is unlikely that her identity and consciousness will be radically transformed by texts. Furthermore, if she does not develop other orientations and constructs of text through participation in other forms of literate practice, she may begin to find the demands of school learning becoming more and more difficult as she proceeds to higher levels. But, perhaps as she learns literacy in school and other contexts she may transform her parents' construction of texts.

In relation to Dineo *as subject*, we think this event shows Dineo's father 'grooming' her for the future. He is consciously developing and modelling certain kinds of navigational capacities which he believes will enable her to 'open the closed doors' to her aspirations. A key navigational capacity is skill in literacy and language. He emphasizes the value of bilingual literacy: she needs to know how to read an indigenous African language as part of maintaining her local ethnic identity, and she needs to know English as part of a global identity, her identity beyond the township. In insisting on *his* language as the language which has value in the home (and not the mother's language, IsiZulu), he is asserting certain forms of linguistic patriarchy in this household. Through his interest in reading as performance he is developing Dineo's navigational capacities in relation to specific local oral cultural practices, which are an integral part of church, schools, and homes.

Speaking more broadly, it seems to us that Dineo's parents are quite comfortable exposing and projecting her into an environment in which diversity is the norm. Johannesburg, the only global city on the African continent, is a cosmopolitan city, replete with a multiplicity of registers in which it is African, European and American (Mbembe & Nuttall, 2004). Dineo and her family are part of this city, and like everyone else, negotiating what it means to be both part of the West and the non-West, the African. Her parents actively encourage her to participate in multiple worlds: it is naturalized practice in the households that the children are exposed to Christian and African traditional lifestyles. Through these hybrid practices, the children are introduced to forms of worldliness, beliefs that the future generation needs to be part of multiple 'elsewheres'. Dineo is not a passive recipient of these ideas: how she will react, resist and transform these ideas and practices remains to be seen. However, how she takes hold of and transforms these forms of linguistic and cosmopolitan capital for a productive future depends to a large extent on the material conditions of Dineo's life: on the day of this reading event, her mother and father were preparing to send all three children to the rural family home in KwaZulu – Natal because there was no money for food.

Case Study 2: Puleng and Her Grandmother

Puleng is an eight-year-old girl who lives with her grandparents, Mr and Mrs Mohale, in the township of Sharpeville in Southern Gauteng, 85 km south of Johannesburg. In accordance with African extended family practices, Puleng's primary caregiver is her grandmother, who pays for her schooling, clothing and other basic needs.

Puleng's mother is completing her studies at a technical college, and she sees Puleng during her study breaks. All members of the Mohale family have qualifications beyond matriculation and are employed. Mrs Mohale's father was a high school principal and her mother a nurse. Mrs Mohale comes from a religious family, and reads the bible every day.

The family can be described as middle class and live in a spacious house in Sharpeville, famous for the 1961 resistance against the apartheid pass laws. The house is located in a low-income area and surrounded by typical 'match box' four-roomed houses built during the apartheid era. There is concern in the family about the 'invasion' of shack dwellings in the area since the ANC government came to power in 1994. According to the family, the high crime levels prevalent in the township are associated with 'foreigners' and 'criminals' who live in these shacks.

Puleng's safety is a source of constant worry for Mrs Mohale.

> Nowadays when you walk out of your workplace you are just panicking, you are in a hurry to be home to see if the child is safe. Everybody is worried about their children's safety ... you know there are so many rapes of little children like this, people have taken to smoking dagga, I don't know if is it frustration or what, it is so unsafe, it is so unsafe.

As a result she does not allow her grandchild to play in the streets, unlike other children in the neighbourhood. She encourages girls in the neighbourhood to play in Puleng's house, where there is a large garage for play and access to a range of resources including television, a computer, toys and books. Boys are not allowed to come and play. Mrs Mohale compares the state of things now to when she was young:

> When I was a child we were free, we could go anywhere ... we nowadays don't let our eyes off our children for less than thirty minutes ... we ask people who are not at work to watch out for our children, so that we can be 'township eyes' for each other. I am trying to teach Puleng how to become my eyes.

Unlike other children in the neighbourhood who go to local schools in the township, Puleng attends a 'town' school and uses a taxi every morning to get there. She is in Grade 2. Puleng likes school, is doing very well there and loves the social life of school. Her school was a segregated whites-only Afrikaans medium school until 1994. It switched to dual-medium in 1995, when English was introduced as a medium of instruction and when the school began admitting children from other languages and races. Lessons are conducted in Afrikaans and English: Afrikaans speaking children attend the Afrikaans classes and mainly black African children attend the English classes. This means that English is taught as a first language, Afrikaans as a second language, and Sesotho is introduced in Grade 5 as a third language.

The family has a rich history in multilingual proficiency in South African languages. Puleng's grandfather is Setswana speaking and Mrs Mohale speaks Northern Sotho. Puleng's great-grandfather was fluent in Afrikaans. The family also speak English. In everyday communication, family members tend to switch between languages, especially Sesotho, Setswana and English. The family values multilingualism: family interaction patterns draw on sophisticated forms of multilingual language play and the children are actively encouraged to learn and use many languages as part of their cultural and intellectual development. This core value of multilingualism is explicitly linked by Mrs Mohale with *ubuntu*, an important concept among South African Africans expressing a sense of caring and compassion for others, a belief that each person's humanity is bound up in the humanity of others. Learning and valuing languages other than your own (including Afrikaans, what used to be the oppressor's language) is part of *ubuntu*, as Mrs Mohale makes clear in this bilingual conversation with Puleng:

Mrs Mohale: So what did you do the whole day [at school] because Mrs Putter [Puleng's teacher] was not around? [Sesotho]

Puleng: They took us to an Afrikaans class. We could not hear a thing. Me and my friends played and made drawings because we did not understand the Afrikaans teacher. [Sesotho]

Mrs Mohale: Puleng, you have to learn all languages. Afrikaans is a language as well. [Sesotho] If you do not know other languages you will become stupid. [English]

Puleng: Mama, I know Afrikaans [English]. But today the teacher used difficult words [Sesotho]

Mrs Mohale takes an active interest in Puleng's education, particularly her literacy and language activities. There is a strong oral storytelling tradition in her family, particularly from Mrs Mohale's father, who believed that 'children can make decisions out of the story and relate them to their everyday life'. Storytelling and story reading at bedtime is a nightly ritual, taking place after Puleng has been bathed, fed and watched some television. Mrs Mohale routinely selects the storybooks for Puleng from the Sharpeville library which she passes on her way home from work. These books are always in English.

In this bedtime story reading event, which takes place in Puleng's bedroom, the grandmother sits upright on the bed with her grandchild either lying down and sitting beside her. The event is being filmed by Puleng's aunt, described below as the camera operator, who is also an assistant researcher on the literacy learning project. The bedtime event is multimodal, encompassing written and spoken language, image, gesture and performance. It begins with story reading in English, followed by oral storytelling in Sesotho or English. We see the two activities as integrated and part of the flow of everyday life in this household. Mrs Mohale's style is strongly pedagogical in orientation, with her controlling the content and the activity of reading and storytelling.

The book chosen for story reading tonight is a picture book called *Fiona the Elephant*. It tells the tale of a little elephant called Fiona who has a problem remembering anything. Her family is very good at remembering things and she asks them for help. They give her some tips which Fiona puts into practice by the end of the story. The grandmother's reading strategies consist of paging systematically through the text, reading it aloud, interspersing the written language and images with different kinds of commentary. She makes clear connections for the child between the visual and verbal text, pointing out the links between the names of the characters and the images of them. For example,

Granny:	Okay Fiona on the picture. You see, she's sitting in the, in the, on the sofa and—
Camera operator:	Se ka sheba nna [Don't look at me.]
Puleng:	(Winking her eyes)
Granny:	Then___they say here Fiona had___(paging through the book) what do they say__they say here Fiona had a problem remembering___(looking at the camera) you see (Puleng seems more interested in the camera than the book at this stage.)
Granny:	(Pointing in the book.) This book is about a little elephant called Fiona. She had a big problem she couldn't remember anything. You see here's Fiona. Fiona's mother always remembered where she put things. Can you see, here's Fiona's mother...

The grandmother consciously tries to recruit Puleng to focus on the text. Her strategy is to begin with the images to arouse her interest, and then to link the visual text to the written text, posing questions about what the verbal text 'says' and then summarizing the gist of the content. Her strategy models a way of talking about, responding to and interpreting information from visual and written texts, all of which are contributing to the development of Puleng's multimodal literacy. Puleng actively participates in this activity by taking charge of one area: reminding her granny to show the camera operator each new visual text as it is revealed.

Halfway through the story reading, Puleng recruits the practice of making these links between the visual and the written text when she also starts to point to the pictures. In the following sequence, the grandmother points out and labels the main characters, using her index finger to identify the words as she articulates them and to frame Puleng's attention. She returns regularly to the main threads of the story, providing the child with a coherent narrative thread and to keep her fixed on the object of study.

Granny: Can you see, here's Fiona's father, he could do all her aunty Sofy's best recipes. Here are eh___Fiona's father is doing a pie the recipe she got from aunty Sofy, can you see?

Puleng: Yes

Granny: mm you can see Fiona's father? Can remember aunty Sofy's best recipes. Here is aunty Sofy Sofy (showing the book to the camera) can you see aunty Sofy?

Puleng: mm

A key strategy she uses is to move fluidly from the meaning of specific parts of the text to how it relates to the text as a whole. She focuses on units of meaning by elaborating on the story, inserting new information, picking up on meanings which are not clear or explicit, and generally acting as a literacy mediator, someone who mediates the text for someone else, in this case, the child. At certain points, she reiterates what the text 'means' in her own words, providing her grandchild with the grounds for knowledge making. Here is an example:

Granny: Her best friend was?

Puleng: Felicity.

Granny: Ja Fiona's best friend was Felicity. They went they signed up to go to Jerry eh uncle Jerry's gym, can you see, Jerry's gym it's called. That's where they are going to play games there at the gym (pointing to pictures). Here's Fiona and her friends Felicity. There they went to the gym. But the day before the class Fiona began to worry. The class was tomorrow, Fiona was now worried. What if she forgot her gym clothes? What if she forgot to go to the class at all? Fiona began to ask her family to help, can you see?

Puleng: (nodding her head)
Granny: She's worried, can you see she's very worried. Here's Fiona she's worried because she knows she has a problem in remembering anything.

This literacy event involves a weaker classification of texts and their meanings than with Dineo's father. The grandmother opens up the boundaries of textual practices by recruiting a wider range of strategies that demand and realize more reader involvement in decoding the text. She carefully paces and sequences the process of reading aloud from the text page by page, moving in and out of the text with explanatory and interpretative comments on the basis of intra and extra textual information. Her comments involve explanations, definitions, recapping of narrative sequence, anticipation of events, reiteration of the main ideas, making the plot and themes constantly explicit, summarizing, paraphrasing and interpreting for the child. Through these practices the grandmother is demonstrating and modelling the rules of talking about, responding to and interpreting images and written texts. She is both focusing on literacy as a set of sub-skills like predicting, summarizing and interpreting, linking verbal text and image, and at the same time showing how written and visual material can be a backdrop for talk and information retrieval. These textual practices model the metacognitive strategies used by experienced readers in making meaning from text.

Although the classification of textual meanings and practices is weaker than those in Dineo's home, and despite the grandmother's stronger control (and thus weaker framing) over the text, classification is nevertheless strong. This is because despite the range of strategies she employs, all are oriented to mediating to Puleng how to crack the semantic code given in the text. Like Dineo's father, the grandmother is oriented to 'the' meaning of the text and communicates the message that the role of the reader is to uncover the meaning to be found *in* the text. Thus the relation between textual practice and meaning remains relatively closed and stable. Furthermore, the grandmother chooses what to focus on, and how to explore it. She regulates Dineo's role, doing most of the talking. Thus Puleng exerts only fractionally more control over interaction with the text than Dineo (like directing her grandmother to include the video camera operator).

Midway through the story reading, the grandmother changes her orientation to the text. Instead of focussing on what the text literally means, she focuses on the moral lessons and implications of the story, demonstrating to Puleng that texts contain messages about how we ought to behave. In the following extract she forges connections between Fiona the elephant who cannot remember her school bag, and Puleng the child from Sharpeville, who also needs help remembering her school books, lunch box and homework. Instead of spelling the connection out explicitly, she does it more implicitly, by asking Puleng a series of yes/no questions much like a teacher might do in class, guiding her to accept the moral lesson. The protagonist of the text subtly shifts from Fiona to Puleng and the message of the text shifts from Fiona the elephant who forgets things to 'you' addressed to Puleng, the subject.

Granny: Fiona had a real problem she couldn't remember anything, can you see?
Puleng: Yes.
Granny: Can you remember all your things before you go to school?
Puleng: Yes.
Granny: (pointing in the book) To pack up everything, to take your schoolbag, to pack up your homework, to take your lunch box before you catch your school bus?
Puleng: Yes.
Granny: You must try to remember everything before you go to school. All your things when going to school (pointing in the book).

Through this process, she communicates the broad message that texts can be invoked for moral and instructional purposes, that they can teach us forms of appropriate conduct. More specifically she demonstrates to Puleng that there are connections between the textual world and the reader's world-in-effect, that she is inscribed in the text. She communicates the message that texts are porous, metaphorical (can stand for something else) and can offer us, the reader, other ways of seeing and being. By establishing a relation between Puleng and the text, she gives Puleng a stake in the act of reading and inserts Puleng's self into the text. This opens up textual meanings and changes Puleng's role as reader, initiating the assertion of a reader's voice. She communicates the message that 'you are in the text and the text is in you'.

The story reading is followed immediately by oral storytelling in which the grandmother relates a version of 'Little Red Riding Hood' in English, called 'Little Red Riding Hood and the Jackal'. She follows this story with a Sesotho version of Tselane, a well-known South African folkloric tale. Both stories are about innocent young girls who unwittingly are led astray by evil forces – jackals or cannibals disguised as mothers or grandmothers who want to devour them. Mrs Mohale ends the tale of Little Red Riding Hood with a strong cautionary note to Puleng:

Granny: And they took out grandmother's body out of the jackal...
Puleng: Mm. (Yes).
Granny: And her mother asked her, 'Did you, why did you not use the road I asked you to use?' ... she did not listen...
Puleng: To her mother.
Granny: To her mother. If she had used the road on her left, she could have gone to her, come to her granny's place quickly, and gave her food before the jackal swallowed her granny. And when she goes to her grandmother, she must not have stopped on the road and talked to ... eh, jackals. Jackals are crooks. They make you their friends, and they are just your ?
Puleng & Granny: (together) Bad friends!
Puleng: And why did the jackal follow Little Red Riding Hood to her grandmother?
Granny: The jackal is a cruel animal.
Puleng: Aowa! (Really!)
Granny: He is cruel. He eats up people. Now Little Red Riding Hood should not have listened to a jackal. A jackal is a bad friend, mm? Okay? That's why you must not listen to any bad friends on the road. When you are sent somewhere, you go there and come back like your mother has sent you. If anybody like your father is sending you, go there and come back. Don't stop on the way and talk to your friends, because they will tell you wrong things, and send you to the wrong place.

Mrs Mohale then explicitly contrasts Little Red Riding Hood with the story of Tselane, who is rescued from danger by the forces of good, in the form of an alert, caring community. In the story of Tselane, the mother has to go to work, and leaves Tselane by herself, locked up in the house. The cannibal giant Dimo comes to the house, knocks on the door and offers Tselane something to eat. She recognizes his voice and refuses to open the door. He swallows an iron and comes back with a 'sweet thin voice'. This time Tselane opens the door, the cannibal grabs her, puts her in a sack and goes to have a drink in a shebeen before feasting on her 'soft meat'. But a group of kindly people in the bar see the sack shaking, realize what's going on, make the giant drunk, free Tselane and fill the sack with scorpions and snakes. The cannibal wakes up, opens his sack and is killed by the scorpions. At the end of the tale of Tselane, Mrs Mohale draws out a different lesson for her granddaughter:

Granny: Ee. E tla re ha o tsamaile, mohlomong, o be o lahleha mo "pole-keng" ye nngwe batho ba a go thusa. A ba swane le jackal. (...When you have gone somewhere, perhaps you get lost at a certain place, some people help you. They are not like jackal).
Puleng: Jackal.
Granny: Mm. A ke re? (Yes. Okay?)
Puleng: (Puleng nods her head.)
Granny: Mo lefatsheng, batho ba bangwe ba "goo". Ha ba bona e le sono ka wena, o le lahlegile, o utswitswe ke batho, ba a go thusa, ba go apese di aparo tse "skoon", ba go ntshe ka mo mokotleng, ba go balehise, ba ho ise ga lena gape, a ke re?(O dumela ka hlogo gape, Puleng) Ba bangwe a ba, a ba "good", a ke re? (Puleng o dumela gape ka hlogo).
(Some people are bad. Some people are... Here on earth, some people are good. When they see that you are in trouble, when you are lost, when you have been stolen by other people, they help you (Puleng nods her head), and dress you in clean clothes, and take you out of the sack, and make you flee back to your home, okay? (Puleng nods her head again). Some are?
Puleng: (Together with Granny) Good.

Mrs Mohale's changes in her orientation during the course of this event from working with the surface meaning of the text to interpreting and recruiting the text for normative purposes. These shifts realize her interests as a grandmother, teacher and guardian of this child. She recruits the norms of behaviour of 'Fiona the Elephant', 'Little Red Riding Hood' and 'Tselane' to communicate her criteria of appropriate conduct that she expects of Puleng. Thus she uses books and oral stories to construct moral lessons about how to act and behave in the same way that the Bible provides instruction to its readers on the 'right' way to live. Like Dineo's father, she works with two languages – English and Sesotho – and is particularly concerned to use Sesotho because Puleng will only learn to read and write her home language, Sesotho, in Grade 5.

Weakening the classification and framing of textual practices increases the potential for textual practices to transform consciousness and identity. On the one hand, since more of the reader/listener is inserted into the process, it may be difficult for the reader/listener to resist being transformed. On the other hand it enables the reader/listener to access other worlds, other ways of being which may in turn enable him or her to change the order of things.

Finally, it is notable that on the one hand the grandmother's practices offer structure and containment, and model important strategies for 'cracking' the code in any text. On the other hand they orient Puleng to sub-texts and implications, and alert her that there are lessons to be drawn from every activity. Traditionally these have been highly valued skills and dispositions in school learning. Thus these textual practices may offer a sound foundation for her learning career in school.

Mrs Mohale is consciously developing Puleng's capacity for care of the self, in the sense of self-regulation and self-surveillance. She has an acute sense of the dangers of township life and wants to instil in her 'a sense of responsibility'. Puleng is Little Red Riding Hood on her way to see her grandmother and the road is full of jackals. Puleng is Tselane, staying at home alone whilst her mother goes to work, a child who has to know how to protect herself against 'cannibals' who disguise themselves as mothers. Like her father before her, Mrs Mohale is determined to make her grandchild aware of the importance of being obedient. She is completely overt in how she uses the text to actualize different forms of knowing, which she manipulates to regulate Puleng. She is intent on developing Puleng's navigational strategies for a circumscribed world of the township in which the child lives, in the belief that these are life skills which she can use anywhere. Drawing on her own deep knowledge of local oral storytelling practices (through her own history of these practices), she uses these representational resources to educate Puleng, to form her character and to socialise her in ways that school do not do. She models the values of the family and the local community: how tales are meant to teach us lessons on how to live. In this potent mix of African traditional storytelling practices, and contemporary Western-style story reading, Puleng is exposed to different forms of knowledge in different modes, in different languages and in different cultures. These are particular forms of worldliness, of cosmopolitan culture, which should stand her in good stead for her future.

Case Study 3: Margot and Her Aunt

Margot is a six-year-old girl, the second child in an English speaking, middle class family living in Yeoville, a suburb bordering on the inner city of Johannesburg. She lives with her parents and her older brother.

Her parents have a history of political activism in the 'white left' and were involved in the ANC (African National Congress) struggle for liberation. They have chosen to live in Yeoville for political and social reasons: it is a strongly multicultural, multilingual suburb, containing white and black middle and lower class families, immigrants from Zaire, Nigeria, and the Democratic Republic of the Congo, and a small group of orthodox Jewish families. Unemployment in the area is quite high and it is notorious for drug-dealing and prostitution.

Margot's parents are well-educated and employed: her mother is an early childhood development educator and her father works for the government in land affairs. Margot is a monolingual English speaker although her ancestry is Setswana. She understands rudimentary isiZulu but does not speak it. She attends a private, well-resourced English medium pre-school close by and is the oldest child in the school. She is very proud of this fact as she is regarded as 'the cleverest' and has a certain kind of status as a result. She has not yet learnt how to read and write, as this begins formally at the age of seven when she enters Grade 1.

Margot leads an active life, following the trends of her peer group, listens to popular music, watches videos and has access to multiple educational and electronic resources. The family read newspapers regularly and the family fridge is covered with schedules, timetables, school notices, children's drawing and notes. Margot is very fond of books and she often reads with her aunt, Kathy, to whom she is very close. She loves listening to stories, jokes and chatter and she is an accomplished conversationalist both with her peers and adults. She knows her way around the computer but does not often choose to play games on it unless inspired by another child. Margot and her friend Sara, who lives next door, spend a lot of time on fantasy play.

The literacy event we focus on takes place around the kitchen table in the family home. There are five participants: Margot, her mother, her brother Sam, her aunt Kathy and her friend Sara, who is four years old. The family is looking at buying a house. Newspapers are spread out. Margot and Sara are seated at the table, paging through the Houses for Sale advertisements. These images form the focus of the children's attention and conversation:

Margot: (points to a photograph in a newspaper advertisement) I think that this house is stupid. It's too small, and it hasn't got a pool.

Sara: Ja, it's stupid.

Margot: (points to another advert with photograph) Look at this one. Look here Sara, look. Hey Mum, this one is okay, see here. Look Kathy, look Sam. Come and look Mum!!
Sara: (Leaning over to see). Why?
Margot: It's got a nice garden. Look at all the trees.
Sara: Those aren't trees. They are too small.

Not only do the children use images as a source of basic information about what a house looks like (its size and attributes) but they also use the images to make critical and comparative judgements on what constitutes a 'stupid', 'nice' or 'okay' house. They are able to retrieve visual information and link it to their background knowledge. What is striking is the confidence with which these opinions are expressed, the sureness of the judgements and the unshakeable knowledge of what constitutes a 'good' house and a 'bad' house.

This is a family activity with adults present, but unlike in Dineo's or Puleng's case, it is not led by the parent, but by the children, principally Margot. Margot regulates everyone's attention, including them in the event by asking questions, commenting on what she sees, and pointing out interesting details. Margot is showing all the practices of a skilful reader without yet being able to decode the written text. In the following extract, Kathy plays a more directive, pedagogical role by helping Margot to understand and locate the generic features of the house for sale advertisement. She playfully scaffolds the interaction by arousing Margot's interest in looking for 'the price' in the text. This leads into an extended conversation on 'the price' and the meaning of the terms 'estate agent'. The tone throughout is playful and witty, led by the children. Here Margot recruits Kathy's attention and calls upon her to make the 'text' the object of her activity by asking her specific questions around the meanings of words, and how to interpret the genre of the text. Margot's aunt is acknowledged as a resource for increasing textual knowledge, rather than an 'authority' who has the last word.

Margot: (Turning the page). Look at this one Mum. (Her mother looks with her). It's good hey!
Kathy: Ja, but I think that it's a bit expensive.
Margot: How do you know?
Kathy: I can see the price.
Margot: Where's the price Kathy? Show me the price Kathy. Does this say the price Kathy? (points to a word).
Kathy: No, that says the name of the estate agents.

Sara and Margot: What's an estate agent?
Kathy: That's someone who sells houses to other people.
Margot: Like a kind of a shop person.
Sara: No, silly (laughs). We don't buy houses in shops.
Margot: I never said we did. But a 'stateagent' is a kind of a person like a person, like someone, like a person who sells things, like, like in a shop. Hey Kathy.

A few minutes later the two girls have fetched pens and paper and are busy writing, constructing their own advertisement for the house they would like. In this seamless switch from reading text and image to producing text and image, the girls show a fluid, comfortable relation to writing as a productive resource for recording, categorizing and making visible (in every sense of the word) important family information. They already have an understanding of what writing is, and the work it can do. They draw on a range of familiar semiotic resources which they playfully and effortlessly transform for their own interests, as they enter into a sophisticated form of fantasy play which is both a parody of reading and writing, and of buying a house. During the course of this transformation, Kathy asks them about what they are writing, demonstrating a much clearer and explicit attention to pedagogical practice. However, she never makes explicit the criteria for writing, which makes her pedagogy invisible. Kathy's relationship to Margot's attempts at writing is particularly significant. Margot is not writing actual words – she is drawing wavy lines or squiggles across the page. And yet Kathy constantly communicates the message to her, that her writing is meaningful and she is 'saying' something.

Kathy: What are you writing Margot?
Margot: I'm writing about the houses.
Kathy: Oh. That's interesting.
Margot: Ja, I'm writing what all the houses have. They've got lots of things. See here (Points to the page she is working on).
Kathy: Oh. If it's got lots of things then it must be a big house.
Margot: Ja it is, 'cos we need a big house. So we have to find a house with lots of things, for all of us. (Continues writing).
Kathy: What does this say? (Pointing to a 'word' on the sheet of paper).
Margot: It says that there is a double bedroom on top.

Sara: And this Margot ? (pointing to another 'word', leaning over Margot's shoulder).
Margot: That says, moooooooove Sara, I can't write properly. It says that you can only have two cars in the front.

Kathy also invokes stronger framing when the conversation turns to money and the way it works. This in fact is the most explicitly pedagogical interlude because Kathy not only orients Margot's attention to particular practices concerning money, she also communicates criteria and privileged practices i.e. the 'correct' way to go about buying a house. In this extract Kathy is consciously developing Margot's 'navigational capacities' in relation to being a future home owner.

Kathy: You've got a line here Margot. What is that line for?
Margot: It's for the price.
Kathy: Oh.
Margot: Ja. You have to put the price on, so that people can know what they much pay. Like in the paper Kathy.
Kathy: Oh ja.
Margot: People mustn't just pay any price Kathy. They have to pay the right price hey. It's like they have to go and get the money and pay the right price.
Kathy: Where do they get the money from Margot?
Margot: They get the money from the bank. They go and ask the bank and then they get the money, and then they pay it to the people.
Kathy: Does the bank just give them money Margot?
Margot: Ja. No problem. They go with they card, and they get the money.
Sam: No. That's too much money for the card.
Margot: No it's not.
Sam: Yes it is.
Margot: No it's not too much money. You can get money with your card.
Sam: No you can't. Hey Kathy?
Kathy: Yes. I think that you have to go inside the bank if you want a lot of money, Margot.
Margot: My mummy gets a lot of money from her card.
Kathy: Yes, she does sometimes. But a house costs such a lot of money that you have to go and specially get it.
Margot: Why Kathy?

Kathy: Because the money goes to the other person in a special way. We don't give the person the money like we do in the shops.
Margot: Oh.

Up to this point, the two girls are working with a strong reality principle around buying a house but at this point, there is a dramatic shift into fantasy play as their imaginations take flight. Both girls take immense pleasure in using the idea of buying a house as a springboard for their fanciful desires and aspirations. Their creativity is praised and encouraged and it becomes a source of amusement for the whole family.

Kathy: Wow. That is an expensive house Margot. I wish we could buy this house. It look like you are writing such a lot, it must be a wonderful house.
Margot: Ja, it's a wonderful house. It's got so many things. It's got a sauna, and a tennis court, and a vegetable garden, and so much bedrooms.
Sara: How much bedrooms does it say?
Margot: It says 27 bedrooms.
Sara: 27 bedrooms! (She and Margot start laughing). 27 bedrooms!
Margot: Ja. There's one for me and one for you and one for mummy and one for Sam, and one for Libby, and one for Timmy, and one for the cats, and one for the rabbit, and one for Kathy.
Sara: And one for everyone!!
Margot: Ja, and there's also a bathroom for everyone.
Sara: Yes, a bathroom for everyone.
Margot: We all have to have a bathroom, even the cats!! (Laughs).
Sara: Yes, (laughing), they have to have a bathroom otherwise they can't clean themselves.
Kathy: Why?
Margot: 'Cos they need to see in the mirror. (Laughs).
Sara: Yes if they don't look in the mirror, they can't do it.
Margot: Yes, they need to look in case they fur goes sqwonk, like this (shows with her own hair, she and Sara laughing all the time).
Kathy: What does it say on your paper?
Margot: It says that they fur will go sqwonk if they don't have a mirror in they bathroom!! (Laughing all the while). They fur will go sqwonk and then they can't go out.

In this literacy event, classification and framing are much, much weaker than in the case studies of Dineo and Puleng. There is an invisible pedagogy operating, but the question is what is the object of the pedagogy? It seems to us that the object of activity is buying a house not reading as such. Even though Margot and Sara are clearly novice readers and writers, reading is such a taken for granted aspect of all activity in this household that the activity is not marked by Kathy as an explicit reading activity at all. She does however mark the writing activity quite explicitly. However, both Margot and Sara externalize practices they have been exposed to in relation to reading both at home and at school as well as IRF (initiate-response-feedback) questioning patterns of school. The notable absence of any messages from Kathy about 'right' or 'correct' ways of reading communicates to Margot and Sara that this genre of text can be read in many ways, there is no specific order of reading the advertisements. In this textual practice, the reading pathways are open, and thus the reader's attention can be paid to different textual features – the images, the logos, the price – at different times.

The multimodal literacy event in this family illustrates par excellence Appadurai's concept of the capacity to aspire as it is enacted in everyday family life. In its orientation towards consumer practices, the 'norms and standards' of buying a house, the talk around the text is full of 'metaphors, justifications, narratives and pathways through which bundles of goods and services are actually tied to wider social scenes and contexts' (Appadurai, 2002: 7). Implicit in these conversations are more abstract norms and beliefs about the 'right' way to live: to have big houses with gardens and pools, to treat pets like people, to have credit cards and bank accounts, to have leisure time to play. Thus what Margot and the other children learn from this fluid, fluent and wide ranging conversation with adult members of the culture, is how to get access to and navigate the world of goods and services, the steps – textual, financial, cultural – to becoming a member of the ruling class. At the same time we must not loose sight of the fact that Margot is also learning how to become part of the literacy club, how to decode, interpret and transform multi-semiotic texts for her own interests and purposes. There is a huge element of pleasure and play in this encounter – literacy is as much about playing games and inventing worlds as it is about getting information about how to function in the 'real' world.

Concluding Remarks

We have called our chapter, 'An eye on the text and an eye on the future' to signal how the 'stuff' of literacy is used by adults in families to teach children both the forms and shapes of literacy, as well as to develop particular orientations towards the future. In each case study, we have tried to demonstrate how the practice of literacy is not neutral but imbued with values, aspirations and attitudes around what textual practices count, for whom, and for what ends. In their relation to literacy learning, adults draw on their own histories of literacy, culture, knowledge and schooling. These histories are different: for Dineo's parents, learning literacy is associated with forms of magic and religious relevation and a particular kind of oral performance. For Puleng's grandmother, literacy is tied to oral storytelling practices which have been part of her history for generations. For Margot and her aunt, literacy is deeply embedded in family life, a natural activity, like eating or playing or sleeping. In all these homes, the 'stuff' of literacy is never one thing: the participants shift from looking at and talking about images to performing the written texts aloud, to producing forms of emergent writing, to telling ancient stories in African languages and in English. These practices are fundamentally multimodal and draw on a range of representational resources available to the participants. These resources are not static: they are socially produced and are part of histories of culturally and historically situated communicative practices which have been developed and transformed through the participants' ongoing interaction with materiality and the shaping of culture. There are examples in these case studies of how the adults and children actively work with historically established conventions in relation to particular ideas of what it means to become literate, but in doing so, reshape these conventions. These transformations occur in different degrees and at different points in the process. They are related to the constraints and possibilities of the resources available in the environment, the interests of each individual sign-maker in relation to the communicative purpose, and the extent to which the sign-maker has a deep knowledge of the practice (Kress, 2003).

The ideological nature of literacy practices is also apparent in how adult members of the culture use literacy to shape social relations and forms of identity (Street, 1993). Our study has shown how each family member uses the practice of literacy to develop each girl child's navigational capacities in relation to possible futures. These capacities vary according to the kinds of access each family has to the nodes and pathways of power and resources. Appadurai (2002) has noted that the capacity to aspire is not evenly distributed in any society. The better off you are, in terms of power, dignity and resources, the more likely you are to be conscious of the links between more and less immediate objects of aspiration. This consciousness comes about because the better off are more 'supple' at navigational capacities through constant practice and concrete experiences. The poor, however, have fewer opportunities for practice. As a result, they have a 'thinner, weaker sense of the pathways from concrete wants to their realization' (Appadurai, 2003: 8). In our case studies, we see this at work in the differences between Dineo, Puleng and Margot's family situations. Dineo's mother and father's aspirations for their daughter take the form of 'being positive', praying and supporting her literacy development. For them, the path to 'worldliness' lies in forms of multilingualism and multiculturalism, giving her access to different languages and literacies, especially English, so that she can move out of her desperate situation into a 'white school' in town. Exactly how Dineo achieves this goal is uncertain because the desperate material conditions in which she lives make it very hard for her to do this. However, the fact that she lives on the borders of the city (as distinct from the rural areas) and is a high achiever in school gives her access to possible scholarships and resources which could help her to realize her potential. But there is no sure road to Dineo's future and there are thousands of children in similar (and worse) situations. For Puleng and Margot, their pathways to realizing their potential are more assured because their families have multiple resources and are more practiced in navigating these nodes and pathways. For Puleng, her navigational capacities include knowing how to look after herself in the face of potential threats and dangers (like being devoured by cannibals), knowing at least four South African languages, having a strong connection to family roots and oral traditions and having a good sense of *ubuntu*. At the age of six, Margot already has a highly developed understanding of what it means to read and interpret images and text, as well as how to produce your own texts in the language of power, English. She is beginning to learn how to be a successful consumer in the age of global consumerism.

These three girls all live in or near the city of Johannesburg, have families who care about them, and are all doing well at school. But they clearly do not have the same life chances. It is 10 years since South Africa achieved freedom and democracy. But for Dineo and her family, living on the edges of poverty, what is the meaning of freedom when there is no food in the house? We wonder how long it will take for the Dineos of South Africa to have a chance to fulfill their dreams, to know what it means to be free.

Acknowledgements

The Children's Early Literacy Learning Project (CELL) was made possible with a grant from the Spencer Foundation and the Anglo American Chairman's Fund. Grateful thanks to the families and children who participated in this study. Many thanks to Mastin Prinsloo, Carole Bloch and assistant researchers, Patrick Baloyi, Pinky Makoe, Marion Drew and Mogobe Moboko.

References

Appadurai, A. (2002) The capacity to aspire: Culture and the terms of recognition. Paper presented at *Wits Institute of Social and Economic Research (WISER) Seminar*, University of the Witwatersrand, Johannesburg, South Africa, 29 August.

Barton, D. (1994) *Literacy: An Introduction to the Ecology of Written Language*. Oxford: Blackwell.

Barton, D. and Hamilton, M. (1998) *Local Literacies: Reading and Writing in One Community*. London & New York: Routledge.

Bernstein, B. (1996) *Pedagogy, Symbolic Control and Identity: Theory, Research, Critique*. London, Taylor & Francis.

Granville, S., Janks, H., Mphahlele, M., Reed, Y. and Watson, P. (1998) English with or without g(u)ilt: A position paper on language in education policy in South Africa. *Language and Education* 12 (4), 254–72.

Gunner, L. (2003) Africa and orality. In I. Abiola and S. Gikannda (eds) *Cambridge History of African and Caribbean Literature*. Cambridge: Cambridge University Press.

Heath, S.B. (1983) *Ways With Words: Language, Life and Work in Communities and Classrooms*. Cambridge: Cambridge University Press.

Hofmeyr, I. (1994) *We Spend Our Years as a Tale that is Told: Oral Historical Narrative in a South African Chiefdom*. Portsmouth, NH: Heinemann; Johannesburg, South Africa: Witwatersrand University Press; London: James Currey.

Kress, G. (1997) *Before Writing: Rethinking the Paths to Literacy*. London & New York: Routledge.

Kress, G. (2003) *Literacy in the New Media Age*. London & New York: Routledge.

Kress, G. and van Leeuwen, T. (2001) *Multimodal Discourse: The Modes and Media of Contemporary Communication*. London: Edward Arnold; New York: Oxford University Press.

Mbembe, A. and Nuttall, S. (2004) Writing the world from an African metropolis. *Public Culture* 16 (3), 347–72.

Prinsloo, M. and Breier, M. (eds) (1996) *The Social Uses of Literacy: Theory and Practice in Contemporary South Africa*. Amsterdam & South Africa: John Benjamins & SACHED Books.

Scheub, H. (1975) *The Xhosa Intsomi*. Oxford: Clarendon Press.

Street, B. (1984) *Literacy in Theory and Practice*. Cambridge: Cambridge University Press.

Street, B. (ed.) (1993) *Cross-Cultural Approaches to Literacy*. Cambridge: Cambridge University Press.

Street, B. (1995) *Social Literacies: Critical Perspectives on Literacy in Development, Ethnography and Education*. London: Longman.

Chapter 7

Crossing the Margins: Literacy, Semiotics and the Recontextualisation of Meanings

CATHY KELL

It has now become something of a truism that we are functioning in a world fundamentally characterised by objects in motion. The objects include ideas and ideologies, people and goods, images and messages, technologies and techniques. This is a world of flows... It is also of course a world of structures, organisations and other stable social forms. But the apparent stabilities that we see, under close examination, are usually our devices for handling objects characterised by motion... The various flows we see are not co-eval, convergent, isomorphic or spatially consistent. They are... in relations of disjuncture... Further, these disjunctures themselves precipitate various kinds of problems and frictions in different local situations. Indeed it is the disjunctures between the various vectors characterising this world-in-motion that produce fundamental problems of livelihood, equity, suffering, justice and governance.

Appadurai, 2000: 5

Introduction

Appadurai's words go to the heart of a central problematic of our times: the relation between the local and the global. Modes and media of communication carry meanings within the streams and flows that make up the texture of the contemporary world, and historically literacy is one of the most important channels through which meanings have crossed space and time. But the contribution of Street and many others working in linguistics, anthropology and history has been to show the flaws in conceptualising literacy as autonomous of those meanings, as a neutral carrier (Street, 1984, 1993; Gee, 1996). Ethnography has provided us with both epistemological and methodological approaches for understanding the problems with autonomous models of literacy, and the studies thus produced have each contributed to the emergence of the 'New Literacy Studies'. But ethnography may also have constrained our ability to focus on the movement of meanings across contexts, through its long tradition of studying bounded communities, groups and sites, where the emphasis has lain on 'production within', rather than 'projection across'.[1] Brandt and Clinton (2002) have usefully opened up such questions by asking:

> But can we not recognise and theorise the transcontextual aspects of literacy without calling it decontextualised? Can we not approach literacy as a technology – and even as an agent – without falling back into the autonomous model? Can we not see the ways that literacy arises out of local, particular, situated human interactions while also seeing how it regularly arrives from other places – infiltrating, disjointing and displacing local life? (Brandt & Clinton, 2002: 343)

The authors are raising what they call 'methodological and conceptual impasses in the social practice approach' which they claim cannot adequately account for the materiality of literacy and the way in which it moves between the local and the global. This chapter is an attempt to argue that we cannot answer 'yes' to Brandt and Clintons' first two questions but that we can offer a definite 'yes' to their third question.

This chapter presents a case study of a meaning making process and sequences of steps in this process as it crosses contexts and shifts modes. 'Crossing the margins' reflects on crossings in a number of different senses: I hope to make these clear as the chapter progresses.

At this stage there are two areas of work which respond to Brandt and Clinton's challenge. First, recent work undertaken in multimodal discourse analysis (Kress, 2003; Kress & van Leeuwen, 2001; Jewitt & Kress, 2003) is starting to address issues of materiality. Secondly, confirming and extending work undertaken within the New Literacy Studies, Street has argued that Brandt and Clinton tend to characterise what they call 'distant' literacies as 'autonomous' (Street, 2003). Street has always maintained (and this lies at the heart of his autonomous and ideological models of literacy) that what might be seen as distant or autonomous literacy needs instead to be seen as always and everywhere ideological, deeply imbued with issues of consciousness and power, identity and control. Street states that: '... we need a framework and conceptual tools that can characterise the relation between local and "distant"' (Street, 2003: 2826–27) and suggests that the shift from studying literacy events to conceptualising literacy practices is one such tool. Furthermore a key theme in many of the anthropological studies in Street's edited collections is the idea that as literacies arrive from other places they are taken hold of in local ways which involve hybridisation and emergence, rather than standardisation and imposition. Street argues that anthropological and educational discourses have shaped these ideas, but that it is important to also argue a response from a sociological perspective. He draws on Giddens' (1991) concept of disembedding mechanisms to do so. He argues that,

> . . . literacy has both potential to disembed, 'to separate interaction from the particularities of locales', and yet at the same time is always instantiated, its potential realised, through local practices. (Street, 2003: 2829)

While I agree with Street's argument, I would like to suggest a further way of developing the framework and conceptual tools that he suggests are necessary. In what follows I will put forward a focus on the concept of recontextualisation (Bernstein, 1996; Sarangi, 1998; Iedema, 1999, 2003; Linell, 1998) which I believe is useful in studying meaning making processes as they traverse social groups, time and space; without falling into the problems of autonomisation or mode-determinism.

Obviously, the way in which one understands *context* lies at the heart of all this. Earlier structuralist versions of context contain at their core a dualism – the idea that context is a container for social action. A somewhat later version of this is the idea of the figure/ground relationship (Linell, 1998) or the focal event/field of action idea (Duranti & Goodwin, 1992). Context thus becomes seen as a frame that surrounds the event being examined and provides resources for its appropriate interpretation. Later versions demonstrate the way in which context is continually created and recreated in sequences of minute interactions. Many writers however, have pointed out the problems with these conceptualisations of context as either 'container' or as 'situationally created experiential spaces' (Engestrom, 1996: 35) and drawn attention to the problems of delimiting what counts as context as well as to the question of who defines context, the researcher or the participants. In a quite radical departure from the above conceptualisations, Engestrom articulates the value of understanding how meaning is mutually constituted in relations between persons acting and activity systems. For activity theory:

> Contexts are activity systems. An activity system integrates the subject, the object and the instruments (material tools as well as signs and symbols) into a unified whole. (Engestrom, 1996: 67)

An activity system is an ongoing, object-directed tool mediated human interaction which is historically conditioned. Discursive tools in particular, mediate between the actors/agents, the motive or direction of the activity and the object of the activity (its outcome).

Russell (1997) argues that activity theory can perhaps facilitate analysis of writing and learning by allowing us to theorise and trace the interactions among people and the inscriptions called texts (and other material tools) without separating either from collective ongoing motivated action over time. This approach seems useful in extrapolating from events to practices – a process which for the researcher seems to carry some of the difficulties encountered in defining 'context'. But a problem still exists in relation to defining activity systems as units of analysis. How big or small are they? Where do they begin and end? In working with the data in the rest of this chapter I hope to raise some possible answers to these questions, as well as suggest further areas for exploration.

Studying Recontextualisation: Units of Analysis

The data for this chapter is drawn from an ethnographic literacy research and intervention project in South Africa.[2] The funded literacy project took place within the context of a participatory development project in which 240 isiXhosa speaking families (who had been living in backyard shacks on the outskirts of Cape Town's black townships), came together in local savings clubs and accessed a government subsidy aimed at supporting the building of houses. I have called the project Tulandivile (Tndv). This particular house-building project occurred within the wider organisational context of a housing association (HASSOC) and the support of a service organisation (SO) and a financial support organisation (FSO).

In amongst an overwhelming welter of semiotic processes and very material actions (my research method was not participant observation, it was at times full-on participation, I remember my back aching as I carried massive concrete blocks and pushed wheelbarrows, sand in my eyes and cement in my fingernails) it became hugely difficult to decide what to focus on and how to define units of analysis.

In my attempts to start refining the quantities of ethnographic data that were collected, I focused on the overall purposeful activity of 'designing and building Tulandivile as a whole' which had taken roughly five years and was about halfway complete. Within that there were literally hundreds of smaller sequences of activities. The timescales and the intensity of these sequences of activities ranged from one day to several months to years, and incorporated numerous semiotic events and practices. I will call these sequences 'meaning-making trajectories'. I have borrowed the term 'trajectory' mainly from the work of Silverstein and Urban (1996) who explore what they call 'text trajectories', implying the involvement of reading and writing. Although the focus of the project was literacy, text trajectories was too narrow a term for my field of study, as I realised that I was not focusing on texts, but on meaning-making processes prior to and after their 'fixing' as texts involving print. Printed text is one moment of codification in the ongoing meaning making process, moment by moment, and meanings may or may not be carried by text. It is difficult to separate the term text from the linguistic written mode and I felt that it was necessary to find a unit of analysis that freed meaning making up from mode, thus enabling the analysis to pinpoint the factors leading to choice of modes and the identification of their affordances.

The data presented in this chapter is from a trajectory which I have called 'writing a wrong'. This trajectory can be broken down into a number of 'strips' over the seven-month period during which data was collected. Within each strip certain moments or events occur, each of which realises another sequential step in the purposeful activity of the trajectory. It is necessary to first narrate the trajectory, and then to pass it through various levels of analysis. These levels of analysis comprise an attempt to build a model for studying recontextualisation.

Narrating the Trajectory

The subject or agent of this trajectory was a woman called Nomathamsanqa, a member of Tndv, who was experiencing great difficulties with her house, at a time of high tension within Tndv and a loss of confidence in, and allegations of, corruptions against the Management Committee (MC) members. Three of these members had become increasingly powerful and insulated from the broader membership; these were called the 'three amigos'. Noma lived alone with her two small children and the family survived on a disability grant. As a result of her disability (the nature of which did not became clear to me until two years later) she had been allocated what was called a 'show house', built as a training exercise in Tndv for the purpose of demonstrating aspects of the building process. Shortly after moving in, Noma appeared to be very distraught and one day she called me over trying to tell me that her house was badly built, and she was having problems as a result. She told me that she had tried to raise her problems with the MC but to no avail. I analyse the 'writing a wrong' trajectory as starting at this point, when Noma seemed to take the first step to raise the problem more formally by putting it on the agenda of Tndv as a whole.

Strip 1: Speaking the problem

In this strip, Noma tried to articulate her problem a number of times in community meetings, over a period of about three months. These meetings (which were called the 'General' referring both to the structure of ongoing events as well as to the nature of the people gathering at these events) were held on a twice-weekly basis in a dilapidated building called 'the Garage' and were run by the chair of the Management Committee (MC), MamaToleni, and attended by around 25 to 40 members of Tndv.

Noma seemed to have planned to raise her problem in these meetings, which she did on perhaps three or four occasions, always in a similar way. It was raised as an individual problem (rather than a collective one). She would start off by raising her hand, and without waiting to be given permission, would say that she needed to raise her problem. She would then launch into it, sometimes rising to a standing position at the same time. There was therefore no space for the issue to be acknowledged formally by the chair. Very quickly, Noma's voice would start to rise, she would start talking more quickly and slightly hysterically, sometimes rocking her body from side to side. She would tend to look into the distance or close her eyes at times. On most of these occasions she would become breathless and start sobbing. The members present would hear her quietly, casting their glances downwards to the floor and making minimal eye-contact.

Over a few minutes (perhaps between about two and six) Noma would intone that the roof was leaking, the wind was coming in the gaps, the walls were unfinished. She would say that this was causing her family to be sick, she had put her trust in the organisation and that she had no way of putting this right herself, and seeing that it was a show-house it needed to be put right for her. The chair usually tried to cut her short, by saying that they would discuss it outside the meeting and that the meeting needed to finish.

Strip 2.1: Writing the problem

About 10 to 12 weeks after Noma had first tried to raise her problems in the general I had managed to pull together a group of about eight people who were interested in reading and writing. This was the very short-lived, neighbourhood-based and informal group called by members 'Masifundisane'. We had experienced difficulties with some of the strategies for this project and as a fairly arbitrary 'stop gap', I had suggested that individuals could write or dictate stories about the building process at Tndv.

The minutes of the first meeting state that Nomathamsanqa was the first to say that she was:

> ... very happy to be part of this process. She would love to be photographed with her children, and to write the story of the building. She is aware that the project is a historical and prestigious one, and that it is important to document it and to share that with others beyond the project. (Msfd minutes, 1/05/00)

There was some discussion about whether there would be any 'benefits' from writing the stories, but Nomathamsanqa said that 'she did not need individual benefit, it is benefit enough to carry the story abroad, and she is proud of the project itself and carries the story close to her heart' (ibid). After the first meeting Somi (a fieldworker) and I walked with Noma back to her house and asked her if she needed any help in writing her story. She said she had an exercise book and she was going to start writing herself, she did not need help.

Over the next week or two Nomathamsanqa wrote her story in isiXhosa in a small school exercise book covered in wrapping paper in a ball point pen. When first shown to me the story was about 10 pages long.

Strip 2.2: Reading the problem

A few days later I was shocked to hear that Noma's story was being read by 'everyone' and that people were 'coming from all over to read it' (Fieldnotes, 12/05/00). I immediately went to Noma's house and asked her if I could see the story. She took it out, and as she read the story to me it was clear that there was no sense of pride in the project, only the overwhelming anger and anguish that she had had to endure living in the house. As she read she gestured again to me the problems with the house. Some neighbours came in and peered over her shoulder at the book, looked at the problems with the house and tried to calm her down.

A few days later I was called to meet with two members (Monde and Thandiwe) who had previously been part of the Management Committee. These two members together with others had decided that Noma needed to take her story to a provincial meeting of the national organisation and read it out.[3]

A few days later I was again told that everyone was reading the story, that 'this thing had spread all over' and that 'everyone is coming and looking at her house and at the problems'. Nomathamsanqa said that 'this writing is good, *because now everyone can see my problem.*' In discussions over the next few days with Monde and other members I was told that the story was 'powerful' and that it contained a critique of the organisation for the way it had dealt with her and her house. One day outside Noma's house I met a man who had come from a group working in house-building about 10 km away. He told me he had heard about the story and wanted to see it. He was waiting to see her so that he could 'read her story and see the problems'. He said it was 'very wrong that she has these problems'. All of this took place in Nomathamsanqa's house, or outside in the open area between the houses and the street.

Strip 2.3: Negotiating the problem

In Strip 2.3 the Masifundisane group had another meeting to talk about the writing of stories. The minutes showed that anxiety was expressed about stories and possible critiques of the organisation. Someone mentioned that maybe there was a need for some 'guidelines' about how to write. Another member said that '... there are tensions' but that 'rules may not help' and that 'we should be free'. The minutes state:

> Nomathamsanqa said that she was also sharing the sentiments, and that she had problems with the idea of sifting what is there. The reality is that people have been through joyful and through bitter times and these should be included. It can help others. I have finalised my story now, now I am waiting for the happy ending. (Msfd minutes, 09/06/00)

Strip 3: Shifting the problem

Strip 3 involved implementing the earlier decision by Monde and Thandiwe that Nomathamsanqa's story needed to be taken to the provincial meeting. This was done, Noma read out the story at the meeting and the response was very sympathetic and interested. A week or so later, Noma was asked to go to the national meeting in the same venue where she was asked to tell the story again (not to read it this time). At that meeting a decision was made that her house needed to be rebuilt.

Strip 4: Materialising the solution

The next time I saw Nomathamsanqa (about two weeks later) she was busy moving into a vacant house so that her house could be rebuilt. This proceeded quite quickly and Noma was able to move back into her house after a month or so.

Monde told me later that 'people had always thought that Nomathamsanqa was *someone that couldn't say anything*, but now they have seen this book and now they have respect for her'. The irony of this is that I had watched over many months (Strip 1) as Nomathamsanqa *said something* (quite a lot in fact) in meetings but with no effect.

The following diagram maps out the trajectory.

Strip	*Timescale*	*Place*	*Events*	*Participants*
1: Speaking the problem	Four months	The garage	Community meetings, Noma raises problem repeatedly verbally	Tndv Management Committee; Noma; between 25 and 40 Tndv members; Cathy
2.1: Writing the story	Two weeks	Monde's house and Noma's house	1. Literacy group meeting 2. Noma writes story at home	1. Ten members of Tndv, Cathy and fieldworker 2. Noma
2.2: Reading the story	Three weeks	Noma's house and street	Numerous readings of story	Noma and numerous others
2.3: Negotiating the story	One meeting	Monde's house	Discussion of how to manage 'critical' stories. Noma asserts her independence	Nine members of Tndv incl Noma; Cathy and fieldworker
3: Shifting the story	Two meetings spread over three weeks	1. Provincial meeting in community hall in adjacent area 2. National meeting in same venue	1. Noma reads out story, discussion in meeting 2. Noma tells story, discussion and decision to rebuild	1. Noma, members of provincial structure; Tndv members 2. Noma; national members; provincial members; Tndv members
4: Building the solution	One month	Noma's house	Rebuilding of house	Builders working on instructions of provincial leader

In the following three sections I analyse this trajectory on three levels. First, I situate each of the strips differentiating the three main activity systems in which they occur. Secondly, I consider the actual communicative events and texts designed and produced by Noma in the first two strips. Thirdly, I relate both of the previous levels to questions of power and control. These layers together represent an attempt to build a language of description for 'crossings'.

Activity Systems

In order to delimit the parameters of what counts as context – I have followed Engestrom's account of context as activity system (Engestrom, 1996: 67). The elements of activity systems suggested by Engestrom and necessary for the understanding of activity are: the division of labour, rules, community; as well as mediational means or tools. At the heart of all these is the actor or agent, and the activity which is being undertaken.

The activity system in Strip 1 is Tndv's meetings structure (the General) which was the main means whereby decisions and tasks around house-building were co-ordinated. This was a deeply unhappy time, with strict control being exercised by the 'three amigos', tight procedures in meetings and general tensions within Tndv. Meetings always took place in the garage and seating arrangements were well-established and quite formalised. The discourse of 'participatory development' circulated within all of the activity systems considered here, yet what was happening in the General and in Tndv more broadly was hierarchical, top-down, verging on the coercive with a general silencing of debate and muffled allegations of financial corruption. This activity system interacted with two main broader activity systems; the national association to which Tndv was affiliated and that of the two service organisations which co-ordinated much of the work nationally. Within these latter two activity systems the participatory development discourse was the dominant one.

Engestrom has defined contradiction as essential to the dynamic of change, and sees activity systems as 'virtual disturbance- and innovation-producing machine(s)' (Russell, 1997: 531). These are often 'fundamental dialectical contradictions about the object/motive of an activity system, the direction of collective activity and they require fundamental choices with long-term consequences . . . which threaten or promise . . . a new form of activity' (Russell, 1997). The contradiction so apparent in the activity system within which Noma's trajectory took place was 'participatory development vs top-down control'.

The mediational means in this activity system were the routines of meetings which were highly structured and formulaic. The dominant mode of communication was verbal, and a limited range of gestural forms of communication could be drawn on. Although paperwork was central in the house-building process (plans, invoices, bank statements, expenditure sheets, savings books, etc.) interaction with paperwork almost never took place in these meetings, as it was undertaken by the three amigos in consultation with members of HASSOC and the SO.

The activity system of Strip 2 was quite different, and I was fully 'implicated' in its formation. Masifundisane can be seen as a micro activity system with its own contradictions operating within the broader ones and engaging with their contradictions. Somi and I were outsiders to Tndv, I was the only 'white', English-speaking person involved. Although I had initiated the process, I was clear that I should not direct it in any way. We had, however, emphasised paperwork in the process, circulating agendas and minutes in both English and isiXhosa, and insisting on informal translations. The intention in Masifundisane was to get members to write their own stories, with the vague possibility that this would form a bottom-up documentation of the house-building process and stimulate debate about its approaches and methods. The meeting referred to and the follow-up one were held in Monde's house, where cups were borrowed from neighbours, Monde boiled up some water on his little brazier, I contributed some sugar and we all had tea or coffee as the discussion started. Routines and practices were very informal.

The remainder of this strip took place in and around Noma's house and in the immediate neighbourhood, although it drew people in from well beyond the neighbourhood. People moved in and out of Noma's house and discussion about the story took place in very informal and unstructured ways, within a wider set of houses and neighbourhood interactions.

The activity system in Strip 3 was comprised of the broader structures of the provincial and national association. Although I did not attend the meetings at which Noma presented her story I had attended numerous similar meetings of these structures and can assume that the formats were similar. Meetings were held in a hall which had been built by the community and were generally attended by 40–100 people representing their areas. They were run by the elected members of both the provincial and national committees. Meetings had some degree of formality with a Chair and minute taker, and people would often call the meeting to order if speakers shifted from the agenda. The discourse of participatory development was more evident in these meetings. Meetings could be interrupted by song or prayer, or impassioned short speeches by members around controversial issues. Agendas but not minutes were sometimes circulated prior to meetings, but minutes, lists, memos, and so on, were sometimes referred to during proceedings.

Noma's trajectory wound its way through these three main activity systems.

Trajectory as Meaning-Making Traversing Contexts and Shifting Modes

In the research from which the content of this chapter is drawn the notion of trajectory corresponds with a sequence of purposeful communicative activities which cross activity systems. These crossings may occur simultaneously or sequentially, but the focus of my research is only on sequential crossings, which I have called semiotic recontextualisations. Linell (1998) points out that two approaches can be taken to the study of recontextualisation: firstly, an approach which has been influenced by Bakhtinian methods in which particular genres and instances of their use are studied and the relation between micro level interactions and macro forces is identified through concepts like polyvocality and hybridity. On the other hand an approach drawing on Fairclough and the concept of orders of discourse, but also approximating the idea of intertextual chains or 'genre chains' (Fairclough, 2003).

Nomathamsanqa, as the subject or actor in this trajectory, designed communicative events in her attempt to achieve her purpose (getting her house fixed). In analysing these communicative events I draw on Kress and van Leeuwen's (2001) strata of communicative practice: discourse, design, production and distribution.

Strip 1

In the first strip, comprised of the verbal attempts to raise her problem in the General, Noma drew on a slightly different discourse and participation structure from that evident in the normal general meetings. She presented her problem as one in which she as an individual was entitled to redress, and that redress was incumbent on the actions of the MC and by extension, the broader Tndv community. However, the general discourse in meetings was one of 'rights and responsibilities'. Rights were constructed as the entitlement to land and house-building opportunities co-ordinated through the government subsidy arrangements and the agreed upon division of labour. Responsibilities were constructed as full participation in all processes and equality amongst members. The sub-text however in this phase of the project was the hierarchical and top-down managerial approach developed by the three amigos, combined with the allegations of corruption and sense of coercion.[4]

Noma's design and production of the communicative events probably occurred simultaneously as spontaneous 'performance', as ritualised expression of anguish and grief. She drew on the communicative mode which was available in that activity system, a verbal presentation, but one that was clearly differentiated from the usual forms of talk in the General. It may well be that she felt driven to this performance as a result of the fact that her earlier attempts to raise her problem with the MC outside of meetings had 'fallen on deaf ears'. Bauman and Briggs' (1990: 73) description of performance describes these events well:

> ... performance is seen as a specially marked, artful way of speaking that sets up or represents a special interpretive frame within which the act of speaking is to be understood. Performance puts the act of speaking on display – objectifies it, lifts it to a degree from its interactional setting and opens it to scrutiny by an audience. Performance heightens awareness of the act of speaking and licences the audience to evaluate the skill and effectiveness of the performer's accomplishment. By its very nature, then, performance potentiates decontextualisation.

I argue that the performance constructed Noma as the 'client' (rather than the 'participant') and the three amigos as the dispensers, acting as an 'appeal' from the client to the dispensers. The ordinary members of Tndv became the audience of this appeal; constructed as silent witnesses. It was unclear to me whether the three amigos were consolidating their authority and the arbitrariness of their power by not responding to Noma's appeal, or whether they simply did not know how to address the problem themselves, perhaps both of these aspects are relevant. Perceptions of Noma's disability may also have been a factor in their responses.[5]

Strip 2

In Strip 2.1 Noma participated in the activity system as an ordinary member rather than as a victim or appellant, and constructed her talk within the dominant discourse of the meeting. She drew admirably on the participatory development discourse – 'the project is a historical and prestigious one', 'it is enough benefit to carry the story abroad', 'she is proud of the project and carries the story close to her heart'. She gave no idea that she would write her story as a critique of the organisation, although the history of her earlier verbal presentations must have been invoked in all of our minds as she spoke.

Apart from my efforts to promote writing in the community over the three to four years that I was involved with Tndv, I had never noticed any attempt to write outside of the day to day tasks that were associated with the house-building process, the vast majority of reading activities that I observed were also of this type. The genre of personal written accounts of life experiences was not at all evident.[6] In retrospect, however, there was a precursor to Noma's trajectory. This was a small booklet, the design and production of which I had initiated at a much earlier stage in the history of Tndv (about a year and a half before this trajectory). This was a small A4 size folded booklet in which a fieldworker and I had recorded the story of the early phase of Tndv, by eliciting narratives from members and inserting photographs. The booklet was produced for a celebratory feast and was distributed at this feast. Our evaluation indicated that the booklet was subsequently widely read and much enjoyed and discussed, although it was certainly not without controversy. It is possible that this process did influence Noma's decision to write her story and her ability to 'imagine' what her story may look like and how it may be distributed.

A further possibility is raised in that the performance mounted by Noma in Strip 1 did give the narrative of her story a certain kind of decontextualisation which she was then able to realise through the writing activity provided by the emergent process (basically the Masifundisane intervention) which constituted the activity system in Strip 2. She had had practice in verbally 'extracting' her narrative from context and participation structure through designing her appeal as performance (see Briggs & Bauman, 1990). Cleverly, however, in the actual written text, she presented herself as an ordinary member of Tndv with great allegiance and loyalty to it at the beginning. In this way she created solidarity with the readers of her story, who were also starting to question their own loyalties at the time.

Lo Bianco and Freebody (1997) refer to the idea of literacy as having three dimensions involving different sets of resources and drawing on different roles in relation to text. The dimensions are the operational (code-breaking), the cultural (using and participating in the meanings and texts) and the critical (analysing texts).

Noma was clearly able to read and write ('code-break') in isiXhosa, she told us she did not need any help. She had written very clear drafts of particular sections of the story in a different exercise book, and had then rewritten them in the main story. There were parts of the final story where she added in bits, using lines and arrows to indicate where they went.

The cultural dimension was brought to bear admirably. Noma's assertiveness with regard to her story grew as she realised that it was 'being heard'. In a highly strategic move, Noma grasped the opportunity provided by Masifundisane and used it to her own advantage. At the same time she did not 'rock the boat' of the first meeting. She 'spoke the discourse' of HASSOC as a whole which I had introduced to set the tone of the meeting, the participatory development speak, the heroic narrative of what people had been achieving at Tndv against all odds, and she kept quiet about the fact that she knew her story was going to be highly critical. Noma's responses represented a sophisticated design process, involving the imagining or picturing of what she was going to do and what it may possibly achieve, how it may possibly 'project beyond'. In this she realised that I, and the texts I was trying to promote, were potential leverage in her struggle.

The second Masifundisane meeting (Strip 2.3) involved an interesting indirect dynamic of critical literacy, where what was happening with Noma's story was clearly uppermost in people's minds yet she was the only one to bring it up directly. Other members discussed elliptically the issue of guidelines, or 'choosing words' (as they put it) so as not to cause problems. But Noma seemed to be growing in strength and clarity about her own position in writing her story, as she said she had problems with 'sifting' what is there, that she had 'written her story and now she is waiting for the happy ending'. Although the genre of written personal testimony was not established or evident in Tndv, the concept of the happy ending certainly was.

It is the public neighbourhood-based reading of the story (Strip 2.2) that is perhaps of greatest interest. Word spread very quickly about the book and Noma was asked to bring it out on many occasions. Reading took place as collective activity. Pairs or groups of people gathered around Noma in her house as she read the story out loud, looking over her shoulder at the words and nodding or tut-tutting as she read. The reading out loud as testimony indexed the physical problems with the house. As she read, she pointed to the problems, which were then visible both as words and as material form. People 'saw' the problems again, they saw the gap between the windows and walls, the absence of the ridge piece, they felt the wind blowing through these gaps, they even saw the rain (on one or two occasions) falling down inside the house!

Monde and Thandiwe's response to Noma's text was emergent. They saw an opportunity provided by the reification of the text into a physical object: 'a story'/'a book'. The silent witnessing of Strip 1 was transformed into action as they interpreted the value of her meaning making process to the developing critique of the three amigos; as well as the value of the material object in 'righting the wrong' for Noma. Here they were drawing on cultural and critical resources which are highly specific to the place and time (when and where else can a small hand-scrawled text in a child's exercise book achieve literally concrete resolution to such an intractable problem?). At the same time there was another kind of emergence, the growing emergence of the realisation that Noma was someone who could 'say something', by this they meant someone who had the courage to 'write something', and this increased her prestige in the community.

The response to the written story in Strip 2.2 was entirely the opposite from the response to the verbal story in Strip 1 (where it was basically ignored). Yet the meaning being conveyed by both texts was almost identical. By way of contrast, in another trajectory which I have studied, the written articulation of an issue was totally ignored in a meeting in favour of an entirely different set of verbal articulations of the issue.

Strip 3

What was very interesting in this strip is the fact that Nomathamsanqa was encouraged by members of Tndv to physically carry her story across to the meeting in the neighbouring area and read it out. Now the physical indexing of the material problems with the house was no longer possible. Yet perhaps a further different layer of indexicality needs to be taken into account – the public discussion and the news which had gone ahead now indexed the story – the climate had changed!

Power and Control

I have discussed design, production and to some extent distribution with regard to this trajectory. Following from Kress and van Leeuwen's model of strata of communicative practice mentioned above, I will now turn to discourse and to more macro questions of power and control.

In applying these concepts to Noma's trajectory I attempt to demonstrate the value of exploring the changes that are generated as meaning making crosses the three main activity systems in the first three strips; what it is that happens in the space between them, the margins, as it were. In order to achieve this I need to identify how each is different from the other, how the discourses operating within each are classified and how the communicative events are framed. In this I am attempting to link discourse and social structure. I will use Bernstein's (1996) concepts of classification and framing for this analysis.

Strip 1 took place within an activity system characterised by a very strongly classified set of discourses and practices. Strong classification is characterised by a degree of insulation from other discourses or practices. The organisational process itself was composed of sequences of individual meetings which were strongly demarcated in relation to other meetings and events at Tndv, and the sequences of individual items within each meeting were also quite strongly divided from each other. Secondly, this sequence of meetings (phase two) was quite distinct from other phases in the history of 'the General'.[7]

Noma's trajectory occurred at the height of the power of the three amigos when the dominant discourse had hardened into fixed routines and rituals. Although there were deep divisions in Tndv and great unhappiness, little of this surfaced directly in the meetings of Strip 1. The general atmosphere reminded me of Freire's culture of silence and my interpretation of this was that members were afraid to raise their unhappiness and criticisms for fear of losing their place on the list for houses. The contradiction between the participatory development discourse and the hierarchical managerial discourse was at its most severe during Strip 1. The design and production of Noma's communicative events in this case was constrained.

In Strip 2 the dominant discourse was that of participatory development and democratic process, notions of struggle but also of rights and responsibilities surfaced. Noma realised that the situation presented her with a possibility, a sense of emergence, and the weak classification of discourses and practices 'allowed' her response to emerge. The mediational means available constructed the form of the response, and this was most definitely 'emergent' in that there was little history of such genres evident in Tndv. Noma's urgency and determination to write/right her wrong was recognised and supported by members of Masifundisane and beyond. 'The moment was seized!' This enabled the articulation of long-suppressed discourses, and the rearticulation of the broader participatory development discourse.

In Strip 3 within the dominant participatory development and democratic discourse of HASSOC as a whole, Noma's appeal was seen as legitimate, she had been wronged and this was to be put right. The reading out of the story had some continuity with verbal presentations in HASSOC meetings in general where the case for issues was often presented, discussed and resolved with some degree of formality. At the same time no doubt, officials in HASSOC realised that this story was dangerous for the reputation of the organisation and they acted to contain this possibility. The response was immediate, people acknowledged the wrong materially by contributing financially.

Many of the discursive practices in these three strips have long histories in South African communities, born of years of struggle and grassroots-level organisation.

	Strip 1	*Strip 2*	*Strip 3*
Activity system characterised by:	Strong division of labour, strong rules, mediational means – only verbal	Weak division of labour, weak rules, varied mediational means – emergence of writing, possible reification of story	Strong division of labour, strong rules, varied mediational means
Discourse (extant in activity system)	Strongly classified (hierarchical, managerial)	Weakly classified (emergent, nexus of tensions between discourses)	Relatively weakly classified (participatory development, democratic)
Communicative mode	Verbal performance (ritualised/de-contextualised)	Writing of story Reading of story (Indexing)	Reading out loud and telling of story; hearing of story; discussion of situation
Discourse emerging and shifting during communicative events	Recognition of constraints	Recognition of emergence	Recognition of possibility
Design and production	Constrained 'victim position'	Emergent (expression of 'empowerment')	Emergent (confirming of 'rights')
Distribution	Not projected to wider audience	Projected	Projected

Conclusion

I would like to argue that there is a need for further studies which focus on the kinds of sequential crossings that I have identified here in order to counter claims for the autonomy or transcontextual nature of literacy. Following on from their first two questions quoted at the start of this chapter Brandt and Clinton (2002) claim that,

> But we want to grant the technologies of literacy certain undeniable capacities – particularly a capacity to travel, a capacity to stay intact and a capacity to be visible and animate outside the interactions of immediate literacy events. These capacities stem from the legibility and durability of literacy: its material forms, its technological apparatus, its objectivity, that is, its (some)thing-ness. (Brandt & Clinton, 2002: 344)

In my view claims like this represent slippage between various concepts, as well as 'mode-determinism'.

Literacy itself cannot travel but when used as a mode of representation in a particular medium it can enable a meaning to travel and that meaning may or may not be 'legible' in the context in which it arrives. A message written in English in a bottle can travel, it will stay intact, have durability, visibility, but if it is washed up on the shores of remote Greenland it may certainly not be legible in that particular recontextualisation. While it may be very legible, a word written on the sand at the beach has very limited durability and certainly cannot travel; its form and its meaning are exhausted in the immediacy of the practice. I hope to have countered the idea that literacy has the capacity to travel, by showing that it was Noma's meaning that travelled at the same time that it traversed modes. And its legibility was entirely dependent on exactly what form the elements took, which constituted the activity system in each recontextualisation, including in particular, the available mediational means and their historical contingency.

At the same time I would like to argue a qualified yes in relation to Brandt and Clinton's third question:

> Can we not see the ways that literacy arises out of local, particular, situated human interactions while also seeing how it regularly arrives from other places – infiltrating, disjointing and displacing local life? (Brandt & Clinton, 2002: 343)

Certainly meanings arrive, infiltrate, disjoint and displace all the time, if we do not recognise this we cannot have a nuanced understanding of the fluidity of mediated human interaction in time and space. But it is not literacy that regularly arises and arrives, infiltrates and disjoints, it is purposeful sequential meaning making activities that are projected, at times taking written form, depending on the contingencies of the context.

I would therefore like to take issue with the binary concept of the local and the global. The value of ethnography is that it clarifies the issue of point of view and ensures that this is always made explicit in research and writing. Ethnography is the attempt to understand and communicate 'insider perspectives'. So I argue that we cannot ever definitively say what is global but that we can perhaps say what is 'not-local' when we understand and make explicit the point of view of 'local'. It may then be possible to collect data starting from 'local' and build up more and more 'non-locals' until perhaps they reach 'global', but this involves the rigorous construction of chains of signification (Walkerdine, 1988), not *a priori* constructions of what the researcher might want them to mean. This brings us back to Street's reworking of the idea of re-embedding, but hopefully making a stronger claim for the ideological model of literacy against the autonomous model (Street, 1984). Literacy can never be autonomous, it can only be activated within each recontextualisation, and depending on vantage point each recontextualisation may be one step further removed from the original 'local' or 'locale' that was studied. In this way hopefully Appadurai's 'vectors' and 'flows' can be appreciated not as abstract concepts but as situated chains of human activity (Appadurai, 2000: 5).

I believe this approach lends itself well to studies of organisational and institutional practices, and to comparative studies across societies. Previous research in this area is revealing but does not focus on the units of analysis themselves (Iedema, 1999, 2003; Blommaert, 2001; Mehan, 1996). I have identified units of analysis (activity systems, trajectories, strips, events) in the study of the recontextualisation of meaning making as it traverses contexts and switches modes. The concepts of strata of communicative practice, the resources involved in literate practice and the use of the concepts of classification and framing to address issues of power and control are brought to bear in analysing specific instantiations of these units. In this I hope to offer elements of a language of description which can be used when undertaking such studies.

Iedema, Mehan and Blommaert each conducted their research in highly industrialised countries and bureaucratised societies. Sequential recontextualisations in their cases follow well-worn paths like rivers that have carved out their patterns on the sub-strata. The stages along these paths represent more durable and less negotiable forms of meaning making, for example: according to Iedema; talk in a meeting becomes nominalised in minutes, minuted decisions become architects' plans, plans become material meaning making as buildings are built. The kinds of spectacular, emergent and contingent processes characterising Noma's trajectory were not evident. Although in Noma's case the trajectory did lead to a more durable form of meaning making (i.e. her house was rebuilt), in most of the trajectories that I have studied in South African informal settlements this did not occur, in fact the opposite occurred.[8] What are the implications of this for theory, research and implementation in development? Mertz (in Silverstein & Urban, 1996) claims that:

> Processes of entextualisation and recontextualisation play a vital role in struggles over social power and modern American society . . . the unfixing and recentering of discourse performs a pivotal role as the semiotic mediation of social transformation. (Silverstein & Urban, 1996: 231)

I suggest that such studies need to be undertaken well beyond American society and can contribute to our understandings of the local and global in new and interesting ways.

Notes

1. This can be seen as a problem more generally within linguistics and particularly schools of linguistics (Rampton, 2000).
2. This project was undertaken by myself while I was based at the University of Cape Town and spanning across four years: 1998 to 2001. Funding for the project was received from the Rockefeller Brothers Fund and is gratefully acknowledged.
3. This discussion gave rise to considerable anxiety on my part, as I had maintained that my project would work within the organisational logic of HASSOC in general, and I was worried that such initiatives might jeopardise my project.
4. I have substantial data detailing these allegations and coercive measures but no space to present this here.
5. It was exceedingly difficult for me to establish the nature of Noma's disability. It was only about two years later that I realised that a term that she used in her story 'Phenytoin' is actually a drug used for epilepsy.
6. I had only observed someone reading a novel, apart from the Bible, once. In 65 questionnaires conducted amongst adult residents, none indicated any reading activities apart from newspapers and children's homework.
7. I make this claim on the basis of extensive ethnographic data collected over the three different phases of the project, but there is no space to report this data here. I hope to avoid the accusation that I am making *a priori* claims about

this process, in the way that these have been made by Blommaert (2001) (I believe, justifiably) about Critical Discourse Analysis, for example. The claims I make in this case are the result of extensive data collection and analysis. Some brief summarising comments on this are: earlier meetings (phase one) were less regular and less differentiated from other events; more permeable, more part of the ongoing texture of life in the organisation. Strict norms governing participation were less obvious. There were frequent comings and goings in the meetings; more bodily movement and crossplay. In contrast and in the latter phase (after the ousting of the three amigos), half to two-thirds of the members would participate in discussions; the position of Chair and minute taker would rotate; minute takers could be members who were not on the committee; there was much bodily movement and at times an almost carnivalesque atmosphere would break out with wild gesticulations, people standing up suddenly, teasing, much humour and irony. On the basis of this data I suggest that sequences of meetings in phases one and three were generally weakly classified while phase two was strongly classified.

8. I learnt a year after these events took place that Nomathamsanqa had died in her house. According to reports, on the day of her death she had appeared well, but that a meeting was held in the community at which Tndv members were told that they would have to replace the roof sheeting of their houses with tiles, as the sheeting did not comply with building regulations. They would have to use money from their own pockets for this. People were most distressed, and I was told that later that night Noma died. I have not been able to return to the site to verify any of this data. This is one of the reasons why I do not quote directly from Noma's story, but tell the 'story of the story'. The story you are reading is dedicated to her.

References

Appadurai, A. (2000) Grassroots globalisation and the research imagination: Globalisation from below. *Public Culture* 12, 1–19.

Baumann, R. and Briggs, C. (1990) Poetics and performance as critical perspectives on language and social life. *Annual Review of Anthropology* 19, 59–88.

Bernstein, B. (1996) *Pedagogy, Symbolic Control and Identity: Theory, Research, Critique*. London: Taylor and Francis.

Blommaert, J. (2001) Investigating narrative inequality: African asylum seekers stories in Belgium. *Discourse and Society* 12 (4), 413–49.

Brandt, D. and Clinton, K. (2002) The limits of the local: Expanding perspectives on literacy as a social practice. *Journal of Literacy Research* 34 (3), 337–56.

Duranti, A. and Goodwin, C. (1992) *Rethinking Context: An Introduction*. Cambridge: Cambridge University Press.

Engestrom, Y. (1996) Developmental studies of work as a testbench of activity theory: The case of primary care medical practice. In J. Lave and S. Chaiklin (eds) *Understanding Practice: Perspectives on Activity and Context* (pp. 64–103). Cambridge: Cambridge University Press.

Fairclough, N. (2003) *Analysing Discourse*. London: Routledge.

Gee, J. P. (1996) *Social Linguistics and Literacies: Ideology in Discourses* (2nd edn). London: Taylor and Francis.

Giddens, A. (1991) *Modernity and Self-Identity: Self and Society in the Late Modern Age*. Stanford, California: Stanford University Press.

Iedema, R. (2003) Multimodality, resemiotisation: Extending the analysis of discourse as multi-semiotic practice. *Visual Communication* 2 (1), 29–57.

Iedema, R. (1999) Formalising organisational meaning. *Discourse and Society* 10 (1), 49–65.

Jewitt, C. and Kress, G. (2003) *Multimodal Literacy*. New York: Peter Lang.

Kress, G. (2003) *Literacy in the New Media Age*. London: Routledge.

Kress, G. and van Leeuwen, T. (2001) *Multimodal Discourse: The Modes and Media of Contemporary Communication*. London: Arnold Publishers.

Linell, P. (1998) Discourse across boundaries: On recontextualisation and the blending of voices in professional discourse. *Text* 18 (2), 143–57.

Lo Bianco, J. and Freebody, P. (1997) *Australian Literacies: Informing National Policy on Literacy Education*. Melbourne: Language Australia and the National Languages and Literacy Institute of Australia.

Mehan, H. (1996) Beneath the skin and the ears: A case study in the politics of representation. In J. Lave and S. Chaiklin (eds) *Understanding Practice: Perspectives on Activity and Context* (pp. 241–68). Cambridge: Cambrige University Press.

Rampton, B. (2000) Continuity and change in views of society in applied linguistics. In H. Trappes-Lomax (ed.) *Change and Continuity in Applied Linguistics*. (pp. 97–114). Clevedon: Multilingual Matters.

Russell, D. (1997) Rethinking genre in school and society. *Written Communication* 14 (4), 504–55.

Sarangi, S. (1998) Rethinking recontextualisation in professional discourse studies: An epilogue. *Text* 18 (2), 301–18.

Silverstein, M. and Urban, G. (eds) (1996) *Natural Histories of Discourse*. Chicago: University of Chicago Press.

Street, B. (1984) *Literacy in Theory and Practice*. Cambridge: Cambridge University Press.

Street, B. (ed.) (1993) *Cross-Cultural Approaches to Literacy*. Cambridge: Cambridge University Press.

Street, B. (2003) The limits of the local 'autonomous' or 'disembedding'. *International Journal of Learning*, 10, 2825–30.

Walkerdine, V. (1988) *The Mastery of Reason: Cognitive Development and the Production of Rationality*. London and New York: Routledge.

Part 3

Crossings in Literacy Practices

Chapter 8

From Boardroom to Classroom: Tracing a Globalised Discourse on Thinking Through Internet Texts and Teaching Practice

SUE NICHOLS

Mrs P:	*Put your green hats on, I'm trying really hard to think but you know my problem?*
Child:	*Not enough green hat?*
Mrs P:	*I didn't have a lot of green hat thinking when I went to school, but I know you do*

(Researcher's fieldnotes)

Stuck in a mental rut? Don't know how to dig any direction but down? ... You may have a problem to solve, or an issue to explore, but you're being pulled in several directions so that you can't focus. Yet you crave creativity.
(Excerpt from 'Put on your thinking caps: Use Six Hats for full-color thinking')

Introduction

Success in the knowledge economy demands that corporations and other market players have the ability to generate knowledge which can be commodifed. This requires workers who can be relied on to produce ideas and to keep producing them in a constant flow. The production of what has been called 'new knowledge workers' requires changes in the processes of socialization (Jessop, 2003). Social agents must develop particular orientations to knowledge, particular subjectivities and identities

(Avis, 2002). They must learn to feel the absence of creativity as a lack and to experience the flow of ideas as positive and natural. Ideas must be brought out of these social agents rather than kept in their heads, in a process that Lyotard refers to as the 'exteriorization of knowledge' (Lyotard, 1979: 4). In these conditions, technologies to facilitate the exteriorizaton of knowledge, and to form appropriate thinking subjectivities, are in great demand.

What one might call 'thinking literacies' are currently high on the agenda for schools which are now charged with the responsibility of producing new kinds of thinking subjects, able to produce ideas at need, responding quickly to whatever contingencies the vicissitudes of the marketplace and the generation of new technologies may throw up (Hartley, 2003). The teaching of thinking is rapidly being incorporated into governments' accountability demands on schools, with an accompanying burgeoning of evaluation practices. In the UK, five thinking skill areas have been added to the National Curriculum: information processing, reasoning, enquiry, creative thinking and evaluation (Gold, 2002). Similar moves are afoot around the world. Teachers, as in all sweeping educational reform movements, are contradictorily positioned as both the obstacles to and the deliverers of change (Ball, 2003). As 'old thinking subjects' socialized in a previous set of conditions, teachers are being required both to recognize their shortcomings and to enthusiastically rise to the challenge of producing the next generation of successful entrepreneurs. This contradiction is encapsulated in Mrs P's representation of herself as someone with a thinking 'problem' who nevertheless has successfully ensured that her students have the skills and resources to do better. Training and resourcing teachers like Mrs P to produce clever thinkers is one of the key challenges of education systems currently.

In this chapter, I will be tracing a discourse of thinking by following a particular technology for producing thinking subjects through cyber and social space, through corporate and educational sites. This discourse on thinking is one, which acts as a carrier for those orientations to knowledge compatible with participation in a global knowledge economy. It circulates through multiple social spaces in ways that are both random and consciously driven by powerful social institutions. Its strength and pervasiveness derives from its promise to deliver competitive advantage to players at every level and in every kind of knowledge game and further, to produce players so that the game can continue. The thinking technology is a pedagogy for thinking which is particularly well suited for exteriorizing knowledge in material social contexts and which claims to produce the flow of ideas that enables successful participation in a competitive knowledge economy. It is the technology known as the 'thinking hats' (DeBono, 2000).

Briefly for now, the Six Thinking Hats approach is based on the categorization of thinking into discrete cognitive orientations.[1] As a form of literacy practice, the Six Thinking Hats exploits multiple modalities and genres. It represents thinking visually, using a different coloured hat to symbolize each thinking orientation (e.g. the black hat signifies an orientation to seeing the negative aspects of a problem or issue whereas the red hat signifies an orientation to the emotional dimension). It provides linguistic texts in a range of genres (e.g. handbook, worksheet, trainer's notes) which describe each of the thinking orientations and guide their use. It prescribes forms of social interaction performed in talk which establish roles for facilitators and participants. It is also performed as embodied participation through the metaphorical or imaginatively enacted putting on and taking off of the 'hats' which encourages participants to change thinking orientations quickly and fluently. Finally, and crucially for this analysis, it proliferates these images, texts and practices through cyberspace using multimodal hypertexts.

The Internet is increasingly being used to deliver thinking curriculum and resources to teachers by state education systems, non-government organizations and commercial entities (Fabos, 2000). It has become one of the prime mechanisms for the globalization of knowledge including knowledge about knowledge. As a key element in the digital technologization of society, it is also one of the justifications cited by those arguing for the need to produce clever citizens (Bradshaw *et al.*, 2002), in effect helping to create the demand for thinking goods and services which it is then used to supply. As an information network which is accessed in every online location, it circulates representations of thinking throughout social space. The Internet also operates as a global marketplace for goods and services which promise to deliver better thinking performance. Thus it is a key mechanism for the commodification of thinking and learning to think.

When teachers access cyber space in their search for resources, they become consumers in this marketplace and part of the network through which circulate discourses of thinking and technologies for producing thinking subjects. I am suggesting that teachers be understood as 'actor-networks' as conceptualized in Actor Network Theory (ANT) (Clark, 2001; Law, 2003). In ANT, distinctions between the inner worlds of social actors and the concrete circumstances of the environments in which they act fall away, as do those between digital and human networks. Networks are understood to operate virtually and materially simultaneously and knowledge to be always constantly circulating through cyber, social and material space. All players in a system are both actors and networks and all technologies for knowledge production and dissemination, whether 'low' or 'high', impact on the operation of actor-networks. Seeing teachers as actor-networks offers an alternative to what has become a deficit discourse of teachers and technology in which teachers are represented as alienated from digital technologies and impervious to globalized knowledge flows (cf. Luke & Carrington, 2002).

ANT encourages ethnographic literacy researchers to look for 'network effects' in local events (Clark, 2001: 5). The local events I examine here are those in which Mrs P employs the six thinking hats pedagogy in her classroom. But as well as locating myself 'in' the local context of Mrs P's work, I enter into the field of digital networks. Imagining myself into the professional context of a busy teacher looking for resources, I search the Internet for the 'six thinking hats', following links where they take me and finding myself in corporate as well as educational sites. As a researcher I am 'in' the network as well as 'in' the classroom. By subjecting internet texts to the same kind of scrutiny as local events I seek to find 'network effects' within networks, both cyber and social. This approach is consistent with cyber ethnography (Miller & Slater, 2000) which Bell describes as 'an itinerant methodological approach that traces connections between on- and off-line milieux' (Bell, 2001: 193).

Another way of describing the approach taken in this analysis is in terms of Fairclough's (1992, 2003) model of critical discourse analysis in which three levels of analysis combine to provide a rich account of the productive workings of discourse: the level of *text*, the level of *interaction* in the specific local context, and the level of *discourse* or in other words knowledge that is circulating through society and reflecting broader cultural and political agendas. My texts here are Web-pages, classroom artifacts, field notes and transcripts of classroom talk. The contexts of interaction are the social and material spaces of classrooms but also the imagined contexts of Internet users searching for information, contexts which I attempt to recreate in my own searching practice. The discourses which I trace are those concerned with the representation of thinking and thinkers.

The Hats at Riverview Primary

My path begins at Riverview Primary School, one of the sites in a research project which investigated early childhood pedagogies and their impact on students of diversity in two contrasting primary school sites over three years.[2] Riverview is an inner suburban state school with a culturally and socially diverse population, which had taken the SHIP (Students of High Intellectual Potential) program which, in most other schools, is restricted to an academic elite, and mainstreamed it across the whole school. Riverview was definitely in the business of creating clever children and the promotion of its thinking skills program had been an element in holding its own against the competition of an expanding private sector in a political climate, which is increasingly favouring private schools (see also Comber & Nichols, 2003).

Mrs P was a key teacher in SHIP methodology at Riverview and an enthusiastic user of the six thinking hats and other thinking pedagogies. She had a large collection of related resources and was constantly gathering more from a variety of sources including the Internet. Her combined Years 1 and 2 class was sometimes visited by local, interstate and international teachers looking for models of these approaches in practice. In Mrs P's classroom, the hats had become part of the pedagogic environment. The bright posters with their sequence of white-black-yellow-green-red-blue were always easy to spot on the classroom wall, like the other posters with the alphabet, sight words or days of the week. One of their key uses was to encourage self-regulation in children. Rather than asking Mrs P how to spell 'the' or what 'red hat thinking' was, a child could refer to the poster.

On the very first day of school, children were introduced both to the hats and the practice of making one's personal knowledge and opinions available to the class collective through an exercise in which they looked at the topic 'school' from the perspective of each of the hats. In the early weeks, Mrs P gave frequent and immediate feedback so that her class learned quickly that a particular coloured hat was intended to trigger a particular kind of response. They were also learning to participate in a long-established interactive routine of classrooms (and an element of 'old way' thinking) the initiation-response-evaluation (Sinclair & Brazil, 1982). At the initiation (e.g. 'Use your white hat') children learned to raise their hands, wait to be identified, offer the appropriate kind of response (in this case, a known fact) and receive from the teacher either an affirmation a challenge ('Do we *know* that?') or a reminder to change to the appropriate hat ('Have you got your white hat on?') and so shift their thinking into the mode required by the collective.

Later in this chapter, we will see Mrs P and her class in action, working with the thinking hats. First though, a detour into cyberspace to explore part of the network through which knowledge about thinking circulates: to appear on the screen on Mrs P's computer, to be downloaded into her hard-drive, to be printed into worksheets and stuck into her children's exercise books.

The Hats in Cyber Space

My data was gathered for this part of the investigation was gathered via search engine Google (popular with teachers) using the key words 'six-thinking-hats'. Predictably, hits numbered in the tens of thousands and the level of repetition of information and terminology across sites was considerable. Clearly discourses of thinking were circulating very widely, through sites of educational governance, curriculum development, all levels of schooling, workplace training, management, resource development, marketing of goods and services not just educational but of many other kinds, lobby groups, homes, media production and others.

From the first 100 sites listed in the search results, 50 were entered and entry pages only were read enabling an overview of producers, audiences and key descriptive categories. This stage of analysis focused on the representation of the six thinking hats, descriptions of their use and modes of address to readers. I noted the ways in which educational and business organizations were constructed in relation to each other: sometimes as different, sometimes as alike and often simultaneously as both. Theories of thinking and learning, metaphors, narratives and indeed the ubiquitous hats constantly crossed between the two.

From these 50 sites, five were selected for close analysis (for descriptive summaries see the Appendix). Each of these sites represents a different category of network point, in terms of: whether their primary audiences were educational, business or both; if educational sites, their relationship to institutions of governance; and whether they were relatively more open or closed sites (as gauged by the number and range of external links). At this stage I followed links from entry pages back to their home pages and from there navigated around the sites to establish the overall intertextual context. A detailed analysis of these five sites is not possible in the confines of this chapter. What I have done is to trace two themes, which recurred across texts and sites, giving brief excerpts in illustration. These two themes have particular relevance to the construction of teachers and students as new thinking subjects: thinking as rational and depersonalized and thinking as productive.

Thinking as Rational and De-personalized

In order for thinking to be productive, it must be available to the collective and in order for this to occur, it must be set free from the personal investments of individuals and sub-groups. The notion that the hats set individuals free from their own subjective investments recurs throughout the texts and sites. In the commercial Learner's Link site 'Franny' a training provider who emphasizes her background in teaching, writes as one dot point in a list of claims as to the hats' effectiveness:

> The game and role-playing nature of the hats allows for the detachment of ego from the thinking: "This is not me, but my red hat thinking." (Example 4, see Appendix)

The red hat is significant here since that is the hat that encourages 'thinking about feelings'. In the Teaching Strategy page of the state education department site this orientation is described as follows:

> Red hat thinking looks a topic from the point of view of emotions and feelings. (Example 1, see Appendix)

The thinking subject is here positioned as detached from the object of thinking, looking at it rather than part of it. From this 'point of view', emotions are also objects to be defined and made available to the collective. The mature thinking subject does not engage in 'me thinking' but achieves distance from the self, assisted by the depersonalizing mechanism of the hats.

The construction of thinking as rational within the context of a corporatized production of knowledge positions children and workers in aligned ways – as potentially irrational subjects who have to be taught self-regulatory habits. An article downloaded from the site of Lynda Curtin, self-titled 'Opportunity Thinker' and provider of thinking training to both schools and corporations contains this moral story:

> Craig Elkins, manager of the Applied Thinking and Creativity Team at Boeing Seattle, not only teaches Six Hats to Boeing employees, but also taught the method to his daughter Chelsea, when she was only four years old. Now an eight-year-old, Chelsea frequently uses Six Hats to solve dilemmas, for instance, whether to eat candy before dinner. Rather than pitching a temper tantrum, Chelsea will sift through all aspects of the problem to arrive at a sensible solution. (Example 5, see Appendix)

In this narrative, parallel relationships are established – manager to employees, father to daughter – which in the educational context would translate as teacher to student. Here the reader is not simply learning that 'anyone' can use the hats but that one group of people with power (managers and fathers) can get another group of people (employees and little girls) to use them in order that the latter group can become self-managing. Considered in the context of these parallel relationships, Chelsea's 'tantrum' is the childish equivalent of the adult 'argument' – unproductive and futile. The relationship also works in the other direction; workers' attempts to argue are, in the terms of this paternalistic discourse, equivalent to a toddler's tantrums. Self-regulation for both groups is the goal of managers, whether educational or corporate.

In the field of education, this discursive strand interweaves with notions of critical thinking and critical literacy, on the one hand, and managerialism, on the other, to produce a particular construction of the thinking subject. This subject is able to be critical on demand, to be critical of those things (s)he may be personally invested in, and to accomplish this without experiencing any damage to self-esteem. In the article 'School adopts De Bono's thinking hats' appearing on the National Literacy Trust Website, a science teacher describes the benefits:

> Very often children cannot criticise their own work because they did it so carefully. Using 'six hats' takes that personal criticism out so that it is not threatening. That means they can start to criticise their own experiment and take it a step further . . . (Example 2, see Appendix)

For teachers, the ethic of care strongly sanctions against putting children in emotionally threatening situations. The push for critical thinking across the curriculum has created tensions for teachers who have felt required to force children into adopting a critical stance towards things they hold dear (particularly popular culture which is a prime target for deconstructive work in the new critical curriculum). Therefore, it is not surprising that a pedagogy, which enables a critical thinking stance to be put on and taken off like a hat, with no permanent ill effects, would be attractive to teachers.

Thinking as Productive

The claim that thinking can be made more productive is common across of texts and sites, although the outcome of this productivity is differently stated: grades and benchmarks in educational sites and profits in business sites. The National Literacy Trust Website emphasizes the measurable results of applying thinking strategies such as the hats. In the focus text, 'School adopts De Bono Thinking Hats', we read that:

> The headteacher credits the tools in part for a big improvement in her pupil's GCSE results.

Indeed, looking at the other news items in the Update section of this Web-page, it appears that any pedagogy or technology can be supported as long as it produces measurable results (and those that do not are of questionable value). Samples of other headings include:

> Reflective pupils lift exam grades.
> Spinning on the spot can boost early academic achievement.
> Formative assessment – the key to raising achievement?

In sites and texts which target businesses, productivity is given a monitory value related to the notion of knowledge as a commodity ('idea banking' is the term used by Lynda Curtin in her Website). These explicitly managerialist descriptions of the hats' use and benefits help us to hear the more understated echoes which occur in educational sites. 'Franny' who markets to both schools and businesses, includes the following statement in the corporate area of her Website:

> The use of the SIX HATS® promotes clearly focused meetings and communication, in turn increasing productivity and profits. Many organizations reported that use of the SIX HATS® reduces meeting time by as much as 50 per cent ... (Example 4, see Appendix)

Because ideas originate within individual human agents, there is a need for a mechanism to draw them out and make them available to serve the corporate goal. In the business world, the traditional mechanism for the production of ideas is the meeting. It is typically claimed that the hats both save time (by making meetings shorter) and make time (for more productive thinking). In this construction of thinking, the mechanism which enables the hats to both make and save time is *focusing*.

Focusing is associated with having a focal problem or topic, ensuring that this problem or topic is not itself open to question and maintaining firm control over the nature of participants' contributions through the mechanism of having everyone wear the same hat at the same time. A corporate trainer quoted by Linda Curtin states:

> The facilitator can say "green hat" and everyone knows what that means. Time isn't wasted trying to understand the question. (Example 5, see Appendix)

In the state education department's six thinking hats Web-page (Example 1), teachers are encouraged start with 'an issue or topic which you would like your students to explore' and to describe each of the hats in relation to the central focus – the topic. For instance the white hat 'identifies the facts and details of a topic'. The role of the teacher, as with the facilitator of a business meeting, is to establish the topic and ensure participants apply all their thinking to this topic. When participants have been taken through the entire typology of thinking orientations, what is then produced is a neutralized assembly of knowledge items. In educational sites, where the product of work is students' knowledge, this assembly is itself taken as evidence of productivity:

> The teacher points to the breadth of views and thoughts, and explains that this is as a result of making ourselves apply a range of different types of thinking. (Example 1, see Appendix)

Note here the reference to conscious effort and to the inclusion of the teacher in the thinking collective. What does it look like when teachers and students 'make themselves apply' each of the thinking types in order to produce a complete assembly of knowledge?

The Hats in Classroom Space

I turn now to some accounts of the hats in practice at Riverview Primary School. My intention here is not to argue that teachers are using the hats like some kind of magic wand to turn children into the idealized kind of new knowledge workers represented in the texts described above. Rather, I am interested in what kind of relationships to knowledge this approach to thinking can enable, support and discourage. What kinds of thinking and thinkers are rewarded in the hats practice? Do we see evidence of 'focusing' and filtering of knowledge and if so, what might be excluded? What purposes do the hats serve for old–new teachers facing multiple and contradictory demands? Two different kinds of classroom practice are examined: whole class discussion and individual student–teacher interaction.

Collective problem solving

In the following extract from a transcript of classroom talk, Mrs P's combined Years 1–2 class undertakes a problem solving exercise. They had begun making up Christmas hampers to donate to poor families, an activity that arose from the Six Hats of Christmas unit that Mrs P found on the Brainways Website (Example 3, see Appendix). This stretch of talk demonstrates how, within the course of a broader curriculum structure (the Christmas theme), Mrs P identifies a problem and successfully focuses the knowledge production of the class collective on working towards its solution, drawing strategically on the six hats language and interaction patterns. The analysis is concerned not only with what is achieved in this process (its intended productivity) but in the possibilities and perspectives present but not recognized or followed through.

The problem involves some individually wrapped chocolate-coated muesli bars which Mrs P had bought in for the hampers. She initiates the discussion by constituting the muesli bars as a problem in the following terms:

1 **Mrs P:**	Now I'll tell you my problem and then you can see if you can solve it. I got these from my pantry. Now they were sitting like this in my pantry. They were obviously sold in a box when I first bought them. Now, one of my children took them out of the box, put them in the pantry and left them like that. On the box would have been the date of when these expire. There is nothing on this now, absolutely nothing, no date. It's sealed, it doesn't need to be put in the refrigerator but I don't know when it expires. I don't know whether I can put them in the box. I don't know what to do. Think about it for a second.
2 **Child:**	I already know.
3 **Child:**	Look where you buyed it from and see the date on the other ones.
4 **Child:**	But it might be different stuff, still different stuff.
5 **Mrs P:**	I could go back to the shop and have a look at the box, but I've had these in the pantry I reckon for about four months. In the shop they've probably got new boxes with new dates, so these dates might not be the same. What else can I do? Do I throw the three of them away?
6 **Children:**	No (multiple responses, all speaking at once)
7 **Mrs P:**	Put your green hat on and let's come up with a creative idea, what can I do?
8 **Child:**	Take one out and test it.
9 **Mrs P:**	That is a good idea.
10 **Child:**	Just taste one bit.
11 **Mrs P:**	Just taste one bit to see if it's off? OK, is there any other suggestions? That was a good suggestion.
12 **Child:**	There might be a box that had the date on it.
13 **Mrs P:**	This is not the box that had the date on it.
14 **Mrs P:**	Now I've unwrapped this muesli bar. Look carefully and tell me whether you think it is still OK.

15 **Child:**	It looks nice and tasty
16 **Mrs P:**	I need another opinion, we've got two. Kelly-Ann, you've got your thumb up. Bryce? You think it's OK? [He nods] The chocolate looks good, it hasn't gone white and there's no signs of green on it.
17 **Child:**	If we send it to 'em, before we send it to 'em, check if there's any green stuff in them.
18 **Mrs P:**	OK. We've got three weeks. Because we don't know the date – it's good today, good idea – we're going to check them as a class in three weeks, to make sure there's no green spots. Oh my goodness, we've got experts here.

Mrs P's opening statement (Turn 1) positions the participants in relation to the problem. The problem belongs to the teacher and so hers is the role of narrating it ('I'll tell you my problem') but the task of solving the problem is assigned to the children ('you see if you can solve it'). In order for this to be understood as a genuine problem, one which elicits new knowledge from the class, Mrs P frames the problem as arising from missing information (there is no use-by date on the muesli bars). In this way she can represent herself as genuinely unknowing without compromising her authority in relation to the problem. In doing so, she takes the role of the facilitator, a role which is focused on producing knowledge flow and so precludes the provision of answers, but does this in a characteristically teacherly way, one which enables her to maintain steerage of the discussion.

Mrs P's initiation is successful in opening the discussion space; children's contributions are immediate and they do not wait for her feedback to comment on each other's suggestions. The teacher's next intervention (Turn 5) is a response the suggestion that she return to the shop to check the date. She acknowledges the possibility ('I could go back to the shop') but establishes this suggestion as impractical by drawing on two kinds of authoritative knowledge: personal knowledge ('I've had these ... about four months') and knowledge of commercial food distribution processes ('In the shop they've probably got new boxes').

Up to Turn 7, there has been no mention of hats. Mrs P's class by this stage of the year had learned a broad range of cues for practicing different kinds of thinking displays. In this case, the cue words 'problem' and 'solve' indicate to the children that this is a situation which requires 'how' thinking rather than recitation of facts or expressions of feeling. However, the teacher's question about throwing the muesli bars away provokes a different response; most children are horrified at the idea and many voices are raised against the idea. The children's strong response halts the flow of problem-solving suggestions and it is at this point that Mrs P introduces the green hat trigger (Turn 7). Here we see the operation of the hats as a focusing mechanism, maintaining collective energy in the service of the particular thinking task. At the same time Mrs P reinforces their respective relations to the problem: Put *your* green hat on . . . What can *I* do?' The class is constructed as a thinking collective (one hat for all) whereas the teacher is the one who owns the problem and has the power to act on it.

This trigger indeed succeeds in eliciting some fresh suggestions, which Mrs P immediately responds to positively ('That is a good idea'). What is left behind in this flow is any exploration of the children's response to their teacher's suggestion that the bars be binned and what this may reveal about the different relationships of children and adults to muesli bars and the whole category of mass produced snack foods. Such an exploration may, for instance, have enabled children to articulate that the idea of muesli bars 'going off' was outside their experience. While the need for a use-by date is a legal requirement arising from regulation of the food industry to prevent food spoilage and bad health consequences for consumers, western children's snack items are generally consumed so rapidly that there is no chance of this happening.

As children cooperatively offer suggestions in response to Mrs P's 'green hat' prompt, a kind of unacknowledged double dialogue is occurring around two different dispositions to knowledge and action, one of them concerned with embodied experience and the other with objective scientific observation. One child's suggestion to 'take one out and test it' (Turn 8) is immediately followed by another's to 'taste one bit' (Turn 10). 'Test' is consistent with a more distanced and rational approach to the muesli bar problem whereas 'taste' invokes an experiential approach, the embodied disposition of one who, seeing a chocolate coated muesli bar, desires to put it in his or her mouth. Mrs P acts on the first of these orientations; rather than taste the bar, she unwraps it and invites the class to observe its appearance (Turn 14). As the discussion continues, the double dialogue continues, one child using the sensory language of consumption ('nice and tasty') while Mrs P is engaged in linking everyday words ('green') to concepts of organic states (decomposition) in order to constitute children as scientific observers. It is only when a child's suggestion is compatible with the scientific orientation (check later to see if the bars are green), that Mrs P signals that the problem's solution has been reached.

The solution is expressed in terms that dissolve the distinction between problem owner and problem solver ('we're going to check them as a class'). Throughout the exchange, the naming of individual children has been minimal and when this occurs it is in terms of the individual's role in contributing to the group task: 'I need another opinion . . . Kelly-Anne you've got your thumbs up'. Knowledge and action are collectively owned and everyone is granted the designation of 'expert'.

Some other uses for hats

While the example above shows the use of the hats to regulate the thinking performance of a collective, Mrs P also employed hats terminology in her interactions with individual children. In some ways, this was less straightforward than in a whole class performance where Mrs P could use her own feedback and response to selectively privilege those contributions, which were consistent with her purpose. In individual interactions, however, conflicts of understanding and purpose were more visible and suggested some of the submerged conflicts which may have been rendered silent by whole class hat thinking. In the following example, Dylan is seen in the midst of a 'green hat' task which had required him to create characters with special powers, different from those in a story Mrs P had recently read aloud. Dylan was considered by Mrs P to be an under-achiever owing to his very slow work rate, despite being a keen reader who liked fantasy novels. This particular task seemed to enthuse him more than usually because he quickly drew figures and wrote adjectives indicating his invented characters were 'imortal', able to 'hipotize' (hypnotize), and 'apparate' (disappear and appear in another place). A fourth word was 'gillyweed' which prompted this exchange between Dylan and Mrs P:

Mrs P: What's a gillyweed?
Dylan: It's a creature from Harry Potter.
Mrs P: Is it real or pretend?
Dylan: It's in Harry Potter.
Mrs P: Is it real or pretend?
Dylan: (silence)
Mrs P: Could you use your white hat for this?
Dylan: (shakes head)
Mrs P: So go for it!
Dylan: (sounds surprised) Great!

From Dylan's perspective, this exchange served no clear purpose except to firstly raise doubt as to whether he had done the right thing and then to allay the doubt with a clear permission to go ahead and do what he had already been doing. From Mrs P's perspective, the exchange reflected a need to ascertain whether Dylan had been engaged in the right kind of thinking. Underlying her questions was the framework of the six thinking hats, which fragments thinking into different and separate cognitive orientations. This exchange suggests the tendency for these different cognitive orientations to form into exclusive binaries, regardless of the originator's intentions. Here the green hat and the white hat stand in oppositional relation to each other, and as is generally the case with oppositional discourses, one term is privileged. Creative (green hat) thinking is the valued orientation whereas factual (white hat) thinking would be wrong. Further, Mrs P's 'real or pretend' question shows how the green/white hat binary easily connects with and maps onto others that are already operating in the site of practice. The dominance of fictional narrative (stories) in the literacy curriculum of junior and primary schooling has often been noted. It is not surprising therefore that a discourse of thinking that privileges creativity and originality should function in school contexts to reinforce an existing textual hierarchy.

That Dylan was a problematic student suggests another function for the hats. As with most routine strategies in a teacher's repertoire, the hats were able to function simultaneously as pedagogic and as regulatory. At times, the latter appeared to be the main function. Amanda was a very speedy child who Mrs P described as 'hyperactive'. She habitually spoke so quickly that she could not be understood easily and was constantly being reminded to slow down. She loved running around and sometimes appeared impatient with sitting and working; once, she was spotted by the researcher looking at the wall and whispering 'Come on clock. Come on clock'. On this occasion, Mrs P had gathered the class into a circle to show and talk about the Christmas objects they had made (part of the 'Six Hats of Christmas unit – see Appendix, Example 3). Amanda volunteered to show her reindeer:

Mrs P (before Amanda can begin):	You need to speak properly, loud.
Jess (to Amanda):	You speak too quickly.
Mrs P (to Jess):	So do you.
Amanda starts to speak quickly:	I made a reindeer but I wanted/
Mrs P (interrupting):	/No. Slow down.

Amanda (spacing out her words): I – made – a reindeer. (speeding up) But I wanted it to be a different reindeer (*continues to describe her creation in detail*) *Amanda, having let out a torrent of words comes to a stop, holding out her reindeer.*

Mrs P: Put your red hat on. Tell me how you feel. *Amanda looks at Mrs P. Mrs P looks back. Amanda knits her brows and looks down as if concentrating. She doesn't speak.*

Mrs P: You can sit down now.

As a thinking performance, this was in hats terms consistent with green hat or creative thinking; Amanda explained she had made a 'different reindeer' and described it in detail. However, it was the red (feelings) hat that Mrs P invoked in her response even though the instructions for the sharing task had not involved any requirement that children talk about their feelings. Given the overall context – that Amanda had been told to 'speak properly' but had reverted to gabbling – it is hard to avoid the conclusion that she was being invited to express a feeling of disappointment in her speaking performance. When Amanda responded with silence, Mrs P did not press further. The disciplinary function of the red hat did not actually require the performance of a feeling statement. The double strategy of withholding praise and implying that there was occasion for some unspecified feeling was enough to signal to Amanda, and to the class, that something was amiss.

Conclusion

In the Internet texts, the six thinking hats read like a manager's fantasy of corporatized knowledge production. Missing from the utopian vision of a workforce or student group that is simultaneously compliant, collaborative, self-regulatory, and generative of top-class ideas is a sense of human beings – adults and children – negotiating multiple relationships in specific local contexts. Missing is any notion of subjective investment in one's own ways of thinking, speaking or representing (except as a management problem). Missing also is any sense of the continuity of 'old' ways of thinking, of histories of practice and their possible impact on social subjects (here, teachers) confronted with the demand to re-orient themselves to new regimes.

In Mrs P's classroom, there was more going on than the production of new knowledge workers. Rather there were many different agendas in complex and sometimes contradictory relation to each other. Food hampers were distributed to poor families as a result of the Six Hats of Christmas activity. Individual children were disciplined using the hats even when this involved impeding the flow of knowledge, an effect that contradicts the hats' intentions if one goes by the Internet texts which are silent on the question of individual power. Children were also able to do their own kind of 'parallel thinking', simultaneously delivering appropriate 'hat' responses and engaging in their own forms of collective or individual explorations which could be tangential, personalized and erratic.

However, this analysis does support the assertion that 'network effects' of a globalized discourse on thinking can be seen in local classroom sites where teachers employ pedagogic technologies such as the six thinking hats, with the aim of producing clever children. When young children learn to put on and take off their thinking hats, they are learning to position themselves in relation to a collective and to exteriorize their knowledge for the benefit of this collective, both of which involve learning to write, speak and otherwise represent knowledge in particular ways. They are also learning not to hold too tightly to personal investments in ideas, that even one's feelings can be held up to collective scrutiny, to be relinquished when the red hat is taken off. The six thinking hats could be described as an 'immutable mobile' that is 'a network of elements that holds its shape as it moves' (Latour, 1990 cited in Law, 2003: 5) through cyber and social space. Wherever it is employed, thinking is fragmented into the same array of cognitive orientations. Wherever it is employed, the same metaphors and interactive scripts allocate to the powerful (facilitators, teachers, parents) the right to focus and channel the knowledge production of others.

Notes

1. While the hats approach is authored and strongly promoted by Edward DeBono, I do not intend to engage in a debate about the author's theories, intentions or academic credibility. It is the circulation of this technology through corporate and educational sites, and its links with broader agendas of productivity, performativity and globalization, which make it an illuminating case for investigation.
2. Funded by an Australian Research Council Discovery Grant *Questioning Development in Literacy* (Chief Investigators: Susan Hill, Barbara Comber, JoAnn Reid, William Louden and Judith Rivalland) and by a University of South Australia Division of Education Arts and Social Sciences Research Performance Fund grant, *Who gets to look clever? Gifted methodologies in the early years* (Chief Investigator: Sue Nichols).

References

Avis, J. (2002) Imaginary friends: Managerialism, globalization and post-compulsary education and training in England. *Discourse: Studies in the Cultural Politics of Education* 23 (1), 75–90.

Ball, S. (2003) The teacher's soul and the terrors of performativity. *Journal of Education Policy* 18 (2), 215–28.

Bell, D. (2001) *An Introduction to Cybercultures.* London and New York: Routledge.

Bradshaw, A., Bishop, J., Gens, L., Miller, S. and Rogers, M. (2002) The relationship of the World Wide Web to thinking skills. *Educational Media International* 39 (3/4), 275–85.

Clark, J. (2001) Using actor-network theories for the study of literacy events and practices in global and local settings. Paper for the *International Literacy Conference*, Cape Town, 13–17 November.

Comber, B. and Nichols, S. (2003) Getting the big picture: Regulating knowledge in the early childhood literacy curriculum. *Journal of Early Childhood Literacy* 4 (1), 43–63.

De Bono, E. (2000) *Six Thinking Hats*. London: Penguin.

Fabos, B. (2000) ZAPME! Zaps you. *Journal of Adolescent and Adult Literacy* 43 (8), May: 720–26.

Fairclough, N. (1992) *Discourse and Social Change.* London: Polity.

Fairclough, N. (2003) *Analysing Discourse: Textual Analysis for Social Research.* London: Routledge.

Gold, K. (2002) Thinking: the next big idea. *Times Educational Supplement*. On WWW at http://www.tes.co.uk/search/search_display.adp?section=Archive&sub_section=Briefing&id=365216&Type=0. Accessed 14.6.02.

Hartley, D. (2003) New economy, new pedagogy? *Oxford Review of Education* 29 (1), 81–94.

Jessop, B. (2003) The state and the contradictions of the knowledge-driven economy. Published by the Department of Sociology, Lancaster University. On WWW at http://comp.lancs.uk/sociology/papers/Jessop-State-and-Contradictions.pdf.

Latour, B. (1990) Drawing things together. In M. Lynch and S. Woolgar (eds) *Representation in Scientific Practice*. Cambridge MA: MIT Press cited in Law (2003) *Materialities, Spatialities, Globalities*. Published by the Centre for Science Studies, Lancaster University. On WWW at http://www.comp.lancs.ac.uk/sociology/papers/Law-Heatherington-Materialities-Spatialities-Globalities.pdf.

Law, J. (2003) Materialities, spatialities, globalities. Published by the Centre for Science Studies, Lancaster University. On WWW at http://www.comp.lancs.ac.uk/sociology/papers/Law-Heatherington-Materialities-Spatialities-Globali ties.pdf.

Luke, A. and Carrington, V. (2002) Globalization, literacy, curriculum practice; discussion: Developing teacher practice. In R. Fisher, G. Brooks and M. Lewis (eds) *Raising Standards in Literacy* (pp. 231–50). London: Routledge.

Lyotard, J. (1979) *The Postmodern Condition: A Report on Knowledge*. Minneapolis: University of Minnesota Press.

Miller, D. and Slater, D. (2000) *The Internet: An Ethnographic Approach.* Oxford and New York: Berg.

Sinclair, J. and Brazil, D. (1982) *Teacher Talk.* Oxford: Oxford University Press.

Appendix: Descriptions of the Five Focus Web-Pages and Associated Websites

Each of these fives sites is described below beginning in each case with the entry text (the page linked to the results of the six-thinking-hats search) and then in terms of the intertextual context (linked pages in and out of the home site).

Example 1: Six thinking hats (http://www.discover.tased.edu.au/english/sixhats.htm)

Text

This page has the standard format and plain unembellished presentation of all Teaching Strategy pages in this state education department site. First are listed the curriculum strands and bands for which the strategy is suitable. Then comes a description of the strategy, a statement of purpose, an example of use and a statement of assessment outcomes. It is addressed directly to teachers using headings in the form of first person questions e.g. 'How do I do it?'

Intertextual context

The page is accessed through the 'Especially for teachers' link from the English Curriculum home page of the Tasmanian Education Department Website (other links are for coordinators, students and parents). From here teachers can link to the 'Teaching Strategies' home page which features a grid displaying over 50 strategies mapped onto curriculum areas and bands. The Six Thinking Hats strategy has the maximum number of dots in the grid indicating it is considered to have the widest possible applicability. There are no external links from this site.

Text 2: School adopts De Bono's thinking hats (http://www.literacytrust.org.uk/database/thinking.html)

Text

This brief text written in journalistic language, presents a hats success story from the perspective of one UK school. The story states that: 'The headteacher credits the [hats] tools in part for a big improvement in her pupil's GCSE results' and mentions that this school is now accredited to provide hats training to other schools.

Intertextual context

This story appears in the 'Accelerated Learning and Thinking Skills' resource pages, a section in the very large web-site managed by the UK-based non-profit organization, the National Literacy Trust. The story is one of several, all sourced from the Times Educational Supplement, which appear in the Update section. Other stories in the update section include: 'Reflective pupils lift exam grades' and 'Spinning on the spot can boost early academic achievement'. Also on this page are links to a bibliography of research titles from journals such as *Nature Neuroscience* and *Cognition*; and to a list of mainly Web-based resources. Many of these links take the user to the Network Educational Press site, a publishing company that produces books with titles like 'Brain Friendly Revision'.

Text 3: The six hats of Christmas (http://www.brainways.co.nz/Chrisweb/hats/hathome.htm)

Text

This page is dominated by a six section grid, in each box of which is a mouse character wearing a coloured Santa hat and a large print question indicating the kind of thinking each represents. The page is headed by the statement: 'Christmas is celebrated by millions of Christians all over the world. What do we THINK about Christmas?' Its graphic presentation, single page format and simple language mean this page would be recognized by primary teachers as a printable worksheet. However each mouse is also hyperlinked to corresponding activity pages.

Intertextual context

This page is accessed through the web-site of Brainways, a New Zealand based company which develops and markets educational resources. The introduction to the Christmas resource explains that it integrates De Bono's hats with Gardner's Multiple Intelligences, provides activities at three reading levels, and addresses essential learning skills. This resource has versions for teacher guided use and student self-paced use. In the 'Teacher Talk' section, large key icons encourage teachers to open linked pages with information on topics such as pedagogy, assessment and professional development. The professional development page links to the site of a US-based company Advanced Practical Thinking which promotes DeBono training to organizations. The student pages offer links to 'live, safe Websites' on the theme of Christmas, one of which takes users to the commercial site KidsDomain which, as well as offering information on Christmas in different countries, has an online shop, and a family holiday planning section.

Text 4: Six thinking hats (http://www.learnerslink.com/Six%20Thinking%20/Hats.htm)

Text

This page is headed by a graphic of six old-fashioned formal top hats sandwiched between two statements: above, the heading 'Revolutionizing Thinking in Schools and Organizations' and below, a quote from Edward De Bono: 'You can analyze the past, but you have to design the future'. Beneath is a list of quoted testimonials e.g. 'Apply the SIX HATS® is a natural for the classroom'. The page provides two sections each describing the hats' purpose and benefits differently, one for schools and one for organizations.

Intertextual context

This page links back to the home page of 'Franny', a training provider whose company is 'Learners Link' and also out of the home site to external commercial sites for the purchase of De Bono products. On every page of Franny's site, a side-bar menu provides links to the range of programs on offer some of which are Gifted and High Ability, Learning that Lasts and Inventor's Workbench. The 'About Franny' page describes her as a parent, teacher K-12, author, consultant, trainer and instructor. From here there is a link to the home page for INVENT AMERICA! – a program for children that is intended to, in the words of its mission statement, '"rekindle the spirit"® of American ingenuity and productivity through national education and public awareness'.

Text 5: 'Six Thinking Hats' for full-colour thinking (http://www.lyndacurtin.com)

Text

This downloadable pdf document is in magazine article format and written in somewhat sensationalist journalistic language encouraging the reader to identify a subjective need for better thinking: 'Yes, nothingness, along with anxiety and frustration, has consumed you. But it doesn't have to be this way. The article then takes readers through a series of mini success stories demonstrating the effectiveness of the hats in different contexts and featuring characters such as 'Alex D'Anci creativity trainer and facilitator'.

Intertextual context

This document is one of several linked to the Six Thinking Hats page on the large Website of Lynda Curtin, self-designated 'Opportunity Thinker'. From this page, teachers can enter the school program section which is headed by the statement 'I am providing you with this information because I always get asked about "the kids". Why aren't we teaching our children how to think at school?' A list of suggested uses for the programs is given, top of which is 'home schooling', and which includes the dot point 'Corporations can sponsor school programs'. On this page, teachers are offered a 50% discount to train as De Bono instructors. The remainder of the services described across this Website are directed at corporations and include such programs with titles like 'management thinking', 'advanced facilitation' and 'accept ideas'.

Chapter 9

Corporate Crossings: Tracing Textual Crossings

JENNIFER ROWSELL

Introduction

This chapter is a case study of publishing corporations crossing into classroom sites. Drawing on ethnographic research conducted over a three-year period, I explore crossings that take place on practical and ideological levels at educational publishing companies in Britain and Canada. To probe the ebbing and flowing of discourses and ideologies, I look to their words through interview data, to artifacts that they create in the form of textbooks, and to my own memories of working in educational publishing in Canada for three years.

Books remain a predominate technology in school. Yet there is a Janus-faced relationship between schooling as in promoting children's intellectual growth, and publishing as in gaining market share and making money. Certainly the form and the meaning of texts disguise a complex hybrid of people, of agendas, of discourses, and of beliefs about how we teach and, in turn, how we learn. Between the author and the reader stand the powerful mechanisms of production. Stages in the development and shaping of educational texts direct readers about how a text should be understood.

Publishing is a complex process with a carousel of actors entering and exiting at various stages. Rather than assuming that texts are originary and monologic (in the sense that only one voice authors a text), the chapter traces the social and material processes that producing textbooks entails. In this way, producing textbooks is seen in the chapter as *an instance of practice.* In relation to the work of Appadurai, the chapter deals with a *financescape* (Appadurai, 1996) in that educational publishing quite clearly concerns the relationship between production and consumption.

The interesting twist here is that schooling carries associations that run against the corporate mentality of many international publishing corporations.

The chapter explores how struggles within crossings play out in texts. I am arguing that text producers, like readers, are active negotiators of meaning. Negotiations are interwoven into texts and as they cross into classrooms, they directly influence how teachers teach and how students learn. Like other chapters in the collection, *crossings* is a central and presiding notion. In the chapter, I explore three forms of crossing that take place between publishers and the educational community: Local–Global Crossings; Workplace–Schooling Crossings; and Multimodal Crossings.

First of all, educational publishers as bricoleurs interpret what educational communities demand and materialize them in texts (crossing from a workplace/corporate space to school/public space). Secondly, textbooks, as pedagogic technologies, acknowledge, transform and communicate key learning principles and have become a primary means of transmitting the curriculum. Given that we have an influx of eclectic materials (textbooks, standardized tests, and educational software), as teachers, there is even more of a demand for consumer savvy. Thirdly, and potentially the most important point here is one that emerges in Davies' (2005) and Knobel and Lankshear's (2005) chapters, *multimodality foregrounds different discourses*: publishers find their own voice and position through the visual. Educational publishers, as bricoleurs, interpret what educational communities (i.e. fields of practice, policy and research) demand and 'mirror' them in textbooks produced for school use. Text production is therefore at once an economic as well as cultural and social activity wherein human subjects guide materials and cross different and often opposing terrains in order to do so. What is more, they use the physicality or materiality of texts to transmit a message.

Crossings as a Heuristic Tool

Early on in the research what became clear was a dearth of studies on the criss-crossing of work domains with school domains. Although schools are indeed workplaces, they are not (necessarily) market-driven work sites with elaborate hierarchies and overall company mission statements guiding work practices. Schools share some of the characteristics of 'new work order' (Gee *et al.*, 1996) contexts, but they, arguably, are far more tied to civic duties and public good than to corporate agendas. Discursively, ideologically and semiotically, work and school are separate and seemingly incommensurable contexts. In reality, however, there are constant and insistent crossings taking place between both contexts – in the case of the study – the domain of educational publishing in Canada and the United Kingdom *and* British and Canadian classrooms. Interpreting crossings taking place among these sites leads us closer to understanding how pedagogic texts like reading programs are produced and in turn deployed and interpreted in classroom practice. In the chapter, I consider three types of crossings:

(1) *Local–global crossings:* This crossing features the increasing local–global tie whereby international publishing corporations (e.g. Thomson Learning Corporation or Pearson Education) buy out smaller, local publishers and place a local overlay on global products for classroom use.
(2) *Workplace–schooling/crossings:* This crossing spotlights the Janus-faced relationship between educational publishers governed by workplace ideologies developing textbooks (CD-ROMs, printed texts, websites) for school use governed by pedagogical, curricular and practical ideologies.
(3) *Multimodal crossings:* This crossing demonstrates how discursive and ideological crossings materialize in a publisher's choice of colour, binding, style of illustration, and trim size of a text.

The study focuses on people who are involved in multiple roles in text making (from editors to executives) and how they embed parts of themselves, their biases and their epistemology into pedagogic texts. Crossings take place as: local practices crossing global practices (e.g. taking a New Zealand reading program and adapting it to a Canadian market); the juxtaposition of workplace ideologies (focus groups with teachers on textbook designs) with schooling ideologies (observing students using educational software); and the degree to which subjectivities (a designer's take on colour) cross corporate agendas (no wiro-bound texts can be manufactured as a mandate by an international corporation). Local/global and educational/workplace crossings are site-specific: *multimodality is the means by which crossings materialize.* For example, a New Zealand program might be adopted by a Canadian publisher and have to be adapted to a Canadian audience. What this entails is not only infusing local terminology, but also visuals that are tied to more of a North American aesthetic. What is more, Canada comprises varying regions that will also require mediation and materializing their own local literacies (Barton & Hamilton, 1998). Such regions as downtown Auckland or regional Saskatchewan need to be accounted for in national textbooks. 'Local crossings' is therefore a problematic concept within the study in that it takes on a different gloss, depending on how regional the crossings are.

In the research, I pay close attention to the notion of crossings as a way of understanding how texts are mobilized in classrooms and materialize in classroom teaching. Crossings, by their very nature, imply hybridity, movement, dynamism because sites are not static, but bring with them, ideas, discourses, modalities which move between and among people and the texts that they create.

Theory and Method of Study

The theoretical perspective of the study is *speech and cognition are mediated by social interaction and cultural practice.* What this means in practice is that language, literacy, and discourse derive from social and cultural practice (Scribner & Cole, 1981). Literacy and learning practices are embedded in various Discourses, or ways of knowing, doing, talking, reading and writing, which are constructed and reproduced in social and cultural practice and interaction (Gee, 1996; Heath, 1983).

Like Davies (2005), data collection in the study has an 'ethnographic texture' in its examination of interpersonal, cultural, social encroachments on text production in Britain and Canada. Data collection was fourfold: ethnographic interviews with people working in publishing; observations of teachers and students using reading programmes in four classroom sites in London and Toronto; textual/semiotic analyses of programmes; and, reflexivity from my own work in publishing.

Dataset

25 ethnographic interviews with people working in publishing
41 observations of four classroom sites in Toronto and London
46 artifacts (publishing artefacts and reading scheme/programme books) analysed as part of the corpus of data
Reflexivity based on $2\frac{1}{2}$ years working at an educational publishing company in Canada

With reflexivity in mind, the chapter evokes my dual role as researcher analysing texts and editor of school textbooks. In my reading of texts, I am guided by a belief that you have to look at practices to understand text meaning. Adopting ethnographic methods allowed me to revisit knowledge and experience accessing a more contextualized and informed understanding of the publishing process. Ethnography, as a methodology, suits the study in that I could call into question, interpret and analyse 'taken for granted' understandings acquired over my time in publishing.

Multimodality in texts carries important messages about programs. Multimodality materializes in modes as in a form of representation, be it colour, fabric, three-dimensions, any 'stuff' (Kress, 1997) that suits the form and the function of a text. Modes within the visual landscape of texts materialize hidden Discourses (Gee, 1996), ideologies, and agendas. For example, creating a guided reading programme with an emphasis on genres of non-fiction in response to new trends in reading, for boys who prefer non-fiction to fiction texts.

As with the rest of the collection, case studies illustrate genres of crossings. My approach derives, in part, from the ethnographic tradition described by Mitchell (1984) as establishing 'representativeness' instead of applying 'enumerative induction'. Mitchell maintains that a case study approach supports 'an argument ... to show how general principles deriving from some theoretical orientation manifest themselves in some given set of particular circumstances' (Mitchell, 1984: 239). Case studies represent instances of practice that can be seen in other studies featured in the collection.

Texts as Traces of Social Practice

What is fundamental to the study is a concept of tracing – tracing people, practices and places within texts. As artifacts, what do textbooks carry with them? Lefebvre's (1991) notion of *spatial practice* is helpful at this moment in that it implies involvement in the production and reproduction of relationships among people, things and practices. Lefebvre claims that space stands on equal footing with social practice wherein one relies on the other in a symbiotic relationship (Lefebvre, 1991). Textbooks represent traces of a model of pedagogy at a certain time, of an editorial teams' set of decisions about how a book should look and sound, and ultimately, of the priorities of a given company (e.g. market-driven vs pedagogical integrity). Things (like texts) can be made in a multitude of ways in certain settings due to the choices and actions made by a given person or people within a given space. With Lefebvre's definition of spatial practice in mind, it is the *space of production*, which affects the *trajectory of practices* that take place during development and production of texts.

Textbooks are artifacts that carry a story of people working within specific spaces. Paying close attention to people and contexts leads us closer to understanding how meanings can be traced as they cross from a work site to a classroom site and perhaps even to a child's home (based on how they are taught literacy at school). Texts record decisions made during production. What happens when a text with a given perspective on literacy crosses a workplace and enters a classroom? In turn, what happens when a teacher, with his or her own perspective and years of experience, mediates its content and crosses into the domain of student learning? The study looks at the interface between crossings and how practices move and cascade into other settings and how they materialize in objects, artefacts or texts as traces of social practice.

Text, as an entity, stands on its own to communicate a separation of domains or spatial practice (Lefebvre, 1991) and local–global publishing companies from the community of schooling. How publishers interpret, transform and materialize these ideologies, systems and ruling Discourses (Gee, 1996) depends on the *interest* (Kress, 1997: xvi) and character of local publishers.

As a set of events, the genesis of a text is in the hands of executives in a publishing company who decide, for example, to produce an intermediate language skills program and, based on teacher feedback, and the program privileges computer skills (see Figure 9.1). The decision to have an electronic overlay affects both content and design in significant ways. In terms of content, the language program uses 'techno' or web-based vocabulary framed by a design that simulates a computer interface. In Figure 9.1, you see the visual and substantive impact of featuring email as a form of travelogue.

The language program has a certain ethos compared to its predecessors, that is staid grammar texts of the past, in contrast Figure 9.1 exudes an interactive, colourful design that makes the acquisition of language skills far more enticing. Textbooks are not made in isolation, but they are tied to different systems that inform their design and content. Invoking Appadurai's notion of *mediascapes* is helpful whereby 'image-centred, narrative-based accounts of strips of reality' – like highly designed language texts – are experienced and transformed by teacher and student creating a different reality.

The Macro in the Micro: Global Spaces Crossing Local Spaces

In the study, language is viewed as fluid and, as meaning-makers, we embed parts of ourselves in our production of texts. Textbooks for the

Figure 9.1 From Nelson Language and Writing 8, Student Text by. © 1998. Reprinted with permission of Nelson, a divison of Thomson Learning: www.thomsonrights.com

school market, whether they are reading, maths or science textbooks, are not only artifacts of political, theoretical and economic agendas, but also artifacts of development and production processes. The current educational climate appropriates teaching through curriculum and instructional commodities, so much so that teachers have come to engage in consumer-like behaviour. Given that there is an increasingly standardized model in the United States (No Child Left Behind), Britain (National Literacy Hour), and Canada (Standardized Testing), we are entering a pedagogy governed by an industrial model, with packages, tests and standardized pedagogic models of teaching and learning.

Equally, we have entered an era of commodification of education, better known as edutainment, with corporations like Disney (Giroux, 1999) entering the domain of education. The creators of content are international corporations, which place local overlays on materials. Such global institutions are crossing the global into the local through educational materials. With these transnational crossings, teachers have an even greater need to bridge the gap between work and schooling. With an industrial model in place, commodities such as packages, tests and standardized pedagogic sequences, teachers need more support on how to mediate consumerism with schooling. There is a much greater need to acknowledge the relationship between transnational corporations and public schooling. The craft of teaching has become a meta-awareness of corporate crossings and facilitating a mediation of consumerism with pedagogy and with practice. As a result, teachers have little room for autonomy in their craft or for envisioning and shaping their practice, given curricular constraints, standardized tests, and pre-packaged materials. Whatever craftsmanship we infuse into our teaching is usurped by the system within which we teach. We therefore teach in an economy of textbooks and 'knowledge work'. What is more, reading programs are shaped by global circulating agendas such as accountability and the push for a technicist approach curriculum.

The Local in Global Publishing

The act of publishing is, for all intents and purposes, an act of *transforming* ideologies, modes and Discourses; combining them with other ideologies, modes and Discourses to make an artefact used by teachers and students. Transformational and materialization processes are ideologically recursive in that they reflect economic, political, social and educational 'realities'. Texts (and the choices they map) relate directly back to a process, a site, and individuals involved in their creation. What separates one publisher from another is *how* they mediate forces on either end of the publishing continuum. That is, where they locate themselves in proximity to larger systems.

Publishing practices and mediations reflect social, political and ideological agendas. For example, 'whole language' and 'phonics' are dynamic in that they adjust to political, social and economic regulations or value systems in place. Whole language in the 1980s was more radical compared with a tamer version in the 1990s. Approaches to literacy development like whole language *tend* to match what is socially, politically, and economically accepted, and prevalent at a given time, in a given place. Equally, publishing practices are dynamic in that they respond to political, social, economic and visual agendas. Again, Lefebvre's (1991) notion of *spatial practice* helps to elucidate the role of space or context in the creation of text – what they look like and how they are tied to the reality of outside institutions. For example, if a program is written by a 'guru' in the field, it will carry that bias into classrooms to be mediated by teachers.

In interviews with people working in publishing, they maintain that it is crucial to interweave dominant curricular Discourses (Gee, 1996) with other, more subordinate Discourses in materials they produce; as one interviewee articulates it, 'What they do now is tailor stuff to meet the curriculum requirements, to fit the language of the curriculum, to put that language directly into teacher books'. By Discourses, I am referring to ways of speaking within specific Discourse communities, for example, the Discourse of local publishing companies versus the Discourse of international publishing corporations. Publishers find, select, and conjoin multiple texts and distinguish themselves in the manner chosen to materialize them.

Local–Global Crossings

Local influences enter the process at pre-production or post-production stages. Meso-level actors are people who consult, review, guide and use textbook content. Such actors do not necessarily work in companies, but test materials to ensure quality, accuracy or even 'pedagogical integrity'. Importantly, dialogues among institutions or systems outside of textbook publishing do not end once texts are manufactured and in classrooms. Dialogues continue when texts are in use, so that changes can be made, if necessary, upon reprint, or suggestions incorporated into future programs.

A local intervention in textbook publishing consists of ideologies, actors, contexts and systems working with publishers, but beyond their direct influence. Meso-level influences are people or places that work for and with publishers to create texts. Examples of meso-level people and places are printing companies, bookbinders, reviewers, teachers (who trial materials) students (who use materials), policy-makers (involved in writing or reviewing materials) and any freelance staff (e.g. designers, illustrators, editors, etc.).

What also lie within such local contexts (although much more linked to the publishing end of development) are printers and book manufacturers. Changes in production and distribution directly affect text production: aesthetically, substantively, and ideologically. On a policy level, curriculum shifts such as an emphasis on phonics catalyse production processes. For example, the National Literacy Hour incited changes to existing reading models such as the *Oxford Reading Tree* model, which were adapted to a Literacy Hour model (i.e. the National Literacy Hour in the UK). Publishers respond to changes at a local level by adjusting programs to befit the new model or through mediation documents.

As Gunther Kress has noted in his work on the motivated sign (Kress, 1997), the interest and agenda of people involved in text production find its way into text content and design. For example, a marketing manager infuses very different ideologies and imperatives into product development compared with an editorial director or pedagogical consultant. Each actor involved in text production leaves a residue or a trace of themselves and their particular agendas in texts produced for school children. Development teams participate in content and design decisions from the wording of activities to cover designs. In the following excerpt from a Thomson Learning (part of the Thomson international publishing group in Canada) interview, a senior author of a spelling series describes her experience developing a large spelling program with a motley group of people:

JR: Did you ever use or discuss your research with the publishing team?

ML: Oh always. It's not like I sat down and said, "Oh, this is important". It was as though the program unfolded. It was like everything was woven together: the concept, the marketability, the design, the content and we met once a week over a six-month period. And John always came down to the university to meet me because it was more convenient for me. So it's not like we divided our time, let's discuss theory; let's discuss marketability. It was an organic relationship, but once John left everything changed. (Margaret Laurence, Senior Author of Thomson Learning Program, Toronto, 8 October, 1998)

The interviewee proceeds to explain how the partnership and meeting-of-the-minds she felt with the first publishing team became a hostile one, which, she argues, found its way into the content of the spelling series. Ultimately, it is due to singular and collective transformational and mediational practices performed by people within specific publishing contexts that texts get made. Texts bear traces of these transformations, negotiations and contestations.

Case Study of Local Crossings

Traditional reading schemes in the UK are a series of readers developed for school children at Key Stages 1 and 2 and they are graded on ability levels. Teacher resource materials, on the other hand, come in a variety of formats (e.g. teacher's resource books, reproducible materials, professional books) and generally accompany programs and schemes as add-on features.

In the UK, the introduction of the National Curriculum caused some havoc to previous forms or models of development. In an interview with Ursula Birken[1] of Addison-Wesley Longman, she described the challenge of negotiating eclectic forces coming from all sides (workplace and schooling) of publishing during publishing processes:

> 'The National Curriculum changed the way publishers worked. Suddenly we had to translate a government document into a usable set of resources. The problem became two-pronged – not only did we have to compete with the structure and format of other reading schemes as we did previously, but also, we had to premise programs on the curriculum'.

In Canada, the same constraints exist only they are compounded by multiple provincial curricula. Although there isn't a disparity among provincial curricula, publishers still have to mediate curricula to meet local and ultimately national needs. By that I mean, alongside placating teachers, corporate heads, senior authors/gurus and reviewers, publishing teams need to acknowledge provincial gate-keepers (the purchasers of educational materials) and their particular views of how literacy should be taught and learned. James Cain of Gage Canadian Publishing (now taken over by Thomson Learning Corporation) echoed Birken's views on negotiating among different parties in different context:

JC: ... there was a time when you could literally walk into a Board of Education in a province and earn an adoption based on

> a publisher's reputation. Often, a province or school board would say, "we like your authors, so we will go with you ...". Today, it is vital to please the customer. If you do not, you are dead in the water. There are not as many gurus around today due to provincial cutbacks ... Essentially, educational publishers have implemented a speculative form of development that is teacher-driven. I would say, in this climate, teachers are more important than philosophy ... What also distinguishes the third and immediate phase of product development in educational publishing is the amount of competition. (James Cain, Gage Publishing Executive [recently merged with Thomson Learning], 14 April, 1998)

You see in the interview excerpt evidence of at least three levels of intervention from meso to macro systems: government intervention; teacher intervention; commercial intervention (the competition). Publishers, in Britain and Canada alike, dilute content with a bit of practice, a bit of curricula, a bit of marketization, a bit of visual mediation, a bit of technology until they have a complex hybrid of multimodal Discourses in texts as signposts for teachers, administrators, policy developers, and so on. Publishers need to cater to Discourses (Gee, 1996) with as much zeal as the competition; this trend has lessened a desire 'to go out on a limb' in a philosophical way, thereby homogenizing the design and content of textbooks. Publishers take account of each layer to mediate, transform, and materialize (in a singular way) their own take on each one. This juggling act is common to the British and Canadian educational publishing markets.

Case Study of Global Crossing

The following case study is based on an interview with a senior editor who has worked in educational publishing in Canada for three decades. Over the course of his time in publishing, Alan Marlowe witnessed the steady erosion of a Fordist model in publishing to an emergence of a 'New Work Order' model (Gee *et al.*, 1996). Alan Marlowe provided one of the more insightful perspectives on the intricate practice of instantiating global–local systems into texts. At several points in our interview, he maintained that, with textbooks, 'form follows function', linking publishing practices to classroom practice to curricular practice and even to global, embodied systems (like race, gender, religion), which lie beyond all three.

During our discussion of publishing processes, Marlowe contemplated the art of imbuing political, social and cultural ideals into texts:

AM: I think that one has to look at the assumptions that are being made and look at how education is delivered. I remember once, several years ago at an International Reading Association Conference, there was a seminar on the development of basal readers in the United States – primarily the southern United States. The reason they were developed was that most of the teachers were killed in the war. So they had a whole lot of young women, delivering the educational system. There wasn't much there in terms of their understanding, their expertise, or their education. So a need was expressed by the United States for foolproof educational materials. Stuff that you could give to anybody. That paradigm and that context in developing language arts and science and math programs is still with us. It comes and it goes, right now they are still doing pre-packaged programs. (Alan Marlowe, Freelance Developmental Editor, 27 July 1998)

Marlowe's recounting of a scholar's interpretation of the evolution of basal readers captures well the transformation of ideologies materialized in texts. According to him, textbooks gained currency over the post-war years in the United States due to a lack of teaching experience – a political, social, gender phenomenon filtered down into the kinds of text produced. Nichols' analysis of teachers' adoptions of DeBono's Six Thinking Hats (Nichols, this volume) resembles Marlowe's discussion of basal readers as pedagogic technologies that teachers pick up, use, and adopt as *a* model of teaching and learning. That is, a particular take on how to teach and, in turn, how students learn transforms pedagogy within classroom and schooling contexts. As a result, to derive meaning from texts, you need to know the assumptions and conditions of their production: 'one has to look at the assumptions that are being made and look at how education is being delivered'. How education is delivered leads naturally into a discussion on the impact of meso-levels of intervention on text production.

Workplace–Schooling Crossings

Educational publishing, as a satellite to schooling, tends to be regarded as more of a business than directly tied to classroom teaching and learning. In light of work experience and the study, it became clear to me that there is a strong nexus between the two domains. They are in frequent contact and the business of making textbooks for students is unquestionably tied to the way teachers teach and think and, ultimately, student perceptions of literacy. The crossings that take place take the form of meetings between publishing teams and teachers, administrators, teacher educators about what contemporary pedagogical needs are at a given time, or, what type of designs they would like to see. Educational publishing companies cannot be created equal and the degree of crossing that takes place relies on where a publisher sits in relation to globalization and marketization. The closer a publisher is to the market, the more contact they will have with the educational community.

What permeates the publishing industry is a need to sell books, yet the processes companies adopt have everything to do with the type of texts they produce. Process and team-based hierarchies in corporations are on a rise whereby publishing corporations engender a loyalty to company values. To illustrate, I refer to a business plan by an educational publisher in Canada. The document typifies ways of being and ways of seeing (Fairclough, 1992) in educational publishing, which resembles mainstream corporations like McDonalds© or Microsoft©. Although it refers to being 'a provider of learning materials' most of the document is devoted to financial matters – 'Business and Finance', 'Customer', 'Environment or Employees'. In fact, it almost sounds as if the writer is converting the reader to the company's cause:

> Drawing on our unique strengths . . .
>
> - Being International *(global)*
> - Being Canadian *(local)*
> - Being the Best *(local–global)*
>
> We will be relentless in our quest to become the publishers of choice for an ever-broadening range of markets and customers. (1997 Business Plan)

Trappings such as 'we', 'our', and 'quest' are hooks for employees to induce a sense of allegiance and belonging to their mission. Adopting company values and corporate imperatives means that context often overrides personal knowledge, experience and belief systems. For example, Cambridge University Press privileges an old-school philosophy of text production. It is a culture in which most of the senior members of product development teams are 'Oxbridge' educated and, as a result, have a more a protracted development and editorial process. Heinemann Publishing, however, provides far more of a characteristic picture of educational materials development. In an interview with a Heinemann executive, she made it clear that Heinemann is guided far more by corporate values than by traditional publishing values:

> When I went to Ginn from children's trade publishing, the design values at Ginn at the time were stodgy and boring. I brought with me a designer from children's traced publishing. One of the things we wanted to do was really improve the whole look and feel and the quality of artwork and illustrations that went into reading programmes and went into educational books... The whole thing changed dramatically because educational books needed to reflect the values of trade books, because teachers are very attracted to trade books, so they need to reflect those values and have something else with them, which is the structure. (Anna Merle, Reed Publishing, Oxford, 18 June 1998)

When Anna Merle speaks of trade publishing, she is referring to books that are bought in bookstores like Chapters or Waterstone's. That is, books on the free market as opposed to educational texts bought through educational publishers. There is a corporate ethic in international publishing corporations that translates into an emphasis on profit and speaking to market trends.

According to Merle, educational materials are produced for a market; this market consists of users; what do most of these users want? They want what they are accountable to teach. In her opinion, you produce books for this percentage of the teaching population. You develop blueprints and templates to service the needs of these types of people. Such a perspective represents the contemporary mentality in educational publishing: an emphasis on markets; dominant or ruling Discourses (Gee, 1996); and economic imperatives.

On the one hand, stands Cambridge University Press, whose books might carry more caché or prestige (by virtue of the name and reputation of the university), but they do not get the market share that Heinemann or Ginn might get. On the other hand, you have corporate/commercial publishers, who generally beat the competition in supplying the market with what it needs exactly when it needs it, but at times jeopardizes accuracy or pedagogy in doing so. It is common knowledge in educational publishing that one cannot always equate quality with profit. As anyone who has worked in the industry can attest, creating a 'solid' product does not guarantee that it will sell. What sells is, as Merle contends, hitting the market at the right time, speaking to educators, and/or tailoring materials to agendas. Based on my experience and interview data, success is tied to the tacit, fine-tuned art of targeting the 'average' user and keeping current with trends.

Some publishers promote the fact that they are ruled by sales and marketing, or actually geared for mass-market sales. Historically, the question has been, does an educational publisher have an eye to the curriculum or an eye to market needs? Publishers may have similar practices, but the manner in which they produce textbooks varies significantly.

Multimodal Crossings

Crossings are materialized in the physicality of texts. What is more, multimodality in texts changes meanings in texts. Publishers differentiate themselves in the way they design their programs. There is a direct link between choices in binding, printing, and trim sizes and a publisher's transformation of curricular, pedagogical, and even socio-economic realities.

What interested me in the study was how publishers materialize disparate ideologies and discourses into texts. Can we construe publishing processes by looking at the physicality of texts? Previous textbook analyses saw production, layout, and representational features of texts as evidence of larger value systems. While acknowledging the importance of these systems in producing meaning, there is a further mediational and transformational level of systems enacted by producers of texts themselves. Publishers transform the interests of the educational community (and the systems being brought to bear on the system of education) and materialize them in textbooks. Stein and Slonimsky (this volume) demonstrate how children within a specific community materialize part of themselves in their texts.

Choices related to template creation and design layout distinguishes one publisher's interpretation of the market from another's. Kress maintains 'makers of signs use those forms of expression of their meaning which best suggest or carry the meaning, and they do so in any medium in which they make signs' (Kress, 1997: 12). In this sense, publishers are makers of signs using whatever means or modes they have at hand to set themselves apart from the competition. Differences among publishers in a market are as important as what unites them.

According to interviewees working in publishing, the issue of enhanced awareness of multimodality and materiality in textbooks represents one of the major shifts in textbook publishing over the past decade. As a Ginn executive expresses it:

JR: What about input in terms of design? How important a role does design play in the development of a book?

JD: Well, I would say an increasingly important one. We are increasingly putting more emphasis into things like typography. One of the things that can also go by the board are things like typography. We would actually like to find people who can come in and talk about it, I mean just like there is very little research done on educational books, we did have some experts come in recently to look at spreads. Typography is something you have to get right, especially with big books. We have developed our 15-foot rule, which is that you should be able to see the print from 15 feet away. We did it and Heinemann, who is our sister company, did it as well. Overall, in terms of design, the key issues are: letter spacing, word spacing, position of text. (Janet D'Arcy, Ginn Publishing, Aylesbury, England, 8 May 1998)

The level of detail paid to design and visual mediations reflects an obvious shift in emphasis from the written to the visual. With heightened emphasis on design features, the relationship among visual, textual, musical, and gestural modalities has changed because they are often mutually complementary, co-constructive, and even conflictual.

Two Case Studies of Multimodal Crossings

Texts, in this way, represent a material realization of systems of people, discourses, ideas and beliefs. Content and pictures in *Our Little Reader* published in 1932 by W.J. Gage & Company reflect another time, and clearly, a more dated value system. In Figure 9.2, the design and content of the 1932 reader resonate with past values, past pedagogy and past ideals.

In *Reading Images: The Grammar of Visual Design*, Kress and van Leeuwen (1996) speak of two different types of participants – *interactive participants* and *represented participants* (Kress & van Leeuwen, 1996: 46). They distinguish between these participants as those who are *interactive* as in participants in the act of communication, or, as those who are *represented* participants who are the subject of communication (Kress & van Leeuwen, 1996: 46). In the case of the 1932 reader below, actions enacted individually and collectively by the two girls, Nell and Baby, and the boy, Tom, are the content of language teaching.

In the illustration, there is very little dialogue with the reader. Most of the angles are oblique, placing the reader/viewer outside of the

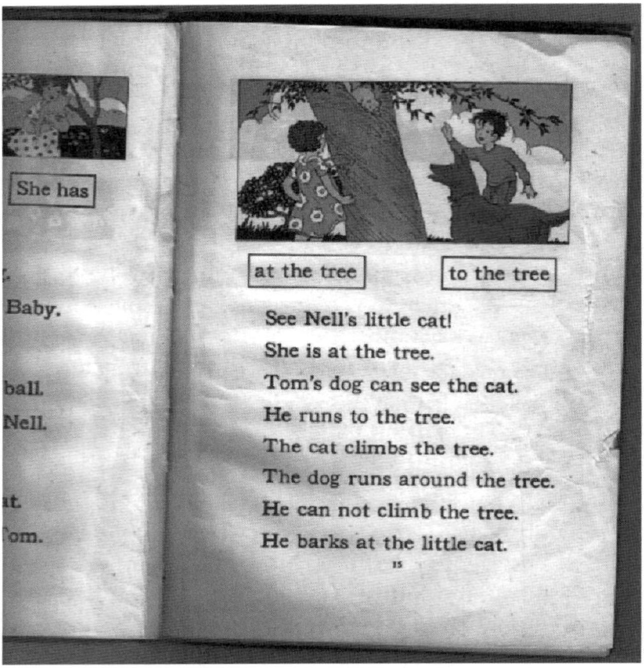

Figure 9.2 *Our Little Reader*

experience (Kress & van Leeuwen, 1996). Pictures function primarily as text support. They are randomly selected images of a cat climbing a tree and a boy, a girl, and a dog looking on. There is a literal picture-to-word correspondence.

Although written text in the 1987 levelled text (Figure 9.3) is equally as bland as the 1932 text, illustrations are far more engaging by infusing creativity and animation into the story. In *I Read*, the illustrator opted for a stylized or cartoony form of illustration, in strong contrast with the naturalistic depiction of childhood in *My Little Reader.*

In Figure 9.3, human and animal alike are anthropomorphized by adopting more an impressionistic style of illustration wherein everyone shares the same bubble-like body parts. The girl, her dog, her mother, her cat, and her fish do not look like human or live things, but instead, like cartoon versions of human or live things. The 1987 Gage text has a

I read to my fish.

Figure 9.3 *I Read*

marriage of text with illustrations when written text and artwork function as separate meaning-making tools.

The shift to a lexivisual approach is obvious in the linguistic/visual divide where pictures add life to banal content. In the 1932 text, the dog and Tom appear on equal footing. There are more frontal angles in the 1987 text, as opposed to the number of oblique angles in the 1932 text keeping the reader outside of the character's domain. The 1932 reader takes a bottom-up/traditional approach to the teaching of reading whereby students are encouraged to understand sentence structure, and, to a lesser extent, grammatical structures as in subject-verb-object. On the whole, within both readers, reading is presented as a fairly passive enterprise through such phrases as: 'Father has the car./It is a big blue car' (1932) and 'I read to my mom./I read to my dog' (1987).

Yet, there is a reversal of the visual and the linguistic in these texts. In *Our Little Reader*, visuals support text and, by extension, they support the model of literacy, whereas in *I Read*, visuals explain and enliven content.

This reversal of the visual and the linguistic carries with it more assumptions than is immediately apparent. That is, a dislocation between text and art reveals a reversal of landscapes: the 1932 text privileging the substantive power of the linguistic over the visual and the 1987 text privileging the substantive power of the visual over the linguistic. From a publishing vantage point, supremacy of visual over linguistic gives publishing companies more jurisdiction over materials and indeed more opportunities for different interpretations or versions of similar content. Although wording can change, there is not as much latitude for creativity as there is with the visual. A sentence like, 'I read to my dog' can be depicted in any number of ways, but can it be worded in as many ways?

In an age of highly prescribed curriculum, which leads to homogenized texts, publishers find their voice and position in the visual. Indeed, through the visual, publishers have on-hand a variety of forms of illustration (stylized, graphic, impressionistic or naturalistic) and they can be designed, formatted, bound (stapled, perfect, sewn) and printed in a multitude of ways. Materializing crossings in texts through multimodality gives publishers a means of differentiating themselves from the competition.

Conclusion

The chapter clearly demonstrates how texts slide across sites. A key strand in my reading of texts has been a view to workplace practices as a space that imbues ideologies and discourses that materialize in textbook content. The movement and cascading of ideas and agendas within texts are performed by people within very particular sites and this concept of ideological crossings fits in well with other crossings presented in the collection. For example, where Nichols (2005: this volume) looks in depth at pedagogic crossing, the chapter probed how pedagogic crossings materialize within print resources produced for teachers. Pastiches of people, their workplaces, and concepts about teaching and learning are palpable in texts published by educational publishers. Like Nichols' study such crossings encroach on the manner in which we teach such subjects as literacy or numeracy or science education.

Deborah Brandt claims that, by the early decades of the 20th century, 'the skills of reading and writing' in North America became 'more deeply implicated in the engines of economic productivity'. Brandt extends these thoughts by describing readers as 'targets both as audiences for advertising and as purchasers of literacy-based commodities'. What surprised me most in conducting a study on educational publishing was the lack of awareness and certainly discussion about the frequent, and I might add, steady crossings among the business of schooling through textbook and educational software production, outside companies manufacturing materials for governments like whiteboards *and* teaching practice, classrooms, and students' development of literacy skills. Brandt attributes the push for 'new thinking, new knowledge, new products, new angles, new markets' to the rise of a knowledge economy (Brandt, 2002: 5–10). Crossings between and among schools and businesses are therefore more frequent and seamless than we might think as educational systems around the world gear for 'knowledge workers' wherein growing knowledge is the primary ingredient to success.

Note

1. I use pseudonyms to protect the identity of individuals involved in the study.

References

Appadurai, A. (1996) Introduction: Commodities and the politics of value. In A. Appadurai (ed.) *The Social Life of Things: Commodities in Cultural Perspectives* (pp. 3–63). New York: Cambridge University Press.

Barton, D. and Hamilton, M. (1998) *Local Literacies: Reading and Writing in One Community.* London: Routledge.

Brandt, D. (2002) Reading, writing, and wealth in the new economy. Lecture presented by the Centre for Interdisciplinary Studies of Writing and the Literacy & Rhetorical Studies Minor.

Davies, J. (2005) Wiccan girls. In K. Pahl and J. Rowsell (eds) *Travelnotes from the New Literacy Studies: Case Studies of Practice.* London: Multilingual Matters.

Fairclough, N. (1992) *Discourse and Social Change.* Cambridge, MA: Polity Press.

Gee, J.P. (1996) *Sociolinguistics and Literacies: Ideology in Discourses* (2nd edn). London: Falmer.

Gee, J.P., Hull, G. and Lankshear, C. (1996) *The New Work Order: Behind the Language of the New Capitalism.* St. Leonards, AU: Allen & Unwin.

Giroux, H. (1999) *The Mouse that Roared: Disney and the End of Innocence.* Lanham, MD: Rowman & Littlefield.

Heath, S.B. (1983) *Ways With Words: Language, Life and Work in Communities and Classrooms.* Cambridge: Cambridge University Press.

Kress, G. & van Leeuwen, T. (1996) *Reading Images: The Grammar of Visual Design.* London: Routledge.

Kress, G. (1997) *Before Writing: Rethinking the Paths to Literacy.* London: Routledge.

Lefebvre, H. (1991) *The Production of Space.* Cambridge, MA: Blackwell.

Mitchell, C. (1984) Case studies. In R. Ellen (ed.) *Ethnographic Research: A Guide to General Conduct* (pp. 237–241). London: Academic Press.
Scribner, S. and Cole, M. (1981) *The Psychology of Literacy*. Cambridge, MA: Harvard University Press.

Part 4

Multimodal Communicative Practices in Pedagogical Settings

Chapter 10

So, What About Multimodal Numeracies?

BRIAN STREET AND DAVE BAKER

Introduction

We would like to put on the agenda, for those discussing multimodal literacies, the issue of multimodal numeracies. The very unfamiliarity of this idea to many in the field may help us see more clearly the assumptions the authors are making as they attempt the task of linking work in New Literacy Studies with that in multimodality. In numeracy the issue of modality is central since numerical principles and procedures are always represented in a variety of modes – from oral and written (using symbols) to visual (in mathematics education terms 'iconic'), including layout and ordering as in a number square or number line, to actional (or 'enactive'), as in the use of concrete apparatus for number or as in the movements across diagrams that we describe below with respect to number squares. We would like to use this opportunity to 'bring numeracy in from the cold', in the sense that for literacy researchers and practitioners, numeracy is often seen as an 'add on' – something to be added to the programme or to the classroom practice or the research questions, once the literacy design and materials have been established. Mathematics educators frequently complain at this Cinderella status and argue that, whilst there may be some similarities between numeracy and literacy, the field of numeracy also has its own distinctive character and requires specialised knowledge and approaches. In order to address these questions, we suggest that we need to make explicit the theoretical and methodological issues that underpin them. We have argued elsewhere (Street *et al.*, 2005) that an ethnographic-style approach (Green & Bloome, 1997) can facilitate our ability to address these questions, to collect the kind of data that speaks self-consciously to both theory and practice in this field and to provide us with a sound 'evidence base' for policy interventions. At that point we especially took account of work in the New Literacy Studies and considered its relevance to understanding numeracy at home and at school, as we detail below. But, in the context of the present volume, we would also like to highlight work in multimodality and to suggest how this field too, can provide a basis for closer observation and better understanding of engagement with numeracy practices, as in the examples we detail below where teachers, pupils and parents move between linguistic, actional and visual modes in the representation of numeracy.

In this chapter we are therefore exploring ways that the concept of multimodality can reveal understandings of critical issues in teaching and learning mathematics. To do this we explain and develop the theoretical background to our approach to mathematical education. We first look at what we mean by numeracy as social practice and what we mean by code switching in formal and informal numeracies. We then seek to illustrate and apply views of multimodality to two pieces of data taken from the Leverhulme Research Programme.[1] The first of these is a numeracy event from a visit to a home and the second is from an observation of a classroom numeracy event. The data are not so much case studies as indicative of how we might connect multimodality and mathematical education. They were selected because of their potential links and salience to these issues and we would anticipate in future ourselves and other researchers following up these insights with fuller case studies.

Throughout this chapter we have distinguished between the terms mathematics and numeracy in order to bring out the 'social' and multimodal features of the practices on which we are focussing. Numeracy, then, is taken as the broader term, including both everyday practices and educational aspects, both of which may have a mathematical dimension. Mathematics, then, we take to be a more specialised and abstract set of practices, usually the domain of professional practitioners both mathematicians in universities and mathematics educators in both higher education and schooling. In the present context, we have tended to use numeracy more precisely, mainly where we want to focus on possible relationships between numeracy and literacy practices. In a volume that reported on research into children's home and school numeracies in the UK (Street *et al.*, 2005), we raised the question as to how far the concepts developed in New Literacy Studies (Barton & Hamilton, 1998; Barton *et al.*, 2000; Heath, 1983; Street, 1984, 1995, 2003; Tomlin, 2002) are relevant to the study of numeracy.

The term *literacy events* derived from the sociolinguistic idea of speech events has, for instance, been adapted by Baker and Street (1996) to investigate *numeracy events.* Shirley Brice Heath, a literacy researcher in the USA, characterised a 'literacy event' as 'any occasion in which a piece of writing is integral to the nature of the participants' interactions and their interpretative processes' (Heath, 1983: 93). Street has distinguished this descriptive concept from the more general notion of 'literacy practices' (Street, 1984: 1; Street, 2000) as a means of focusing upon 'social practices and conceptions of reading and writing', focusing upon the social models of literacy that participants bring to bear upon those events and that give meaning to them. Consideration of the relation between *literacy events* and *literacy practices* provides a useful basis from which to engage in field research on literacy as a social practice. We have provisionally adopted the concepts of *numeracy events* and of *numeracy practices* on analogy with *literacy events* and *literacy practices* (Baker, 1996, 1998; Baker & Street, 1996). By focusing on *numeracy events* as units of inquiry in both home and school, we were able to observe those 'occasions in which a numeracy activity is integral to the nature of the participants' interactions and their interpretative processes' (Baker & Street, 1996: 80). Likewise, in parallel to literacy practices, we might see numeracy practices as more than the behaviours that occur when people do mathematics/numeracy – more than the events in which numerical activity is involved – and so explore the conceptualisations, the discourse, the values and beliefs and the social relations that surround numeracy events as well as the context in which they are sited. One key application of these concepts concerns the explanation of underachievement in mathematics by many pupils, whether children or adults, when they encounter formal teaching of the subject, in schools and programmes. An acknowledgement of the existence of multiple numeracy practices, each framed and sited in the context in which it occurs, suggests an explanation that differs from the dominant concerns with 'lack of motivation' or with 'deficit': instead the recognition of different numeracy practices in school and out of school and the emerging hypothesis that the differences between *schooled numeracy practices* (following Street & Street, 1991; Cook-Gumperz, 1986 on 'schooled literacy practices') and out-of-school numeracy practices may be a factor in the under achievement in formal numeracy of some learners. From this perspective, for instance, the underachievement of children from less affluent homes may have to do with the boundaries and barriers such children face between formal and informal literacy/numeracy practices; likewise, the underachievement of adults on literacy and numeracy programmes may be to do with the differences between the everyday numeracy and literacy practices in which they are skilled and the specialist numeracy and literacy practices required in formal education. How, then, can we investigate these hypotheses and what might their relevance be to the understanding of broader issues concerning multimodality raised in the present volume? We would like to suggest that we need to clarify the language of description that we are using to understand these processes. In particular, we would like to suggest a way of characterising the relationship between literacy and numeracy, between home and school and between/across modes within school mathematics that will then enable us to address these issues.

The questions raised above have been addressed in yet another book that privileges literacy but provides scope for comparison of the two fields, Street's recent edited *Literacies Across Educational Contexts* (Street, 2005). Here, international contributors challenged researchers and practitioners to apply to diverse educational contexts the principles entailed in viewing literacy as a social practice. Colleagues working in mathematics education have been more reticent in applying to that field the principles entailed in viewing mathematics as a social practice. This paper begins to take on that challenge and considers how we might apply these perspectives to diverse educational contexts involving mathematics.

The challenge involves firstly exploring what does it mean to think of mathematics as a social practice – how does a 'social' view alter taken-for-granted assumptions about mathematics? For instance, a social view questions the assumption of universality built into many accounts of mathematics – that it is the 'same' everywhere; and it challenges the top down view of learning associated with such assumptions about secure knowledge – that people simply have to be taught the rules and procedures. Both theoretically and in terms of pedagogy, the social view then, offers a new approach that would start from the rich variety of engagement with mathematical principles evident in people's ordinary lives – from pigeon racing, to building a sand-pit, to table setting to managing home accounts.

In the present volume the authors address the relationships between literacy, visual communication and actional modes in a variety of fields but they do not embrace numeracy (Millard *et al.*, this volume). We would like to ask what would be involved in locating numeracy too in the discussions about multimodality? We describe below some data from a recent project researching numeracy at home and at school that indicates the significance of multimodal forms of meaning making in the learning and use of numeracy. In teaching numeracy to school pupils, teachers tend to shift between linguistic modes as in the speaking and writing of sentences or signs associated with mathematical systems, to visual mode as in the layout of diagrams such as the number square or number line to actional mode – getting pupils to trace movement across the square, moving down a grid and across lines or to use concrete apparatus that represents numbers. Much of this is addressed at an implicit level, as though such mode switching were naturalised for all learners in all contexts, whereas the attention or lack of it evident from our observation of pupils in such situations suggests that for some at least the switches are not self evident and may indeed be problematic. There may be explanations here for student under performance in numeracy but before we address such pedagogic issues, we need to develop a language of description and a methodology for addressing mode switching in numeracy, just as researchers in this volume are doing with respect to literacy. The examples below represent an initial attempt to bring these two fields together with respect to issues of multimodality and to overcome some of the separation that generally characterises their relationship.

Numeracy as a Social Practice

We start with the premise that numeracy is a social practice (Baker, 1996, 1998; Baker & Street, 1996), an analogy with literacy as social practice, as a way of then thinking through what it means to also address multimodality as social practice and its role in the practice of numeracy. The gains in describing literacy as a social practice have been well documented (Street, 2005) – and the gains in linking literacy and numeracy in this way are beginning to be addressed (Baker & Street, 2004a; Street *et al.*, 2005; Street, forthcoming), for example, in contrast with viewing literacy and numeracy simply as skills or as universals that everyone should learn and acquire in the same way. But there are also some losses. Mathematics educators will want to argue for a specialist dimension to the use and understanding of number and associated concepts that is not fully captured by this analogy (Tomlin *et al.*, 2000). Furthermore, the analogy does not yet distinguish between the formal meanings of mathematics usually cited by mathematics educators and the informal everyday uses of the skills associated with such number and conceptual work on which ethnographers have focussed (Ginsberg *et al.*, 1997) (for a psychologist's view on the role of 'informal mathematics' in attainment in schooled mathematics see Nunes *et al.*, 1993). We would like, therefore, to suggest a model of 'numeracy' that takes account of these variations in meanings and dimensions, thereby both maintaining the analogy with literacy where it is appropriate but also recognising the distinctiveness of the field of mathematics and building in understanding of the relationships, and differences, between formal and informal mathematics. The model attempts to provide a language of description for these variations.

At the broadest level, then, we can begin with the premise that numeracy, like literacy, is a social practice. To some mathematicians this is too general and vague a concept, since in one sense 'everything is a social practice'. However, for our purposes it is important to distinguish between different kinds of such practice and at the same time to hold onto the acknowledgement that all such practices are rooted in social conditions, thereby facilitating analyses that explain differences in performance according to those conditions. From the perspective of some mathematics educators, there is a universal dimension to such practices – 'maths is the same everywhere' e.g. two plus two always adds up to four. Within the logic of given systems and conditions this is, of course, true – but only according to that logic and what the anthropologists have told us is that such logics may vary from one cultural context to another (Bishop, 1988; Knijnik, 2000; Restivo, 1992). Nevertheless, within its own terms, there is a 'mathematics dimension' to numeracy as social practice – this dimension privileges certain kinds of operation and procedure and certain specialist language and skills. For instance, multiplying numbers or providing a proof of a mathematical result can be thought of as a mathematical practice privileged by the community of mathematics educators. It may be possible to describe everyday numeracy practices in this way, but that would not exhaust their meanings and significance for participants, for whom such informal numeracy practices as doing the shopping or racing pigeons or timing videos are salient in other ways and are rooted in different logics of practice.

The important point for the concern with multimodality is that many of these procedures and practices, whether formal or informal, can be performed without writing them down – they can be done 'in the head' or with the use of images or perhaps mnemonics that are not the same as a fully developed writing system. Mathematics, then, can go on without recourse to literacy. Much practice in mathematics calls upon different modalities, such as use of signs, whether in the form of number symbols or words or use of diagrams (like number squares) and inserting them into texts, with sequences, juxtapositions that indicate meaning, and so on (for a further discussion of the mathematics of road signs see Baker & Street, 2004b). In this sense, the analogy of numeracy with literacy is not uniform, there are distinctive features of mathematics that cannot simply be reduced to those of literacy and some of these may be rooted in its multimodal forms of representation. Having discussed what we mean by numeracy as social practice and looked at the possible links between literacy and numeracy, we can now begin to call upon work in multimodality to describe and explain these features of numeracy practice. Later we describe some events where there is salient evidence of such multimodal numeracies.

Mode Switching in Formal and Informal Numeracies

Likewise, when we look more closely at the uses of literacy and numeracy, we find a further distinction, between formal and informal practices that may also be applicable to multimodality. In the field of literacy such informal practices have been well documented in recent years in the many ethnographies of literacy (Barton & Hamilton, 1998; Barton *et al.*, 2000; Heath, 1983; Street, 1984). Such informal uses include at one extreme the writing of graffiti in forbidden places, whilst at a less contentious level it includes the everyday notes, memos and scribbles that we all employ for functional as well as symbolic purposes. In numeracy such informal uses are less well documented, although researchers in ethno mathematics have provided some telling accounts of, for instance, the use of mathematical principles for navigating by Pacific sailors, the uses of 'street mathematics' by young sellers in urban areas of Brazil (Nunes *et al.*, 1993) and the skills of classifying and ordering milk bottles into crates amongst dairymen in Boston (Scribner, 1984). Such evidence often includes use of a variety of modes besides the linguistic and we cite here one such example from our own research in the Leverhulme Home-School Numeracy Project in the UK, which focuses on the uses of finger counting by a young Pakistani girl whose family had migrated to London[2] (Baker & Street, 2004a). Tomlin, a researcher on this project, had asked the girl, Aayesha to tell her how many children were in her class and received the following response:

> I said the class didn't have many children. Aaysha tried to count them by silently running through them in her mind, totting up numbers on fingers. I noticed she finger-counted in threes, three to a finger or thumb. I asked about this: Mr Anwar [her father] says "we" count three to a finger, so 15 to a hand, 30 in two hands. Mr Anwar's description included folding over two fingers and saying six. (AT/Tarnside/Aaysha 1, 21.11.00)

The multiplicative potential of the three to a finger counting scheme, familiar in parts of Asia, may have enabled him and his daughter, Aaysha, to perform some functions more effectively than using the UK system of one finger to each item. According to some mathematics educators, the potential of the procedure of counting three to a finger might have different affordances than counting one to a finger. Three to a finger shifts attention towards patterns and relationships between numbers and thence towards the processes of calculating rather than those of counting. The use of this informal home based procedure may therefore also be useful pedagogically in classrooms in facilitating its users to move on from counting to more formal numeracy practices, such as addition, multiplication and other ways of calculating.

The pedagogic point is important here as it indicates the relationships between such informal practices and the formal dimension of mathematics and brings out the extent to which the boundary between them is not fixed or static. In a classroom, wishing to introduce students to ways of calculating, a teacher will often not know about or not make use of the students' own informal numeracy practices, such as finger counting, and instead begin with a variety of representations, from body counts to use of concrete mathematical structural apparatus to oral commentaries and use of writing on a black or white board. In the latter case, which is of particular interest to literacy educators and to our present concern with multi modality, some numbers and the appropriate signs e.g. $21 \times 3 = (20 \times 3) + (1 \times 3)$, will be inscribed on a board and the teacher may also make use of conventional layouts, such as putting the numbers to be processed above a line and the 'answer' below. Perhaps even more striking here is the meaning that teachers attach to the sign '=' in the number sentence $3 + 7 = 10$. An oral description of it may be that three plus seven *makes* 10 with the flow or argument from left to right. The use of the word 'makes', makes the sentence irreversible. Yet teachers may also want the students to reverse the sentence in order to break 10 into 3 and 7. They then have to redefine '=' to mean 'the same as'. Such situations demonstrate features of mode switching, where teachers shift between oral, visual and written modes, and between sign systems in the written mode (words, notation signs, layout), a theme elaborated more fully in the forthcoming book of the Leverhulme Project (Street *et al.*, 2005). To many students of mathematics, whether adults or children, such conventions and procedures may be entirely unfamiliar and there might be a significant drop out amongst those members who quickly got left behind. If, on the other hand, the teacher started from where the students were and asked them in culturally sensitive ways to indicate the methods they used for addressing problems, then they would be more likely to facilitate their learning of new procedures. In terms of mode switching, explicit attention to the changes between oral, visual, written and actional might help the children track the teacher's meanings across these different communicative contexts.

There is, therefore, a complex relationship between the formal and the informal dimensions of both literacy and numeracy and how these relate to the larger distinction between the mathematics and the literacy dimension of numeracy practices. We might, for instance, begin with the informal practices of the mathematics dimension of numeracy and use them as a scaffold to the formal features of mathematics (e.g. multiplication). At the same time introduce the multimodal dimension by moving from finger counting to writing down the numbers and signs associated with that procedure, making explicit the shifts of mode as we do so. Keeping the language of description clear – that we are moving from informal mathematics to formal mathematics to literacy and multimodality – avoids the confusion that would attend our calling all of these practices 'numeracy' or all of them 'literacy'.

We learn from this account the importance of the ethnographic attention to people's own meanings and practices – if people learn best by building on what they already know rather than denying, rejecting or even denigrating such local knowledge, then studying such practices and using them as a basis for androgogy and pedagogy provides a positive way forward to helping more to achieve. Such an account may also help us to explain why so many underachieve. But whilst the practical implications for the design and delivery of programmes of literacy and numeracy are considerable, we would also like to pursue further here the broader questions regarding multimodality that these initial insights suggest.

Mode Switching in a Primary School Numeracy Class

Having discussed theoretical views about multimodality in numeracy we now will extend and apply these ideas to a classroom numeracy event. We describe here this event that was observed in the Leverhulme Numeracy research on home and school numeracy practices (DB, Mountford, 13 November 2002). The class of seven- to eight-year-old children was in a school sited in a city on the south coast of England in a white working class housing estate, which was seen locally as a financially deprived area. There were about 30 children in the class. The room was a fairly large, newly decorated, airy and fully carpeted room with five groups of tables. There were two computers in the room. There was quite a lot of number apparatus in the room and a number square on the wall. (A number square is a large square with the numbers 1 to 100 arranged in 10 rows of 10 squares starting with 1 in the top left and 100 in the bottom right, see Figure 10.1.)

Extracts from field notes of numeracy event from a school visit to Mountford, 13 November 2002

The children arrived in the class and gathered on the mat in front of the teacher. Next to her was an easel with a large number square attached and facing the children. The teacher wanted them to develop strategies for doing "add nine". She wanted them to be aware that to add nine they can add ten and then take away one. She first asked them to add thirty-six and nine to think about this as a class and then to put their hands up with both their answers and their strategies. Some seemed to do it immediately; some tried count up from thirty-six; others tried to add ten and take away one; others tried to use the number square; and others did not do much.

The teacher asked orally: "What is thirty-six add nine?"
Child: "forty-five. Added ten took off one"

Once one child gave the answer the teacher discussed the strategy. She told them orally that they could first add 10 and then take away 1.

1	2	3	4	5	6	7	8	9	10
11	12	13	14	15	16	17	18	19	20
21	22	23	24	25	26	27	28	29	30
31	32	33	34	35	**36**	37	38	39	40
41	42	43	44	**45**	46	47	48	49	50
51	52	53	54	55	56	57	58	59	60
61	62	63	64	65	66	67	68	69	70
71	72	73	74	75	76	77	78	79	80
81	82	83	84	85	86	87	88	89	90
91	92	93	94	95	96	97	98	99	100

Figure 10.1 Number square

> She then put a written representation of the strategy "+10 – 1" on the board. She also showed them how they could use the number square. They could go down one line from 36 to 46 in order to add 10 and then move to their left to 45 to take away 1. (See numbers in bold on Figure 10.1.)
>
> She then moved onto another example of the same thing.
>
> Some like Vincent knew how to solve the problem from the start already. Kay was fully attentive and compliantly held up her hand with the answer. Lenny and Seth were looking away from the board and were not engaged. Kerry and Jaz were sitting next to me to the side of the mat, they seemed to have no clue what to do.

In this event the teacher had shown the children three different modes for representing the problem and her preferred strategy. First she presented the problem to them orally. In a sense this is 'in their heads' and can be used for what is termed 'mental mathematics'. Then using symbols, she wrote a mathematical sentence and finally she used the number square to give a visual representation. There is considerable distance between these modes. The oral use of the number '36' does not reveal immediately that that number could be broken up easily into separate numbers of tens and units to allow the adding of 10 to get 46 and then subtracting one. Indeed the use of several operations within this process and the order they are done in may cause confusions. The move from the oral to the representation in symbols in the second mode where the number nine is seen as '+10 – 1' is more clearly a large shift for some of the children. The symbols are a very dense and compact way of carrying meanings. The children would have to select between their potential meanings for example instead of seeing +10 as an operation to add 10 it could be seen as the type of a number on a number line that is plus ten. Lastly, as teachers of mathematics we tend to see diagrams like the number square as a rich aid for our teaching without necessarily being aware of some of the complexities involved. The idea that when we add numbers we move to the right or down on a number square is not necessarily obvious. So to add nine to 36 we could count along the square and would at some point have to jump from the 40 at the right-hand end to 41 at the left-hand end. Alternatively we would need to accept that to add 10 we would move down one line of the square from 36 to 46. Then to subtract one we would move to the left to 45. The number square, as attractive as it might be pedagogically in mathematics education, is not without its problems. The visual and actional modes being called upon here require learning and practice and may not be familiar to many of the pupils – hence perhaps the inattention by some pupils that we noted above and the problems some have with the learning.

In the numeracy event above the children were therefore involved in three different modes of representation. This use of multiple representations in teaching of numeracy is encouraged in schools in England (DFEE, 1999). It is thought that being exposed to several ways of thinking about mathematics problems will help children with their school numeracy. For some of the children in this class like Vinny, the multiple modes used may have helped their learning, perhaps by reinforcing these children's already successful understandings by providing them with enriched images of the situation and even providing them with choices. Some children, such as Kay, may have been helped by being able to choose the representation they felt most comfortable with and reject the others. However, for other children perhaps Kerry and Jaz, this switching of modes could well have been a problem itself. We could suggest that trying to understanding links between such different representations of a task, instead of providing enrichment and choice, could confuse some children particularly those struggling with the concepts.

The conclusions that we could draw from the incident might not be to abandon the notion of presenting children with multiple ways of representing a problem, but rather to be aware that some children may find such mode switching problematic. Teachers could then seek ways of making the switching less problematic perhaps through more culturally sensitive selections of the modes and then making the switching process between modes more explicit and accessible and therefore allowing the children space to decide what use they could make of the different modes.

We would also point out the lack of any evidence here of links between this event and the children's experiences out of school. The event is sited firmly in what we have called school numeracy practices (Street *et al.*, 2005). Given that this is at the moment an unchallenged and an established part of schooling then the question remains as to how can we modify pedagogies to ensure the most effective learning of these practices. As we, and others have pointed out elsewhere (Baker & Street, forthcoming), out of school numeracy practices may provide a foundation for pupils' encounters with such schooled numeracy and some bridging of the two domains makes educational sense.

Conclusions

In this chapter we set out to consider ways in which views of multimodality could be applied to understandings of issues in teaching and learning formal mathematics in schools. By using our understandings of theoretical ideas such as switching and numeracy as social practice to both home and classroom data we have shown that multimodality as a model has salience and significance in mathematics and mathematics education. We have identified different modes of representations of mathematical ideas that could be seen in some instances as actional, diagrammatic and/or symbolic. We have suggested that problems of switching between such modes may be a source of some children's difficulties in the subject. In adopting this approach, the chapter can make some claim to novelty, in attempting to extend to the field of numeracy ways of analysing such issues that are more familiar in the field of literacy, of the kind evident throughout this volume.

The data we have discussed can, then, contribute to debates about pedagogy and offer explanations for pupils' underachievement in schooled numeracy. However, before we move too far down the policy line, we feel it is important to develop a methodological and theoretical frame within which to consider such numeracy practices. We have suggested elsewhere that treating numeracy as a social practice and researching such practices through ethnographic perspectives may provide a valuable starting point for such an approach. In this paper we have elaborated on these issues with respect specifically to the modes of communication involved in such practices, and suggested that the field of multimodality may also have much to offer to such thinking. However, in the context of a volume mostly addressing literacy practices, we would also like to urge researchers in the field of multimodal literacies to take into account the domain of numeracy, which already, perhaps more obviously than literacy, engages with multimodal representations. We have indicated how some of this might be of interest to multimodal studies, with reference to a few examples drawn from our recent research and look forward to exploring these issues further with colleagues in numeracy, literacy, multimodality and ethnography. There is great scope here for further research in the new field of multimodal numeracies.

Acknowledgement

With thanks to Alison Tomlin for the finger counting example and comments.

Notes

1. The Leverhulme Numeracy Programme is a five-year research programme (1997–2002), that focuses on pupil attainment in numeracy and is based at King's College London. The research consists of a core longitudinal project and five focus projects linked to it and to one another. Each of the five focus projects seeks to explore in depth explanations of pupil underachievement in one or more of the broad areas of classroom, teacher, school and home, using subsets of the schools involved in the longitudinal core project and supplemented by other schools as appropriate. Focus 4, 'School and Community Numeracies' has three researchers, Alison Tomlin and Brian Street (King's College London) and Dave Baker (University of Brighton).
2. In parts of Asia, a four-to-a-finger counting scheme is also known, sometimes including or excluding the thumb from the calculation and using whole hands for totals.

References

Baker, D.A. (1996) Children's formal and informal school numeracy practices. In D. Baker, J. Clay and C. Fox (eds) *Challenging Ways of Knowing in English Maths and Science* (pp. 80–88). London: Falmer.

Baker, D.A. (1998) Numeracy as social practice: An adult education context in South Africa. *Journal of Literacy and Numeracy Studies* 8 (1), 37–50.

Baker, D.A. and Street, B.V. (1996) Literacy and numeracy models. In *The International Encyclopaedia of Adult Education and Training* (pp. 79–85). Oxford: Elsevier Science.

Baker, D.A and Street, B.V. (forthcoming) Navigating schooled numeracies: Explanations from the UK for the low achievement in math of children from a low SES background. In M. Allexsaht-Snider (ed.) Special Issue of *Mathematical Thinking and Learning* on Parents' Perceptions of their Children's Mathematics Education: Considerations of Race, Class, Equity, and Social Justice.

Baker, D.A. and Street, B. (2004a) Mathematics as social. *For the Learning of Mathematics* 24 (2), 19–21.

Baker, D.A. and Street, B.V. (2004b) Mathematics as social: A comment on Barwell 24(1). *For the Learning of Mathematics* 24 (2), 19–21.

Barton, D. and Hamilton, M. (1998) *Local Literacies: Reading and Writing in One Community.* London: Routledge.

Barton, D., Hamilton, M. and Ivanic, R. (eds) (2000) *Situated Literacies: Reading and Writing in Context.* London: Routledge.

Bishop, A.J. (1988) *Mathematical Enculturation: A Cultural Perspective on Mathematics Education.* Dordrecht: Kluwer Academic.

Cook-Gumperz, J. (ed.) (1986) *The Social Construction of Literacy.* Cambridge: Cambridge University Press.

Department for Education and Employment (DFEE) (1999) *The National Numeracy Strategy.* Sudbury, Suffolk, UK: DFEE.

Ginsburg, H., Elsie Choi, Y., Lopez, L.S., Netley, R. and Chao-Yuan, C. (1997) Happy birthday to you: Early mathematical thinking of Asian, South American and U.S. children. In T. Nunes and P. Bryant (eds) *Learning and Teaching Mathematics: An International Perspective* (pp. 163–207). Hove: Psychology Press, Taylor & Francis.

Green, J. and Bloome, D. (1997) Ethnography and ethnographers of and in education: A situated perspective. In J. Flood, S. Heath and D. Lapp (eds) *A Handbook of Research on Teaching Literacy Through the Communicative and Visual Arts* (pp. 181–202). New York: Simon and Shuster Macmillan.

Heath, S.B. (1983) *Ways With Words: Language, Life and Work in Communities and Classrooms.* Cambridge: Cambridge University Press.

Knijnik, G. (2000) Ethnomathematics and political struggles. In D. Coben, J. O'Donoghue and G.E. FitzSimons (eds) *Perspectives on Adults Learning Mathematics: Research and Practice* (Vol. 21) (pp. 119–33). Mathematics Education Library. New York: Springer.

Nunes, T., Schliemann, A. and Carraher, D. (1993) *Street Mathematics and School Mathematics*. Cambridge: Cambridge University Press.

Restivo, Sal P. (1992) *Mathematics in Society and History: Sociological Inquiries.* Dordrecht: Kluwer Academic Publishers.

Scribner, S. (1984) Studying working intelligence. In B. Rogoff and J. Lave (eds) *Everyday Cognition: Its Development in Social Contexts.* Cambridge MA: Harvard University Press.

Street, B. (forthcoming) Applying New Literacy Studies to numeracy as social practice. In A. Rogers (ed.) *Urban Literacy: Communication, Identity and Learning in Urban Contexts.* Hamburg: UIE.

Street, B. (1984) *Literacy in Theory and Practice.* Cambridge: Cambridge University Press.

Street, B. (1995) *Social Literacies: Critical Perspectives on Literacy in Development, Ethnography and Education.* London: Longman.

Street, B. (2000) Literacy events and literacy practices. In K. Jones and M. Martin-Jones (eds) *Multilingual Literacies: Reading and Writing Different Worlds* (pp. 17–29). Amsterdam: John Benjamins.

Street, B. (2003) What's new in New Literacy Studies. In *Current Issues in Comparative Education*, Teachers' College Columbia: NY 5(2) May 12, 1523–1615. On WWW at http://www.tc.columbia.edu/cice/.

Street, B. (ed.) (2005) *Literacies Across Educational Contexts: Mediating Learning and Teaching*. Philadelphia: Caslon Publications.

Street, B. and Street, J. (1991) The schooling of literacy. In D. Barton and R. Ivanic (eds) *Literacy in the Community* (pp. 143–66). London: Sage.

Street, B., Baker, D. and Tomlin, A. (2005) *Numeracy Practices at Home and at School* (Vol. 4 of series on Leverhulme Numeracy Research Programme). Dordrecht: Kluwer.

Tomlin, A. (2002) Fieldnotes on school and home visits for Leverhulme Home-School Numeracy Project – referenced by author/place (e.g. school), subject (e.g. child), date e.g. *AT/Tarnside/Aaysha 1, 21.11.00.*

Tomlin, A., Street, B. and Baker, D. (2000) Home/school relations and their significance for effective learning and teaching of numeracy. BERA: September 2000, Cardiff ms.

Chapter 11

Transformative Pedagogy: Teachers Creating a Literacy of Fusion[1]

ELAINE MILLARD

Introduction

This chapter draws from four particular cases of teacher/pupil interactions in which each of the teachers, who were at the time involved in separate small-scale research projects into home influences on children's understanding, supported their classes' learning by drawing on individual pupil's informal knowledge to support formal and indeed, national curriculum requirements. In doing so, I argue they created powerful contexts for learning by drawing on what children brought in with them from their experience of globalised, multimodal literacy encounters in the home. I have used the concept of *fusion* to describe the deliberate intention of teachers to make use of what have variously been called their cultural capital (Bourdieu, 1977), funds of knowledge (Moll *et al.*, 1992) or literacy assets (Tyner, 1998). The teachers, in drawing these new aspects into the established teaching and learning patterns of schooling, were responding to what have frequently been described as 'New Times' in education (New London Group, 1996).

New Times Old Solutions

We might expect that any education system in tune with its young people and their cultural experiences would wish to develop the means to enable them to make productive use of their prior experiences and understanding. However, this does not seem often to be the case. Children are becoming multimodally literate whilst their schools' more explicit practices remain stubbornly print-bound. The emphasis nationally is on a firm control of tracked stages and targets and a timed delivery of key skills. In Bernstein's terminology, it can be seen that the curriculum is both strongly classified and framed, that is, control is exerted both over what is taught and the manner in which it is taught (Bernstein, 1996) so that teachers feel they have little opportunity to introduce new ideas. Moreover, the imposed literacy curriculum carries with it strict regimes of national testing which also impact heavily on what gets taught. This is not only the case in the UK, but appertains in all societies seeking to improve their competitiveness in the global arena through improved literacy performance. Here is a comment from a Trinidadian teacher, from a published dissertation, on her perceived loss of autonomy in curriculum matters:

> While a few students do exceptionally well, the majority of our graduates from secondary school are not equipped to fit into the modern globalised economy. Students are being bombarded with "National Tests" and the "Secondary Entrance Examination", both are supposedly measurable criteria that would attain defined standards of proficiency. However, subjecting students at ages seven, nine and ten to the rigorous preparation for "National Tests" and (S.E.A.) has only overloaded both the teachers and students. Children become frustrated and embarrassed about their inability to master the work while the teacher may be going ahead trying to deliver the curriculum in time for the Ministry's tests. (Primary teacher, Trinidad)

Curricula devised and tested in this way correspond to what Street calls an 'autonomous' model of literacy 'a single thing with a big L and a single y' (Street, 1993: 81). It is a literacy that assumes the precedence of written over spoken texts with a hierarchy of importance topped by the analytical and expository skills of essayist literacy, which still dominate modes of assessment in higher education (Lillis, 2001). It is based on the reaffirmation of a standard, written, national language, transmitted largely through a print-biased, linear pedagogy. It requires the replication of knowledge able to be tested through examination systems which are still recognisably those developed in the 1960s for what was a very different generation of labour.

Lankshear and Bigum (1999) have shown clearly how teacher practices work to domesticate children's relationship to new technology in their account of a government-funded study of literacy, technology and learning in the Australian states of New South Wales, Queensland and Victoria. They suggest that much of the applications of technology they observed conformed to, 'old wine in new bottles' syndrome. The teachers seemed often to be looking for technological applications that resonated with their pedagogical styles and, generally, with fitting new technologies into classroom business as usual – encouraged, of course, by syllabus guidelines which lend themselves precisely to this kind of thing. (Lankshear & Bigum, 1999: 456)

In such classes, the pupils remain seated in desks, focused on either a board or on a teacher doing most of the talking and serving a diet of pre-set tasks which ask them to feedback as individuals information transmitted to them as a group. Where new technologies are employed in school, the effect is often as Lankshear and Bigum go on to suggest, to render the connection with mature or out-of-school purposes 'entirely mysterious', citing 'Seymour Papert's wry observation that 'someone from the nineteenth century could step into contemporary classroom and know at a glance where they were' (Lankshear & Bigum, 1999: 457).

The disjunction between the multimodal world of communication which is available in the wider community and the conventional print modes of the standard curriculum has resulted in an increasing alienation of many pupils from what schools have on offer. Alienation increases as they progress through their education. It makes older pupils, particularly large sections of boys, more difficult to engage in the learning process and is at the heart of the disparity of attainment within the standard assessment tests and final examinations between boys and girls. In earlier research into gendered literacies (Millard, 1997; Millard & Walsh, 2001), I have argued that it is a 'difference' in how boys and girls conceptualise what is important in communication, not laddishness *per se*, or any detectable biological difference in intelligence, which lies at the heart of the continuing disparities in achievement. Moreover their learned dispositions towards literacy events are largely created outside of classroom settings and are much more influenced by peer group interaction than engagement with adults.

Because of their pupils' perceived lack of relevance of what is offered in class to their present and future interests, many schools have experienced high levels of disaffection that makes the role of the teacher an unattractive one. Ultimately, the over-riding aim of national programmes to devise teacher-proof methods of delivery seems increasingly misguided as it becomes more and more evident that the old inequalities of access to full educational opportunity and ceilings on attainment are as culturally and class-bound as they ever have been.

Moreover, much of the current work on home to school literacies which feature in all the education policies of developed Western economies have systematically pursued policies to persuade families to accommodate to the systems, practices and emphases of the school curriculum. This has resulted in a plethora of interventions directed at bringing school values and practices into the home [see e.g. the SHARE project created by The Community Education Development Centre (CEDC), Bastiani, 1997]. It seems increasingly important that the 'one-way traffic' from educational institutions to home (Marsh, 2003) should throw into reverse and that teachers be enfranchised to take meaning from what their pupils bring with them into the classroom. This might shift the binary relationship between home practices, watched over by parents, and school practices, dominated by teachers. As children mature and take greater control over their own consumer and leisure interests, they become more self-determining. Children's cultural exchanges with other children are of prime importance to them and are dominant in the negotiations of interests between home, school and peer groups, influencing the kind of literacies that have meaning for them. Traces of children's engagement with the new technologies can be found in almost every aspect of their self-selected reading and writing (see e.g. Dyson, 1997, 2001). By this I do not mean only to designate the actual time children commit to playing on and working with computers and related technology themselves, but the pervasiveness of technological design features on all their texts, the multimodality of communication processes and methods of access to other texts which have been made possible by technology. It is becoming increasingly important for schools to engage with these new ways of meaning making.

Transformative Work in Schools

In working on action-based projects supported by researchers at the University Sheffield (Marsh, 2000; Marsh & Thompson, 2001; Millard & Marsh, 2001; Millard, 2004, 2005) teachers have been prompted to consider questions such as:

- What use can be made of the knowledge which children bring with them in the classroom contexts devised for reading and writing?
- How can their personal, current knowledge be transformed to facilitate a more critical understanding?
- What might the making explicit of the transformative process look like?
- How can school literacy be framed to develop the habits of critical consciousness that are at the heart of a productive literacy responsive to changing times?

They have been involved in a process which I have called a transformative pedagogy founded in a *literacy of fusion* which is characterised by the blending of aspects of school requirements with children's current interests (Millard, 2003). The metaphor is taken directly from the concept of fusion cuisine that combines disparate elements without homogenising them. It has its roots in Kress's (2003) concept of transformation whereby the available materials for any discourse create the possibility for new meanings which always harbour elements of negotiated change and transformation (Kress, 2003: 46–47). Further 'in such a theory all acts of representation are innovative, and creativity is the normal process of representation for all' (Kress, 2003: 121). The 'newly designed' is always the 'redesigned' and bears a unique aspect arising from that particular moment of meaning making.

Narrative Framing

I have described in detail elsewhere (Millard, 2003) how children's narrative interests can be openly imported directly into their school work (i.e. not 'found' as smuggled in references to an otherwise school-formulated meanings) allowing both boys and girls to work with personal preferences. In *The Castle of Fear* (Millard, 2005) and *Writing of Heroes and Villains* project (Millard, 2004), pupils aged nine-to-ten years old were encouraged to incorporate their individual knowledge of narrative characterisation and plot structure taken from more visual modes, into the planning and creation of new print-based narratives, which had embedded within them elements of the imposed curriculum objectives set for their stage of education. The teacher's planning encouraged pupils to move between drawing and writing in a seamless flow, allowing personal preferences for different modalities to be selected in arranging individual texts, creating characters and in generally designing a new work. To support creative work, pupils were encouraged not only to draw on examples from the school texts they were sharing which were, *The Lion the Witch and the Wardrobe* and *The Hobbit*, but also from the selections of video clips they watched at home which featured villains and their schemes to undermine the protagonists.

Out of this work I have selected a particular text, which I use when working with other teachers to argue for the importance of pupil choice in the affordances (Bearne & Kress, 2001) for meaning making. It was produced by a boy who had always appeared eager to write and who was considered an exemplary pupil in this aspect by his teacher but who revealed his real preferences when allowed choice to plan in drawing as well as words. He drew a scene from *The Hobbit*, which he presented in a film frame after hearing me read a section of the story to the class. I will reproduce here my comments given in an earlier account:

> I'm not into writing. I like organising my ideas in pictures. Whenever Miss J. (the classroom teacher) asks Chris to draw his ideas I want to do that too. When the Misty Mountain song was read to us, I got a picture of a dark moon and I swooped in over the mountains to a castle and then deep down into the dragon's lair.
>
> His picture sequence is clearly drawing from his understanding of film action, shot in perspective with the focus moving slowly in on the dragon's lair. Designated a 'clever' boy, he has not often been encouraged to sketch out his ideas for writing in images, however, his response on this occasion shows clearly how the affordances of the visual mode enables him to articulate ideas of narrative structuring by means of the image, acquired through his preference for filmed narratives. (Millard, 2003: 6)

It is perhaps easy to see how the development of an understanding of narrative and fictional composition may be helped by drawing from pupils' individual interests in other popular forms of storytelling (see Figure 11.1). I have shown how elements take from material as disparate as James Bond movies, chivalric quest stories and computer games can all be transformed in the classroom to support school learning. The next two examples, however, focus on other genres that are set as requirements for this stage of learning.

Writing Persuasively

My second example of what a *literacy of fusion* looks like is taken from a piece of work planned to teach persuasive/discussion writing, which is a required genre for Term 2 of Year 6 in English primary schools. The framework asks teachers to 'teach' children to identify the features of balanced written arguments, that is to 'summarise different sides of an argument; clarify the strengths and weaknesses of different positions; signal personal opinion clearly'. Schools are accustomed to draw from a range of conventionally school favoured topics to encourage such work, such as cruelty to battery hens, fox hunting, parents' parking near school and the perennial question of school uniforms.

Many teachers work with writing frames that show how to incorporate the salient features of the appropriate genre (Wray & Lewis, 1997). In my example, children had begun not from instruction on the genre or with

Figure 11.1 The dragon's lair

abstract use of the frames for writing, but with several children's demonstration of a set of Pokémon cards which had been 'allowed into the classroom' for discussion and explanation, as they were the object of heavy school restrictions at that time. I doubt that there are many teachers of this age group who are unaware of this phenomenally successful trading game. However, Pokémon is a Japanese creation based on a card trading game in which 63 fantastic creatures are collected and classified. The game is further supported by a plethora of supporting merchandise, which includes many different computer games, a film and its video, and plastic and soft toys in a variety of sizes. The class had already formed very strong opinions as to the fairness of their head teacher's actions in banning the cards from the playground. This restriction on this popular culture craze was a common phenomenon in English primary schools in the academic year 1999–2000, following a 'moral panic' in the popular press about how the fad was corrupting the young by leading to stealing and bullying. The class I was studying had also brought in passages from tabloid newspaper reports for their shared reading to add to one found by the teacher in the TES (Lockwood, 2000) explaining how children might learn from the cards. They used these articles to search for the phrases and words that expressed strong opinions on one side or the other. Then, having looked at ways in which opinions could be expressed, they wrote letters of protest against or in support of the ban. Here are good examples of both sides, the first against the ban:

> Dear Mr S,
>
> I would like you to consider lifting your ban on Pokémon cards. I have several reasons for asking this. One of them is it helps you develop your Maths, because you are taking the attack damage away from the Pokémon's life. So surely if it helps maths it can't be so bad. Furthermore, I would like to ask you, did you not have crazes when you were at school?
>
> Pokémon also helps small children learn about animals. Weedle is a caterpillar, Seaking a fish, Growlithe a dog and Mankey a monkey. I would like to emphasise that if you let us keep our cards we would soon get bored of them but barring them just prolongs this. Finally I want to say that if we are allowed Pokémon cards people will have something to do and it will keep them out of mischief. I hope you will think carefully about this matter.
>
> Yours faithfully.

The next supports the headteacher's decision

Dear Mr S,

I am in total agreement that you banned Pokémon in school.

Some people might argue that the Pokémon ban in this school should be lifted, but I think they cause arguments, theft, bullying and violence.

One reason is that it encourages bullying and violence when somebody tries to take someone else's Pokémon cards and when that person doesn't let them have them the bully resorts to violence. Secondly there have been a few incidents in other schools where Pokémon cards have been stolen from bags and coats.

Furthermore, arguments often erupt when children are playing with them and they are arguing who has the best Pokémon cards.
If you hadn't banned Pokémon cards some children who didn't like Pokémon would have been left out because all the other children were playing with the cards.

Finally lots of children have stolen money from their parents to buy Pokémon cards because they didn't have any money of their own. Therefore, although some people think that Pokémon cards should not be banned. I believe you have made the right decision in banning them.

The pieces neatly fuse the concerns of the teacher, who wishes to develop the features of the genre expected, by using a persuasive writing framework, and is reflected in the children's use phrases such as:

- I would like you to consider
- Therefore although some people think
- Furthermore, I would like to ask you
- Arguments often erupt
- Finally, I would like to say

and the pupils' strong, personal feelings, based on their experience;

- Pokémon also helps small children learn about animals. Weedle is a caterpillar, Seaking a fish, Growlithe a dog and Mankey a monkey.
- If you hadn't banned Pokémon cards some children who didn't like Pokémon would have been left out.

- When somebody tries to take someone else's Pokémon cards and when that person doesn't let them have them.
- One of them is it helps you develop your Maths, because you are taking the attack damage away from the Pokémon's life.

The work therefore has taken its meaning from both classroom and out of school contexts and has enabled the teacher to facilitate complex discussions of different aspects of the cards noted by different writers. The teacher's interest in finding out more about the ways in which Pokémon cards were used had also helped the children to value their knowledge and become explicit in explaining their views and preferences.

My third example was also created within the same literacy framework requirements. In this case, however, the teacher who was becoming increasingly confident in drawing on children's funds of knowledge (Moll *et al.*, 1992) encouraged the class to identify an issue which they wished to persuade someone in authority to do something about. They were then asked to explain the problem in either words or pictures. One girl drew a cartoon which showed their head teacher, ensconced in the warmth of his study, with a mug of tea and buns labelled 'staff special teas' to hand (see Figure 11.2). He is pictured casually swinging the whistle which he will blow when he considers it is time to let Class 6 in from the playground. A speech bubble reads, 'Ahh! Just another half hour more'. The children are shown outside in a rainstorm, getting drenched, coughing and groaning. The cartoon's caption reads: 'Y6 aren't a line. They're a class'. The written work, which was developed from this satirical drawing, is in the form of a letter to the headteacher. It reads:

> Dear Mr M,
>
> I am writing to ask that Y6 should not line up at the start of the day and after break time.
>
> Firstly, do you know when you were talking about rights in your assembly? I think this should be our most important one because Y6 aren't that keen on lining up. I know you're doing it for us and we respect that, but we say we should be allowed in because we are more mature.
>
> A further issue that you should consider is since it is only a few months before we go to the High School and we are lined for the rest of school. Why can't we just walk in sensibly on our own now? A third point I would like to make is that we are nearly in High School and our last

Figure 11.2 Cartoon: Year 6 aren'y a line. They're a class

> year should be the best. And it would show how nice a headmaster you are. Also people come past and say whose class are taking the responsibility coming in. I understand that people are concerned we might block the doorway and maybe knock small children down but I think we will set a good example if we were trusted.

The writer is once more using the connectives suggested by the frameworks as appropriate to persuasion such as 'firstly', 'a further issue', 'a third point' which have been given as part of a model writing frame for persuasion (see Figure 11.3). These are fused with the child's own rich context for communicating her own opinions:

- Y6 aren't that keen on lining up
- It would show how nice a headmaster you are
- We say we should be allowed in because we are more mature

In both of these examples the teachers involved have been attentive to their children's interests and allowed them freedom of content choice. The second piece however, is remarkable in its enabling of different modes

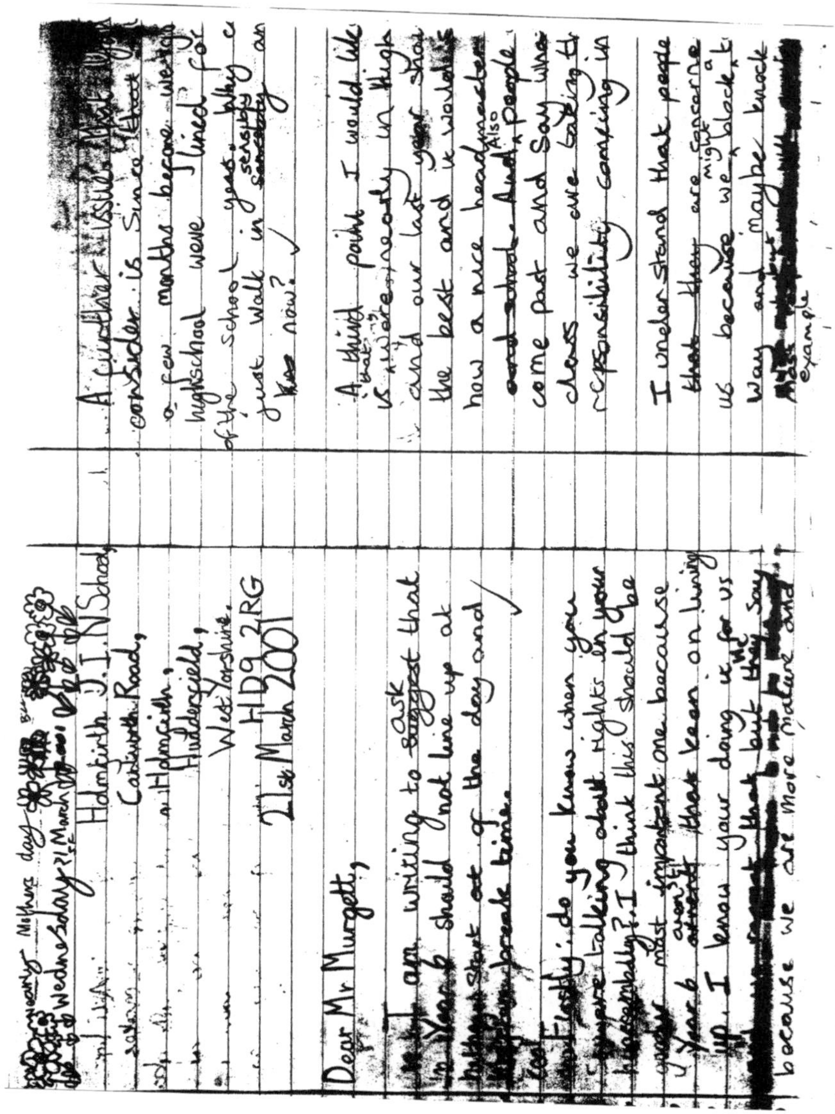

Mothers day
Wednesday 21st March 2001

Holmfirth J.I.N School
Cartworth Road,
Holmfirth,
Huddersfield,
West Yorshire.
HD9 2RG
21st March 2001

Dear Mr Murgett,

I am writing to ask that Year 6 should not line up at start of the day and break time.

Firstly: do you know when you were talking about rights in your assembly? I think this should be most important one because Year 6 aren't that keen on lining up. I know your doing it for us but we say because we are more mature and

A further issue consider is since a few months before we highschool were lined for of the school year. Why just walk in sensibly and now?

A third point I would like is that we're nearly in high and our last year the best and it would how a nice headmaster And also people come past and say class we are taking responsibility coming in

I understand that people are concerned us because we might block a way and maybe knock example

Figure 11.3 Letter to headteacher

which enabled a whole class discussion of which form, cartoon or letter of protest seemed most effective. In this case, the cartoon was certainly what the headteacher took most notice of.

My fourth example was produced as a response to the request in a Y6 science lesson to make notes on 'Preserving' in a way which would make the facts memorable for the individual. Its author was part of a class who took particular pleasure in cartoons and illustrations (see Figure 11.4).

In the mapping out of what he has learned, he instinctively supports Kress's perception that the left hand side of any text represents the given while the right hand side creates the new (Kress, 2003: 70). In this case, the left hand side is dominated by the teacher's title and the right has the boys representation of the content of the lesson, transformed into humorous visual puns and comic style speech bubbles. The information might simply have been presented as a numbered list.

Methods of preserving fish

(1) Refrigeration
(2) Deep Freezing
(3) Smoking
(4) Salting
(5) Tinning
(6) Drying
(7) Bottling

Or as a sentence: 'Fish can be preserved by refrigeration, deep freezing, smoking, tinning, drying or bottling'. The boy's representation using spatial disposition and humour has allowed him to make the task his own and arguably the material more memorable. In thinking about the role of these and other texts in fostering what Luke and Carrington (2002) describe as,

> ... the potential of literacy education as a curriculum practice for the generation of 'student' dispositions, positions and position-takings for viable and powerful life pathways through new cultures and economies, pathways that wind through globalised and local, virtual and material social fields. (Luke & Carrington, 2002: 233)

These are large claims for such small steps in the creation of texts; however all four examples have been chosen to illustrate how pupils given sufficient autonomy and enjoying a sense of command of the content of text can make effective transformations of personal meaning for a public forum. The work they have been doing takes meaning from

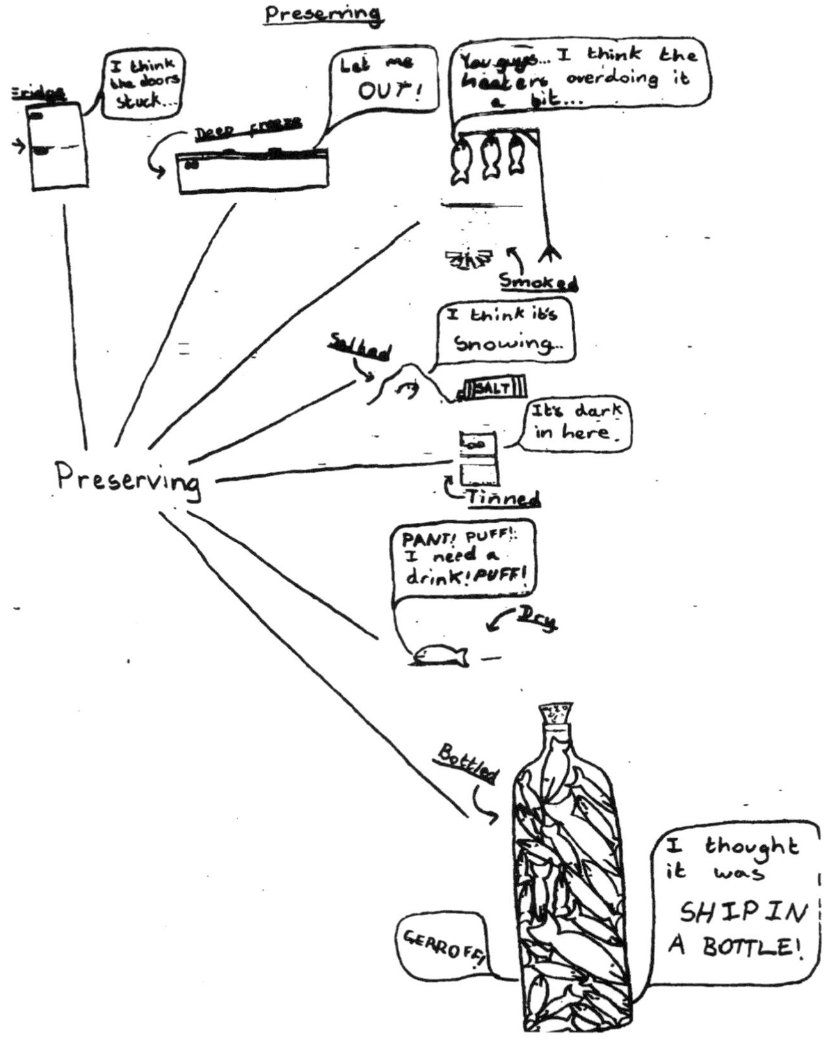

Figure 11.4 'Preserving' notes

the life they are living but also gives them tools for understanding and critiquing other texts. There are, I admit, several disadvantages to the use of supporting genre frameworks; not least in that the 'genres' they purport to formulate have been framed as abstractions and treated as far more constant forms than in practice they turn out to be. Moreover, the writing frames can simply be used in the way of an old worksheet to force pre-discussed information into a straight jacket of organisation. However, used wisely, they can enable children to remake both their own ideas and the ways of expressing them more critically. The intention is, as Kress has described, to encourage a more 'generative' notion of text which, 'encourages and normalises "design" of text in response to the perceived needs of the maker of the text in a given environment' (Kress, 2003: 121). In this case the environment is that of the school in which pupils fight for agency against all the controls that constrain their activities.

Defining a Literacy of Fusion

I have begun to formulate the processes involved when teachers help in a structuration of pupils' creation of personally meaningful texts within their teaching objectives as a literacy of fusion (Millard, 2003). I use Barthes' concept of structuration (1974: 200) rather than that of structure to signify an ongoing process that is not fixed into a given and inflexible entity but which is open to transformation and therefore allows the child full agency in manipulating both codes of meaning and the stuff of modality. Each aspect of this process which enables the weaving of adult and children's voices into new texts is described below.

Access

The role of the teacher in this aspect is to make decisions about what might be worth studying with a particular class of children and how underlying meanings and structures can be made accessible. For example, in choosing to teach, 'persuasive writing', the teacher is following a curriculum objective, but focusing on a debate about Pokémon gives the children more authority over the material. Access also requires a consideration of whose meanings will be given space in the classroom. For example, will interests and views on Pokémon or the imagined world of the Bat Cave be accorded equal attention with more received opinions on Fox Hunting or the more school-friendly fantasy world of Narnia? In selecting and welcoming in different sources, teachers need to be aware of both their pupils' passions and preoccupations and how these can be productive in enabling new meanings to be created.

The arena

Arena is the word I use for an appropriate context for learning. Kress has shown how all texts require a 'site of appearance' (2003: 48) and that this has an effect on the texts, which appear in particular sites. The arena requires the teacher's attention to the purpose and audience for a particular kind of communication that would make aspects of writing or oral presentations meaningful to the children. The letters written to head teachers were seen to have an effect and demand a response, the quest stories were produced as small books and shared with classmates and many opportunities were provided for them to swap ideas for particular puzzles and problems and to read and critique positively each other's work. The cartoon notes were an element of an individual's learning process.

Agency

Agency requires the teacher's focus during the development of work in class as to who is allowed to shape and transform meanings. Much of current literacy curriculum asks the teacher to be the model of good practice by composing in front of the children or by accepting and reshaping their contributions to fit a particular genre. A transformative pedagogy allows the children to explore aspects of their out-of-school identities and be provided with spaces where they can choose whom to persuade or entertain on their own terms. A particular example of a child's voice being given power was provided by one boy in the *Castle of Fear Project* who brought in an account from a James Bond movie to show that villains could be defeated without killing. The teacher involved confessed to wanting to have disallowed his contribution as unhelpful because of the adult nature of the material. In fact, the boy had chosen a very appropriate clip to show to the others.

Affordance

It perhaps appears that the transformative pedagogy, which I advocate is nothing more than a rehash of the child-centred learning of Dewey and Bruner. Bruner (1997) has in fact revisited his earlier concept of child-centred learning and suggests 'mutualist' as the main characteristic of a respectful pedagogy. This involves 'an exchange of understanding between the teacher and the child' and the ability 'to find in the intuitions of the child the roots of systematic knowledge' (Bruner, 1997: 57). It does share with an earlier take on child-centred pedagogy an interest in children's own resources for learning. However, to achieve fusion it also requires that teachers develop a more complex understanding of the affordances of particular modes of communication and the implications of these for the development of critical awareness. For example, the discussion of whether letter or a satirical cartoon was better able to express the children's views allowed consideration of the different affordances of spoken, written, and visual text. Affordance is also connected directly with the next aspect, which I wish to include in the mix.

Appropriacy

This requires that teachers help children make their selections as to which modes and genres are best suited for the task in hand. Will a satirical cartoon prove more effective than a formal letter? Which of the aspects of Pokémon play can be used to effect in the classroom? It focuses on how to help children to select and best use the stuff, which they have to hand. For, as Dyson's work has shown, children already engage in recontextualising processes which link textual practices derived from a diversity of social worlds to the official school curriculum (Dyson, 1997, 2001). Dyson makes visible the interaction of the child's growing personality and the semiotic resources that are brought into play in the act of making meaning and describes how children deploy their own textual stuff to, 'amuse, please or just pass muster' (Dyson, 2001: 34). It is the role of the teacher to recognise such preoccupations and to initiate discussion of what might work best for particular tasks. This brings me to the final ingredient, which is linked directly to critical awareness.

Accountability

Effective fusion relies heavily on a teachers' attentiveness to the interests and skills brought into the classroom and their ability to help children to transform what they already know into stuff that will give them greater agency in a wider world. They also need to encourage children to become more critical of their own and others' meanings. With this critical awareness comes the possibility of accountability whereby teachers enable children to trace who is accountable in and outside texts and also to account for their own responses and choices in making them. For example, when working on creating quest narratives based on aspects of computer gaming with a class of 10-year-old children (Millard, 2005), I shared with them a table I had compiled of the gendered narrative choices they had made. My table showed clearly that the boys had used more adventure and space narratives in their work whilst girls had taken many more elements from fairytales. A group of the boys mocked the girls' choices as babyish. Their teacher and I then asked all the class to think about fairytale parallels with the characters and events in films such as *Star Wars* and *Lord of the Rings*, recording their responses on a white board and helping them to see a commonality in all the fantasy genres. The discussion of narrative problems and their resolutions also led to lively debate about whether there were ways of overcoming evil empires other than zapping them with weapons.

Conclusions

It is perhaps appropriate now to remind ourselves of the founding principles on which my concept transformative practice has been created. Giroux (1993) for example, has argued powerfully that it is most important to begin to engage literacy 'not just as a skill or knowledge, but an emerging act of consciousness and resistance' (1993: 367). He suggests that literacy cannot be viewed as a neutral skill but should be defined in political and ethical terms. It is political because to 'read' the world always brings in relations of power, and it is ethical because we read the world differently depending, for instance, on circumstances of class, gender, race, and politics. Giroux's position informs those practices which we call 'critical literacy' and which inform much of our current debates about pedagogy and curriculum (Lankshear & Bigum, 1999; Luke & Carrington, 2002).

However, I want to stress that the development of critical literacy will remain only a theoretical ideal unless connected to a pedagogical practice that ensures that it becomes embedded in children's own modes of responding to and producing all manner of texts and artifacts. Children will not be able to develop a critical awareness of their own and other's preferred modalities and ways of expressing meaning if they have been given insufficient experience of using them for their own purposes and critiquing aspects of their choices, in the ways I have described above. Before critical literacy can take root, children need to be given opportunities to employ a wide variety of ways of telling, designing and making texts and to engage in meaningful and explicit dialogue in relation to their preferred modes and dispositions of expressing thought. Because each new act of meaning is at one and the same time a product of an individual creative impulse and an echo of the inherited social and cultural practices of a particular community or group, there is a need to foster an understanding of both personal and public elements of that meaning. It is this process that I am putting forward as a means of *transformative pedagogy* based on a *literacy of fusion:* that is, a literacy characterised by movement and change and which demands attentiveness from teachers to the worlds their students experience outside of the classroom.

Note

1. An abridged and less developed version of the theory described in this chapter was first published in *Reading, Literacy and Language* (2003) 37 (1), 3–9.

References

Barthes, R. (1974) *S/Z: An Essay* (R. Miller, trans.). New York: Hill and Wang.

Bastiani, J. (1997) *Share: An Evaluation of the First Two Years* (September 1996–July 1998). Coventry: CEDC.

Bearne, E. and Kress, G. (2001) Editorial. *Reading, Literacy and Language* 35 (3), 89–93.

Bernstein, B. (1996) *Pedagogy, Symbolic Control and Identity: Theory, Research, Critique.* London: Taylor & Francis.

Bourdieu, P. (1977) *Outline of a Theory of Practice* (R. Nice, trans.). Cambridge: Cambridge University Press.

Bruner, J. (1997) *The Process of Education.* Harvard: Harvard University Press.

Dyson, A.H. (2001) Where are the childhoods in childhood literacy? An exploration in outer school space. *Journal of Early Childhood Literacy* 1 (1), 9–40.

Dyson, A.H. (1997) *Writing Superheroes: Contemporary Childhood, Popular Culture, and Classroom Literacy.* New York: Teachers College Press.

Giroux, H. (1993) Literacy and the politics of difference. In C. Lankshear and P. McLaren (eds) *Critical Literacy: Politics, Praxis, and the Postmodern* (pp. 367–77). Albany, NY: State University of New York Press.

Kress, G. (2003) *Literacy in the New Media Age.* London: Routledge.

Lankshear, C. and Bigum, C. (1999) Literacies and new technologies in school settings. *Curriculum Studies* 7 (3), 445–64.

Lillis, T. (2001) *Student Writing, Access, Regulation and Desire.* London: Routledge.

Lockwood, M. (2000) Playing the name game. Creative writing. *TES*, 6 October, 2000.

Luke, A. and Carrington, V. (2002) Globalisation, literacy, curriculum practice. In R. Fisher, M. Lewis and G. Brooks (eds) *Raising Standards in Literacy* (pp. 231–50). London: Routledge/Falmer.

Marsh, J. (2003) One-way traffic? Connections between literacy practices at home and in the nursery. *British Educational Research Journal* 29 (3), 369–82.

Marsh, J. (2000) But I want to fly too! Girls and superhero play in the infant classroom. *Gender and Education* 12 (2), 209–20.

Marsh, J. and Thompson, P. (2001) Parental involvement in literacy development: Using media texts. *Journal of Research in Reading* 24 (3), 266–78.

Merchant, G. (2003) Email me your thoughts: Digital communication and narrative writing. *Reading, Literacy and Language* 37 (3), 104–10.

Millard, E. (2005) To enter the castle of fear: Engendering children's story writing from home to school at KS2. *Gender and Education* 17 (1), 57–63.

Millard, E. (2004) Writing of heroes and villains. In J. Evans (ed.) *Literacy Moves On: Using Popular Culture, New Technologies and Critical Literacy in the Primary Classroom* (pp. 121–45). London: David Fulton.

Millard, E. (2003) Transformative pedagogy: Towards a literacy of fusion. *Reading, Literacy and Language* 37 (1), 3–9.

Millard, E. (1997) *Differently Literate: The Schooling of Boys and Girls.* London: Falmer Press.

Millard, E. and Marsh, J. (2001) Sending Minnie the Minx home: Comics and reading choices. *Cambridge Journal of Education* 31 (1), 25–38.
Millard, E. and Walsh, J. (2001) *Improving Writing at Key Stage: Getting it Right for Boys and Girls.* Huddersfield: Kirklees School Effectiveness Service.
Moll, L.C., Amanti, C., Neff, D. and Gonzalez, N. (1992) Funds of knowledge for teaching: Using a qualitative approach to connect homes and classrooms. *Theory Into Practice* 31 (2), 132–41.
New London Group (1996) A pedagogy of multiliteracies. *Harvard Educational Review* 66 (1), 60–92.
Street, B. (ed.) (1993) *Cross-Cultural Approaches to Literacy.* Cambridge: Cambridge University Press.
Tyner, K. (1998) *Literacy in a Digital World: Teaching and Learning in the Age of Information.* Mahwah, NJ: Lawrence Erlbaum.
Wray, D. and Lewis, M. (1997) *Extending Literacy: Children Reading and Writing Non-fiction.* London: Routledge.

Afterword

DEBORAH BRANDT AND KATIE CLINTON

We are thrilled by a volume of studies that brings together two vital strands of literacy research, New Literacy Studies and multimodality, to explore how the two perspectives challenge and complement each other. As two readers who tend to lean in two directions (Katie toward multimodality and Deb toward New Literacy Studies), reading this volume has led to fruitful discussions between us. So we are grateful to the editors for allowing us a chance to have a final reflective word in this space.

In 'Limits of the Local: Expanding Perspectives on Literacy as a Social Practice' (Brandt & Clinton, 2002), we suggested that social practice theory was too human-centered and called for forms of ethnographic inquiry that included attention to the role that non-human actors play in meaning-making. We introduced Latour's (1996a) translation model of action, his idea that we act by mediating the actions of other mediators. We wanted to see NLS bring the technology of literacy back into literacy theory. The huge advantage of the multimodality perspective as we see it is the language it provides for talking about technologies as actants at the scenes of reading and writing, as active and ideological social agents toward which readers and writers orient. What we did not discuss in the article is how this model of action would replace the more common metaphor used to organize our ways of thinking about action: causality.

As Kress (2003) notes in his book *Literacy in the New Media Age*, causality is an artifact of the English language (other languages, too, but especially English). Specifically, he notes how 'causation is just about built into clauses in languages such as English, with their noun–subject–verb–object structures' (Kress, 2003: 57). We can see this S-V-O logic as defining a structural feature of the shift from the autonomous model of literacy to the social practice model. The autonomous model put the technology of literacy in the active subject position, and the human in the passive acted-upon position. The key idea was that the technology of literacy enacts powerful changes on humans. The model sought to explain how when people learn to read and write they learn new forms of thinking and reasoning. So, in the autonomous model, the technologies of reading and writing cause the ways of thinking and reasoning that these technologies support. But, then, ethnographic investigations, notably by Scribner and Cole (1981), shifted the equation, showing that the consequences of literacy arise from the human uses of literacy. Now it was humans in the active subject position, and the technology of literacy in the passive position. These studies recognized that technologies enable us to do things that we cannot do without them, but the capacities of technologies were carefully talked about in terms of potentials, for how-people-used-literacy was the lens for explaining the consequences.

Mediation models escape the S-V-O constraints. They provide a way of talking about technologies acting without suggesting that somehow technologies are back in the control seat. The mediation theory of action avoids defining what is acting on what. Rather, 'to act is to mediate another's action' (Latour, 1996a: 237). If you are acting with another person, say if you are having a conversation, then the places you go, and that which transpires, is emergent from the interaction. Similarly, when you act with a technology, you act by mediating the actions of the technology as it does yours. So, you can see how we are now in a position to ask what kinds of actions technologies accomplish. In accounting for these actions, Lemke (2000) makes a key insight when he calls for multiple timescale analyses. That is, he observes that meaning-making happens on different timescales, and suggests how 'it is the circulation through the network of *semiotic artifacts* (books, buildings, bodies) that enables coordination between processes at radically different timescales' (Lemke, 2000: Introduction). When we think about meaning-making happening on different timescales, we can note how literacy technologies (or literacy materials or objects) potentially act in different ways and on different scales from other participants in a literacy event.

In particular, when it comes to new technologies, and as we try to understand the new forms of meaning-making they enable and how these new forms shift current ways of thinking, subjectivities, and notions of 'what exists, what is good, and what is possible' (Berlin, 1993: 103) the concept of affordances is key. In line with the idea of mediation, the idea of affordances suggests that we can orient to technologies as providing possibilities for action. If we think of literacy technologies as having affordances and if we think of people mediating these affordances, then we have a model for thinking about both human and non-human action that is neither technologically deterministic (as the autonomous model is) nor anthrocentric (as the social-practice model is). In Katie's work on videogames, she seeks to define the new kinds of experiences they enable and to think about how these experiences provide new kinds of resources for education. Drawing on ecological psychology (Gibson, 1979) and the phenomenology of Merleau-Ponty (1979), she is developing what she calls the *literacy experience* construct. This allows a way of thinking about the interaction between people and technology (as the interaction occurs in the time-span of the moment of use), as a dialogue between the person and the technology.

Specifically the *literacy experience* construct brings the perspective of multimodality in on the ground level of meaning-making. The key idea is that it is our interactions with technologies that provide the resources for meaning making. Yes, these resources become used in social ways and we can define them in social ways (as the literacy events and literacy practices constructs do well), yet it is our interactions with technologies that make these social uses possible. In other words, we might say, as Heidegger (1962: 98) does, that we cannot use a technology without experiencing it, and therefore we need a way to account for how it is our experiences with technologies that enable us to do things with them. To define 'resources' as the outcome of the interaction between humans and technologies (where technologies provide possibilities for action and conditions for perception) makes salient how a resource is a particular experience. It suggests that a person can't use a particular resource a technology enables unless he or she is able to experience the 'timings, tempos and properties' (Latour, 1996b: 268) of the technology in the particular ways called for by the literacy event.

This might be a good place to explain our appeal in 'Limits of the Local' for seeing literacy technologies and objects as in some way 'autonomous'. We wanted to emphasize that the technologies of literacy enter a dialogue on their own terms, sometimes in conflict with those that take them up but always worthy of analysis for what they contribute in their own right. We did not mean to suggest that literacy technologies or literacy objects are ideologically neutral. It was wrong on our part to use the word 'autonomous', as that term, since Street (1984), has had a particular history and meaning in literacy theory. In hindsight, we would have framed our call as a need to bring the 'thingness' of literacy into an ideological model.

Just as *Travel Notes* tests the concept of multimodality for enriching New Literacy Studies, we see this volume as testing the conceptual wherewithal of the New Literacy Studies to remain relevant in a post-print era. New Literacy theory was a product of the age of print. As it developed in the 1970s and 1980s, NLS focused its ethnographic gaze often on geographically isolated, often economically overlooked communities where the technologies of paper and ink were absorbed into local ways of life in ways that tended to enhance rather than disrupt local practices and values. Yet there is something quaint about many of these studies now as communication revolutions of the late 20th and early 21st centuries have blasted concepts of place and space and proliferated social interactions and involvements that were nearly impossible in the past. In the age of the Internet, genres still circulate for local use and innovation but also may stay more firmly tethered to centers of origin. Unlike Bibles that were set to sea in the holds of sailing vessels, electronic texts now reside at specific addresses – homes we must visit in order to read them – where writers or their sponsors can keep close tabs on readers. In 'Limits of the Local' we recognized that all reading and writing are local events but not necessarily localizing events. We called for analysis of both localizing and globalizing activity involving literacy and for systematic comparison of literacy events in terms of the proportions of both. Such analysis becomes especially crucial in these times, especially for uncovering new structures of inequality and the role of literacy in them and for remembering that the forms of literacy individuals or communities practice may not be the forms they would prefer to practice.

In its ethnographic dimensions, *Travel Notes from the New Literacy Studies* captures the enormous changes in communication that have marked the past 20 years yet also shows the vitality and validity of the NLS perspective for these new times. With attention to social practices, values and routines, NLS provides above all a critical historical perspective, reminding us that new forms of literacy do not necessarily dislodge the old. Rather old and new often operate together and affect each other, often creating the ideological density that marks contemporary reading and writing.

What do these chapters suggest is being carried over from the old? We see that adolescence is still a time of intense use of literacy for affiliation and identity experimentation. We see that home and leisure uses of literacy especially seem linked to traditional socialization by gender, race and class, as families use reading and writing to pass to their children orientations crucial to competition and survival. We see the continued importance of literacy intermediaries in bringing together people and resources. We see how literate skills and preferences are exploited by market interests. And – for now – we see the authority that the written still wields over the oral.

What is new? One thing is the rise of writing and the development of mass authorship, an intensifying focus on writing as part of economic and social production, even at young ages. Indeed it may be in the identity of the writer that the tensions between old and new forms of literacy are at their most salient. Writing is moving from an ability to persuade an audience to an ability to attract an audience, to an ability, at its most 'powerful' to attract a market. With its steady eye on literacy in its particulars, NLS not only forces attention to the ideological meanings of literacy but cumulatively will be able to tell the story of ideological transformations in those meanings over time.

References

Berlin, J.A. (1993) Composition studies and cultural studies: Collapsing boundaries. In A.R. Gere (ed.) *Into the Field: Sites of Composition Studies* (pp. 99–116). New York: MLA.

Brandt, D. and Clinton, K. (2002) The limits of the local: Expanding perspectives on literacy as a social practice. *Journal of Literacy Research* 34 (3), 337–56.

Gibson, J. (1979). *The Ecological Approach to Visual Perception.* New York: Houghton-Mifflin.

Heidegger, M. (1962) *Being and Time* (J. Macquarrie and E. Robinson, trans.). NY: Harper & Row (original work published in 1927).

Kress, G. (2003) *Literacy in the New Media Age.* London: Routledge.

Latour, B. (1996a) On interobjectivity. *Mind, Culture, and Activity* 3 (4), 228–45.

Latour, B. (1996b) Pursuing the discussion of interobjectivity with a few friends. *Mind, Culture, and Activity* 3 (4), 266–69.

Lemke, J.L. (2000) Across the scales of time: Artifacts, activities, and meanings in ecosocial systems. *Mind, Culture, and Activity* 7 (4), 273–90.

Merleau-Ponty, M. (1979) *Phenomenology of Perception* (C. Smith, trans.). London: Routledge & Kegan Paul.

Scribner, S. and Cole, M. (1981) *The Psychology of Literacy.* Cambridge, MA: Harvard University Press.

Street, B.V. (1984) *Literacy in Theory and Practice.* Cambridge: Cambridge University Press.

Biographies

Donna E. Alvermann is Distinguished Research Professor of Language and Literacy Education at the University of Georgia. Formerly a classroom teacher in Texas and New York, her research focuses on youths' multiple literacies in and out of school. From 1992 to 1997 she co-directed the National Reading Research Center, funded by the US Department of Education. With over 100 articles and chapters in print, her books include *Content Reading and Literacy: Succeeding in Today's Diverse Classrooms* (4th edn), *Popular Culture in the Classroom: Teaching and Researching Critical Media Literacy*, *Bridging the Literacy Achievement Gap, Grades 4–12*, and *Adolescents and Literacies in a Digital World.* Past president of the National Reading Conference (NRC) and co-chair of the International Reading Association's Commission on Adolescent Literacy, she currently edits *Reading Research Quarterly.* She was elected to the Reading Hall of Fame in 1999, and is the recipient of NRC's Oscar Causey Award for Outstanding Contributions to Reading Research, the Albert Kingston Award for Distinguished Service and College Reading Association's Laureate Award and the H.B. Herr Award for Contributions to Research in Reading Education.

Dave Baker is a Reader in Adult Numeracy and Post 16 Mathematics at the Institute of Education, University of London. He studied mathematics before becoming a teacher of mathematics in schools. He taught on teacher education programmes and then undertook research into teaching and learning mathematics with a particular focus on issues of social justice in mathematics. His most recent research was on social explanations for children's low achievement in mathematics. This resulted in a book, due out in 2005, on *Navigating Numeracies: Home/School Numeracy Practices.* He has published two other books, presented at many conferences and published academic papers on mathematics education.

Deborah Brandt is a Professor of English at the University of Wisconsin, Madison, where she teaches undergraduate writing and graduate courses on literacy and contemporary writing studies. She is author of *Literacy as Involvement: The Acts of Writers, Readers, and Texts* (Southern Illinois University Press, 1990) and *Literacy in American Lives* (Cambridge University Press, 2001) as well as many articles and book chapters. Her work focuses on the social conditions of literacy and literacy learning, including issues of access and equity. She is at work on a new project, tentatively called *Writing Now: New Directions in Mass Literacy,* which is tracing the rise of writing as a means of production since about 1960.

Katie Clinton is a Doctoral Student in the Department of Curriculum and Instruction at the University of Wisconsin, Madison. Her research focuses on identifying how digital technologies' capacities for interactive representations solicit and support particular capacities of humans, which enable people to experience the digital worlds of games in embodied ways. In particular, she is seeking to describe the distinct resources interactive representations introduce and to suggest how they enable a form of communication which shares more in common with acting and interacting in the physical world than to alphabet-based writing systems.

Barbara Comber is a key researcher in the Centre for Studies in Literacy, Policy and Learning Cultures and Professor in the School of Education at the University of South Australia. Her professional passions include pedagogy, critical literacy, social justice and teacher's work. A major priority is working with radical innovative teacher-researchers. She has recently co-edited three books – *Turn-around Pedagogies: Literacy Interventions for At-risk Students* (Comber & Kamler, 2005), *Look Again: Longitudinal Studies of Children's Literacy Learning* (Comber & Barnett, 2003) and *Negotiating Critical Literacies in Classrooms* (Comber & Simpson, 2001).

Julia Davies is a lecturer in Education at the University of Sheffield, where she co-directs the MA in Literacy and Language. Her research predominantly focuses on on-line communities. She has written about teenagers' uses of new technologies to explore issues of identity and the articulation of gender through online formations. She has also focused on changes in literacy and language, looking at ways in which spellings, word choice and emoticons are used to help mark out affinities across individuals with shared interests. She is also looking at the role digital technologies are playing in the development of visual Literacies. Julia also works with teachers in schools looking at ways in which digital Literacies can be embedded more closely into official curricula and is also involved in a school-based longitudinal study, looking at gendered patterns of behaviour and achievement of pupils. She has forthcoming chapters in Marsh and Millard's *Popular Literacies, Childhood and Schooling* and Buckingham and Willett's *Digital Generations*.

Hilary Janks is a professor in the School of Education at the University of the Witwatersrand, Johannesburg, South Africa and an adjunct professor at the University of South Australia. Her teaching and research are in the areas of language education in multilingual classrooms, language policy and critical literacy. Her work is committed to a search for equity and social justice in contexts of poverty.

Cathy Kell currently works as a Learning Designer in the Centre for Flexible and Distance Learning at the University of Auckland, New Zealand. She previously lectured at the University of Cape Town in South Africa in adult education and literacy studies, and has been involved in the field of adult literacy for more than 20 years. She has published widely in the field, particularly in the New Literacy Studies and development, ethnography and policy.

Michele Knobel is an Associate Professor of Education at Montclair State University (USA), where she co-ordinates the graduate and undergraduate literacy programs. She is also an Adjunct Professor of Education at Central Queensland University, Australia. Her research at present focuses on the relationship between new literacies, social practices and digital technologies. Michele's most recent book is *A Handbook for Teacher Research* (with Colin Lankshear). She is currently working on a new literacies primer, *Technoliteracies* (with Colin Lankshear and Angela Thomas), as well as co-editing *The Handbook of Research on New Literacies* (with Donald Leu, Julie Coiro and Colin Lankshear).

Gunther Kress is Professor of Education/English, and Head of the School of Culture Language and Communication, at the Institute of Education, University of London. He has a specific interest in the inter-relations in contemporary texts of different modes of communication – writing, image, speech, music, gesture – and their effects on shapes of knowledge and forms of learning, and in the changes – and their effects and consequences – brought by the shift in the media of communication from the page to the screen. Some of his recent books are: *Reading Images: The Grammar of Graphic Design* (1996) (Routledge); *Multimodal Discourse: The Modes and Media of Contemporary Communication* (2001) (Edward Arnold) (both with Theo van Leeuwen); *Before Writing: Rethinking the Paths to Literacy* (1997); *Early Spelling: Between Convention and Creativity* (2000); *Literacy in the New Media Age* (2003) (all published by Routledge); *Multimodal Teaching and Learning: The Rhetorics of the Science Classroom* (2002) (Continuum); edited (with Carey Jewitt), *Multimodal Literacy* (Peter Lang, 2003); and *English in Urban Classrooms* (FalmerRoutledge, 2004).

Colin Lankshear is a freelance Educational Researcher and writer based in Mexico where he is a permanent resident. He is currently a half time Professor of Literacy and New Technologies at James Cook University in Cairns, Australia, an Adjunct Professor of Education at Central Queensland University, Australia, and teaches short courses in Mexico, Canada and the US His current research and publishing focus mainly on literacy and other social practices involving new technologies. Recent books include *New Literacies: Changing Knowledge and Classroom Learning* (with Michele Knobel), and *Cyber Spaces/Social Spaces: Culture Clash in Computerized Classrooms* (with Ivor Goodson *et al.*), and he is joint editor of a forthcoming work, *The Handbook of Research on New Literacies.*

Jackie Marsh is a Reader in Education at the University of Sheffield, UK, where she co-directed, with Elaine Millard, the ESRC Research Seminar Series *Children's Literacy and Popular Culture* (2002–2004). She recently edited, along with Nigel Hall and Joanne Larson, the *Handbook of Early Childhood Literacy* (Sage, 2003) and is an editor of the *Journal of Early Childhood Literacy.* Jackie is involved in research which examines the role and nature of popular culture and media in early childhood literacy both in- and out-of-school contexts. Her latest publication in this field was the edited text, *Popular Culture, New Media and Digital Literacy in Early Childhood* (RoutledgeFalmer, 2005).

Elaine Millard is a Senior Lecturer in Education at the University of Sheffield and a founder member of the Sheffield Literacy Research Group. She has worked with a large number of LEAs on evaluation projects and courses related to literacy. She was previously a teacher and advisory teacher in comprehensive schools in Sheffield and Nottingham. Her main research interests concern the changing patterns of literacy and the relationship of out of school interests to students' work in school, particularly in relationship to their gender differences and preferences. She researches in collaboration with teachers and their pupils in school to investigate pupils' perceptions of the literacy work they undertake both at home and in school.

Susan Nichols is a Key Researcher at the Centre for Literacy Policy and Learning Cultures at the University of South Australia. An experienced teacher before becoming an academic, she is involved in promoting teacher inquiry and in developing online resources for teacher-researchers. She is currently conducting a critical inquiry into web-based educational resources for parents and investigating on-line and localized information networks. She has published chapters and articles on a wide range of topics including literacy curriculum and pedagogy, parent involvement, gendered literacies, learning difficulties and higher education. Her research orientation combines ethnography with critical discourse analysis and is informed by feminist and post-colonial theories.

Kate Pahl is a Lecturer in Education at the University of Sheffield. She is Director of EdD in Language and Literacy at the University of Sheffield. She has written several chapters and articles on the theme of texts and practices in families, and is interested in the educational fields of family and community literacy. She is the author of *Transformations: Children's Meaning Making in a Nursery* (Trentham, 1999) and, with Jennifer Rowsell, *Literacy and Education: The New Literacy Studies in the Classroom* (Paul Chapman, 2005). Her current research, funded by the Arts Council of Great Britain via Creative Partnerships, will use ethnography to study the work of visual artists in educational and community settings in the context of regeneration in South Yorkshire. She has also been involved in research on children's literacy and popular culture and has published chapters in that area.

Jennifer Rowsell is an Assistant Professor of Literacy Education at Rutgers University. Her research interests include: looking at texts as traces of social practice by viewing multimodality as integral to understanding the way children, youth and adults make meaning; and teachers' mediation of their identities (and those of their students) in teaching. In addition, she is conducting a research study that examines ways of bridging home and communities with schools in the New Jersey area. She has co-authored two books, one with David Booth entitled, *The Literacy Principal* and one with Kate Pahl entitled, *Literacy and Education: Understanding New Literacy Studies in the Classroom.*

Lynne Slonimsky lectures in the School of Education at the University of Witwatersrand, South Africa. She is interested in the psychology and sociology of knowledge and pedagogy, and the relation between them. She has brought this gaze to bear on academic disadvantage and curriculum responsiveness in higher education, youth development and service learning, curriculum development in both formal and informal settings, teacher education and literacy. Her current research focuses on the dynamics of authority relations in some South African classrooms and their constitutive implications for the development of knowledge, identity and democratic values.

Pippa Stein is Associate Professor in Applied English Language Studies at the University of the Witwatersrand, Johannesburg. She has a PhD from the Institute of Education, University of London, in the field of social semiotics, literacy and multimodal communication, from a social justice perspective. As a literacy educator and researcher in post-apartheid South Africa, her work explores children's access to, and participation in literacy education within the context of democracy and human rights. Recent publications include chapters in C. Jewitt and G. Kress (eds) (2003) *Multimodal Literacies* (Peter Lang), S. Anderson, P. Attwood and L. Howard (eds) *Facing Racism in Education* (2004) (Harvard Educational Review Reprint Series) B. Norton and K. Tooney (eds) (2004) *Critical Pedagogies and Language Learning* (Cambridge University Press), and B. Street (ed.) (2005) *Literacies Across Educational Contexts* (Caslon Publishing). She is currently working on a research project with colleagues in London, Delhi and Johannesburg investigating the construction of the subject English in secondary schools in these three cities.

Brian Street is Professor of Language in Education at King's College, London University and Visiting Professor of Education in both the Graduate School of Education, University of Pennsylvania and in the School of Education and Professional Development, University of East Anglia. Professor Street undertook anthropological fieldwork on literacy in Iran during the 1970s and taught social and cultural anthropology for over 20 years at the University of Sussex before taking up the Chair of Language in Education at King's College London. He has written and lectured extensively on literacy practices from both a theoretical and an applied perspective, with 13 books to date and over 80 articles. He recently wrote up a research project on home/school literacy and numeracy practices (forthcoming – co-author with Dave Baker and Alison Tomlin, *Navigating Numeracies: Home/School Numeracy Practices*, Kluwer) and has just published a collection of essays on applications of New Literacy Studies to educational work under the title *Literacies Across Educational Contexts: Mediating Learning and Teaching* (Caslon Press: Philadelphia).

Index